# Framing Software Reuse:
## Lessons from the Real World

ANDREWS AND LEVENTHAL   Fusion: Integrating IE, CASE, and JAD
ANDREWS AND STALICK   Business Reengineering: The Survival Guide
AUGUST   Joint Application Design
BASSETT   Framing Software Reuse: Lessons from the Real World
BODDIE   The Information Asset: Rational DP Funding and Other Radical Notions
BOULDIN   Agents of Change: Managing the Introduction of Automated Tools
BRILL   Building Controls into Structured Systems
COAD AND NICOLA   Object-Oriented Programming
COAD AND YOURDON   Object-Oriented Analysis, 2/E
COAD AND YOURDON   Object-Oriented Design
COAD WITH NORTH AND MAYFIELD   Object Models: Strategies, Patterns,
    and Applications
CONNELL AND SHAFER   Object-Oriented Rapid Prototyping
CONNELL AND SHAFER   Structured Rapid Prototyping
CONSTANTINE   Constantine on Peopleware
CONSTANTINE AND YOURDON   Structured Design
CRAWFORD   Advancing Business Concepts in a JAD Workshop Setting
DEGRACE AND STAHL   The Olduvai Imperative: CASE and the State of Software
    Engineering Practice
DEGRACE AND STAHL   Wicked Problems, Righteous Solutions
DEMARCO   Controlling Software Projects
DEMARCO   Structured Analysis and System Specification
EMBLEY, KURTZ, AND WOODFIELD   Object-Oriented Systems Analysis
FOURNIER   Practical Guide to Structured System Development and Maintenance
GARMUS AND HERRON   Measuring the Software Process: A Practical Guide
    to Functional Measurements
GLASS   Software Conflict: Essays on the Art and Science of Software Engineering
JONES   Assessment and Control of Software Risks
KING   Project Management Made Simple
LARSON   Interactive Software: Tools for Building Interactive User Interfaces
MCMENAMIN AND PALMER   Essential System Design
MOSLEY   The Handbook of MIS Application Software Testing
PAGE-JONES   Practical Guide to Structured Systems Design, 2/E
PINSON   Designing Screen Interfaces in C
PUTNAM AND MYERS   Measures for Excellence: Reliable Software on Time
    within Budget
RIPPS   An Implementation Guide to Real-Time Programming
RODGERS   ORACLE®: A Database Developer's Guide
RODGERS   UNIX®: Database Management Systems
SHLAER AND MELLOR   Object Lifecycles: Modeling the World in States
SHLAER AND MELLOR   Object-Oriented Systems Analysis: Modeling the World in Data
STARR   How to Build Shlaer-Mellor Object Models
THOMSETT   Third Wave Project Management
WANG (ed.)   Information Technology in Action
WARD   System Development Without Pain
WARD AND MELLOR   Structured Development for Real-Time Systems
YOURDON   Decline and Fall of the American Programmer
YOURDON   Managing the Structured Techniques, 4/E
YOURDON   Managing the System Life-Cycle, 2/E
YOURDON   Modern Structured Analysis
YOURDON   Object-Oriented Systems Design
YOURDON   Rise and Resurrection of the American Programmer
YOURDON   Structured Walkthroughs, 4/E
YOURDON   Techniques of Program Structure and Design
YOURDON AND ARGILA   Case Studies in Object-Oriented Analysis and Design
YOURDON, WHITEHEAD, THOMANN, OPPEL, AND NEVERMANN   Mainstream
    Objects: An Analysis and Design Approach for Business
YOURDON INC.   YOURDON™ Systems Method: Model-Driven Systems Development

# Framing Software Reuse:

## Lessons from the Real World

**Paul G. Bassett**

*To join a Prentice Hall PTR Mailing List, point to:*
http://www.prenhall.com/register

YOURDON PRESS
Prentice Hall Building
Upper Saddle River, New Jersey 07458
http://www.prenhall.com

**Library of Congress Cataloging-in-Publication Data**

Bassett, Paul G.
   Framing software reuse: lessons from the real world / Paul G.
Bassett.
      p.  cm. -- (Yourdon Press computing series)
   Includes index.
   ISBN 0-13-327859-X  (case)
   1. Computer software--Reusability    I. Title.    II. Series.
QA76.76.R47B37  1996
005. 1 -- dc20

                                               96-15821
                                              CIP

Acquisitions Editor: *Paul Becker*
Editorial Assistant: *Maureen Diana*
Editorial/production supervision and
   interior design: *Diane Heckler Koromhas*
Art Director: *Jerry Votta*
Cover Designer: *Anthony Gemmellaro*
Manufacturing Buyer: *Alexis R. Heydt*
Editorial Liaison: *Patti Guerrieri*

© 1997 by Netron Inc.
Published by Prentice Hall PTR
Prentice-Hall, Inc.
A Simon & Schuster Company
Upper Saddle River, New Jersey 07458

The publisher offers discounts on this book when ordered in bulk quantities.
For more information, contact;
        Corporate Sales Department
        Prentice Hall PTR
        One Lake Street
        Upper Saddle River, NJ 07458
        Phone: 800-382-3419; Fax: 201-236-7141
        e-mail: corpsales@prenhall.com

Printed in the United States of America

10  9  8  7  6  5  4  3  2  1

ISBN 0-13-327859-X

PRENTICE-HALL INTERNATIONAL (UK) LIMITED, *London*
PRENTICE-HALL OF AUSTRALIA PTY. LIMITED, *Sydney*
PRENTICE-HALL CANADA INC., *Toronto*
PRENTICE-HALL HISPANOAMERICANA, S.A., *Mexico*
PRENTICE-HALL OF INDIA PRIVATE LIMITED, *New Delhi*
PRENTICE-HALL OF JAPAN, INC., *Tokyo*
SIMON & SCHUSTER ASIA PTE. LTD., *Singapore*
EDITORA PRENTICE-HALL DO BRASIL, LTDA., *Rio de Janeiro*

# Contents

# Foreword

What began as a casual dinner conversation nearly ten years ago has finally emerged as Paul Bassett's important book on software reuse. Paul and I and the publisher have been somewhat frustrated by the slow gestation of the ideas you're about to read. Perhaps it's for the best: I'm not sure the world was really ready for a serious, in-depth treatment of the concept of software reuse back in 1987.

Today, with the industry buzzing about components and objects and applets, perhaps we are ready. There is an increasing demand from business executives for higher levels of productivity, dramatically shorter development schedules, and higher levels of quality. More and more organizations are concluding that reuse is not just a "Boy Scout virtue" like loyalty, bravery, and thrift—but a serious engineering approach yielding enormous practical benefits.

Of course, every software engineer has heard of reuse—and many will claim they've attempted it, in one form or another. But as Bassett describes it, the reuse that actually occurs in the typical organization is "ad hoc," or accidental. Indeed, most organizations are entirely unaware of the level of reuse that occurs within their organization, as I've been able to confirm from numerous informal surveys around the world. Bassett optimistically suggests that the level of "ad hoc" reuse can vary from 0% to 40%; in most of the metrics investigations I've seen of such organizations, the actual number is closer to 20%.

One reason for the increased level of reuse that we've begun to see throughout development organizations is the appearance of a number of application development environments like Smalltalk, Delphi, Visual C++, and Visual Basic—which come with a rich library of reusable components. Indeed, it's so rich that most developers don't have a chance of learning or using all of the vendor-supplied components, but that's a different story. Bassett refers to this form of reuse as "latent reuse." While it has indeed had a positive impact on productivity, especially in the building of fancy GUI windows that our users love so dearly, the vendor-supplied components are relatively low-level "grains of sand." With little or no connection to the application domain in which the developers are immersed.

The next level of sophistication involves intra-project reuse, which typically results in 80-90% reuse; and this is typically the level that "ordinary" advocates of reuse achieve. What's significant about Bassett's work—and the material in this book—is the emphasis on achieving a higher level of reuse known as "systemic" and a level beyond that known as "cultural reuse." In organizations practicing the most advanced forms of reuse, reuse is typically at the 95–99% level; productivity levels are almost two orders of magnitude above the "ad hoc" reuse organizations.

To make this work requires some technology, and some significant organizational changes. The technology introduced by Bassett is the technology of frames. A completely new concept to most software engineers, it may cause a certain degree of bewilderment on the part of programmers who thought object-oriented programming provided all the mechanisms we would ever need to support reuse. But as you'll learn in Chapters 12 and 13, there are a number of subtle problems with conventional OO methods and tools. On the other hand, Bassett reassures us, that "the good news is you can practice an advanced form of OO using frame technology, and do it with any 3GL." That's an incredible statement—you can practice an advanced form of OO, and achieve astounding levels of reuse—without abandoning COBOL and jumping into what many business-oriented application programmers regard as the alien and unpleasant world of C++, Smalltalk, or (to be au courant) Java. Indeed, such a statement would seem so outrageous and politically incorrect (for today's computer community is highly politicized, as evidenced by the ongoing debates over languages and methodologies!), were it not for the convincing case studies and examples Bassett describes in this book.

The technological aspects of frame technology are indeed important, but for most organizations, the management issues will spell the difference between success and failure. At the very least, these organizational and cultural issues will determine whether the organization remains rooted at the ad hoc level of reuse or has a reasonable hope of reaching the systemic or cultural level of reuse that Bassett describes. I've done a reasonable amount of consulting work in this area, and I know that the organizational changes required to support systematic forms of reuse are difficult to accomplish; but it's also evident, from the discussion throughout "Framing Software Reuse" that Bassett has thought longer and deeper and harder about the issues than I have. The fact that he has explained the issues cogently, and often quite eloquently, won't necessarily be enough to accomplish miracles in your own organization. But it's an important start.

Indeed, that's what Bassett's book really represents: an important start, for most of us, on the road to "serious" reuse. Most of us are rank amateurs when it comes to reuse. It's analogous in many ways to the amateur tennis players who watch Wimbledon matches on television and then wonder why they can't play as well as Pete Sampras or Steffi Graf. Unfortunately, even if you had the physique of these world champions, and even if Sampras and Graf patiently explained the strategies of winning tennis, it wouldn't be enough. It takes years of hard work, and most of us don't have the discipline or persistence.

When it comes to reuse, we're in a similar position. The good news is we have a world-class expert, Paul Bassett, who has written the best book about reuse I've seen in my career. The bad news is if you're really serious about reuse, be prepared for a lot of work and a lot of practice. On the other hand, the really good news is that if you digest the book and apply its principles diligently, it really does work.

*Ed Yourdon*
*April 1996*

# Preface

This book shows software developers, analysts, and managers how to make reuse work. The book highlights frame technology: a language-independent way to manufacture software from components that can adapt each other. Why should you read this book? Because of what adaptive reuse can do for you.

Example: One Fortune 50 company's entire information systems development staff numbers only 40 people (with no outside contractors). Yet they satisfy over 28,000 user requests for software changes and enhancements each year.

Further example: A major retailer developed and deployed its mission-critical purchase-order management system in 80% less time and effort than development projects used to take them before they embarked on adaptive reuse. The project was enormous—over 1300 programs and 5 million lines of code. On the last four subsystems alone they saved $11 million in development costs, and $12 million in early deployment benefits.

Frames solve thorny, long-standing software industry problems. Finally, we can combine high productivity with high quality, preserve flexibility without sacrificing performance, port systems to multiple platforms with native look-and-feel functionality, reduce complexity (in addition to hiding it), and, most importantly, reduce the cost of so-called maintenance. Sounds like magic, right?

Wrong. It is not magic. Reuse is so fundamental to all mature engineering disciplines, it is not even part of their jargon! But effective software reuse is harder, because nonphysical things have more degrees of freedom available to them. Physical parts are reused as is. Software parts often need unpredictable modifications before they can be reused.

Software practice has begun to mature, to acquire some of the substance and rigor that are the hallmarks of an engineering discipline. As with all new paradigms, there has been an initial period of healthy confusion. Software's "craft" phase has been an exciting half-century of brash precocity, experimentation, fads, buzzwords, religious wars—an on-going turmoil. Emerging from this pandemonium are principles that can effectively lead us out of the wilderness.

## Origins

I have a very clear memory of that fall day in 1978, standing at the greenboard in my York University office, talking to my colleague, professor Gunnar Gotshalks, about the frustrations of code generators. In addition to teaching computer science, I had recently founded a software house, called Sigmatics Computer Corporation, to serve the needs of local businesses. Gunnar was under contract for Sigmatics; we were installing a custom software system for the city of Barrie, Ontario. We were using code generators I had created to automate the tedium of writing screen and report programs.

The report generator, for example, certainly avoided a lot of drudgery by automatically coding the details of report layouts, providing subtotals, and the like. Over 90% of a typical report program was generated from its WYSIWYG (what you see is what you get) specification. The rest was the "fine-tuning," always necessary to adapt generated code to the specifics of the system. The frustration was not the fine-tuning per se, but the aggravation of having to manually retune it every time so much as a one-character change was made to the WYSIWYG specification. Most people would simply give up at this point and resort to patching the generated code. But I had built those generators and I was determined to use them!

On the greenboard I drew a state transition diagram, representing a program. "We should be able to cut any line of the graph and splice a subgraph into the cut automatically," I said to Gunnar. Then I erased a line and drew more circles and lines, in place of the erased line. "Of course, we need to be able to nest the splices, and we should also be able to delete subgraphs as easily as add them."

That was the genesis of "frames."[1] As hoped, I could modify my screen and report definitions, regenerate the programs, and recustomize them automatically. To my pleasant surprise, I also could modify frames without affecting programs already containing those frames. This smooth meshing

---

[1] By the summer of 1979, I sorely felt the inadequacy of my terminology. I was calling the components "chunks." My technical staff at Sigmatics discovered engineering insights that were hard to articulate because of a lack of precise terms. After some casting about I recalled Marvin Minsky's use of the word "frame" in artificial intelligence, and it quickly caught on. The richly intuitive connections to car frames, window frames, frames of reference, and so on, provided a "frame of mind" for understanding software engineering.

of frames with generators and existing programs produced a palpable sense of untapped power.

It was immediately obvious that even without code generators, frames could be reused in interesting ways. They were a universal way to package information into components—any text in any language (including natural languages such as English) could be constructed entirely from frames. During the assembly process, frames automatically adapted, and were adapted by, other frames. But the real proof of the pudding has been in the eating. Hence this book.

The rules of chess are simple, but master-level play is not. Just so, frame technology is simple, but its implications become simple only when we change the way we think about software development. In my own case, for example, it was to take me over a decade to reach my present, still limited, understanding of why frames work as well as they do.

## Overview

This book is intended for both practitioners, especially those involved in business application software, and their managers. They will learn how to overcome many of the frustrations plaguing current practice. Students of software engineering will find a conceptually integrated, easy-to-learn software design and construction process.

You can understand reuse, and how to make it work, from this book. To use frame technology in practice, as is the case with any technology, requires a tool set. Netron, Inc., provides such tools, but describing them exceeds my purpose and scope.

This book is divided into four parts, and interspersed with case studies of practical applications.

**Part I**, called Executives' Overview—Reuse That Works, provides an executive's overview of reuse: concepts, technology, methodology, infrastructure, and culture. But theories, no matter how intriguing, must be backed by tangible results. Those who have applied the ideas in Part I have reduced project costs and time-to-market by an order-of-magnitude or more.

**Part II**, Frames Enable Reuse, goes into details[2] about component-based software engineering and frame technology, including analysis and design issues. Frames are compared to other software constructs, including an explanation and discussion of object orientation.

[2]See "Paul Bassett's Book" on the World Wide Web: http://www.netron.com for an animated explanation of frame commands.

However, technology merely enables. Reuse, to achieve its greatest effectiveness, must also involve the appropriate processes, infrastructure and cultural attitudes. Managers can, if they wish, proceed directly from Part I to Part III.

**Part III,** Reuse Changes the Software Engineering Process, explains how reuse changes the software development process: how to develop and standardize adaptable components, and, in parallel, how to develop systems that reuse those components.

**Part IV,** Managing the Transition, returns more thoroughly to the challenge of transforming organizations into ones that obtain two orders-of-magnitude advantages from adaptive reuse.

## Acknowledgments

My primary intellectual debt is to Gunnar Gotshalks, who built the first prototype "chunk" processor and with whom, in the early days, I had many fruitful collaborations. To the principals of Netron, Inc., especially Willie Kisin and Roy Hughes, I owe my gratitude for a robust implementation of frame technology in NETRON/CAP™ and Netron Fusion™ and for its myriad trials by fire in a diversity of computer hardware and application development environments.

To Ware Myers, thank you for your critical help in making revisions to my manuscript.

To Michael Rehkopf, thank you for being so willing to volunteer huge amounts of your valuable technical and editorial criticism. (Without the Internet, this book would still be in gestation.)

To Ed Yourdon, thank you for encouraging me to get started, and for suggesting Ware Myers to me so I could get finished.

To Paul Becker, my publisher, thank you for your efforts getting the book into readers' hands.

And to Penny, my wife, who suffered up close with my interminable writing and rewriting, thank you for your patience and support.

*Paul G. Bassett*
*January 1996*

# PART 1

# EXECUTIVES' OVERVIEW— REUSE THAT WORKS

The historic engineering disciplines, such as civil or mechanical engineering, learned long ago that they can save themselves much design effort, as well as improve the quality of the finished project, by reusing already designed components. Obviously, software engineering can do the same. For decades, it has reused subroutines, macros, objects, and so forth. And it has set up libraries, repositories, and interchange standards for accessing such reusable components. So far, with these approaches, reuse ranges between 10% and 50% of the code in a project.

Component-based frame technology does better. It does better

1

because the frames I will describe are adaptable. Being adaptable, they can be reused in many more situations than components that have to be reused as is. With these reusable, adaptable designs and components, reuse routinely achieves 90% and often can reach better than 95%. At this level of reuse, software development is far more efficient than traditional develop-from-scratch or other reuse approaches. In a study of 15 projects from nine organizations, a leading metrics company reports that reuse of these adaptable frames reduced schedules by 70% and development costs by 84%, on average, compared to industry norms.

While technology is certainly necessary for effective reuse, it is not nearly the whole story. Reuse affords a new perspective on analysis, design, and development, for both applications and their components. And to maximize the benefits of reuse, we must attend to its infrastructural and cultural aspects as well. Organizations that have done so, well exceed the already significant results reported in the study.

Lest you be carried away with the exciting possibilities, reuse is neither a silver bullet nor a magic weight loss pill. It is a diet and exercise program, which Part I presents in executive summary form.

# Reuse: Its Time Has Come

## CHAPTER 1

> From harmony to heavenly harmony,
> This universal frame began:
> From harmony to harmony
> Through all the compass notes it ran.
>
> John Dryden, 1687

As the power of computer hardware has multiplied in recent years, software systems to run on these more powerful systems have grown in size, development schedules have lengthened, and costs have risen. One of the lessons people are painfully drawing from the effort to build these systems is that they are too complex to be built from scratch. The alternative is to build them from reusable parts that have already passed the test of workability.

That is not a very original thought, you might object. Of course it is not. The hallmarks of every mature engineering discipline are its engineering handbooks. Without these thick bibles of proven components and design models, modern society simply could not exist. In software, too, reusable components have been a goal for almost half a century, starting with macros and subroutines and continuing with skeleton code, fourth-generation languages, code generators, and CASE (computer-aided software engineering) tools. Currently, many have pinned their hopes on object-oriented languages.

All these techniques have merit. They have contributed to the slow improvement in software development productivity that we have experienced over several decades. But they have not delivered the oft-promised reuse breakthrough. People who have been around for a while are skeptical. "Is reuse an idea whose time will never come?" they ask.

Reuse mechanisms have simply not been sufficiently adaptable. Correcting this deficiency not only delivers breakthrough benefits, but offers a window on why this correction works and what it takes to obtain those benefits.

I'll get to that, but first, some of you may still be understandably skeptical. The results obtained by the metrics company, Quantitative Software Management, in its objective study of practical software reuse might dent your skepticism. Then, with your skepticism in check, you will be ready to read on.

## Major Organizations Participated

Netron's clients report very good results from using frame technology, but their reports are anecdotal. Because people believe that software vendors hype their products, vendor claims are heavily discounted in the marketplace. Netron wanted something more solid. It decided to take the unusual step of inviting an independent auditor to do a cross-sectional analysis of the Netron customer base and let the chips fall where they may.

The independent assessor is QSM Associates, Inc. of Pittsfield, Massachusetts, an affiliate of Quantitative Software Management, McLean, Virginia, founded in 1978. Ira Grossman and Michael C. Mah conducted the study using techniques pioneered by Lawrence H. Putnam, president of the parent organization, a former nuclear physicist, and renowned metrics expert [1].

Nine client organizations elected to fully fund and to contribute project data to this research study on a pledge of confidentiality of the raw data. Seven of the organizations, listed in Table 1-1, agreed to be publicly identified. They include a large telephone company, a major bank, an important retailer, a manufacturer, a government department, a third-party package software reseller that services the casualty and general insurance industry, and a gas utility.

All the contributed projects fall within the business/management information systems category of QSM's database of more than 4,000+ completed business systems projects. The database lists development time, effort, size, number of defects, productivity, and other relevant data for each project. And the database includes projects that used all manner of software development tools, including none at all.

**Table 1-1  Nine organizations in seven industries funded and participated in the QSM study (two wish to remain anonymous)**

Ameritech
Chemical Bank (now Chase)
Hudson's Bay Company
Noma-Cabletech
Revenue Canada
Teleglobe Insurance Systems
Union Gas

The 15 projects range in size from 4574 SLOC (source lines of code) to 9,300,715 SLOC (without blanks and comments), averaging 133,000 SLOC.[1] So, this set of projects is broadly based in different industries, though all are within the business category. It also represents a range of sizes, and the median size (74,563 SLOC) is approximately the same as that of the QSM database.

## Process Productivity About Ten Times Better

That finding—process productivity is 9.4 times better on average in the frame-technology projects than in the QSM database—is very specific. Before I explain how QSM arrived at this result, Figure 1-1 provides a broader picture of what it means. The open bars toward the left end of the productivity-index scale represent the percentage of information-systems projects at each productivity level in the QSM database. The black bars toward the right end of the scale are the projects accomplished using frame technology.

You can think of the open bars as similar to the IQ bell curve (or normal curve). On the IQ curve, the mean is 100; in Figure 1-1, the mean of the open bars is 16.9 on the process-productivity index scale.

What is this scale? Technically, the process-productivity index is produced by the equation in Figure 1-2. The equation looks a bit formidable, but we need concern ourselves with only two points here. (In their book [2] Putnam and Myers explain how the formula was derived from a statistical analysis of thousands of actual projects.)

---

[1] QSM excluded the two largest projects from this average because otherwise it would have been 840,730 SLOC, a value above all 13 projects in the quoted average.

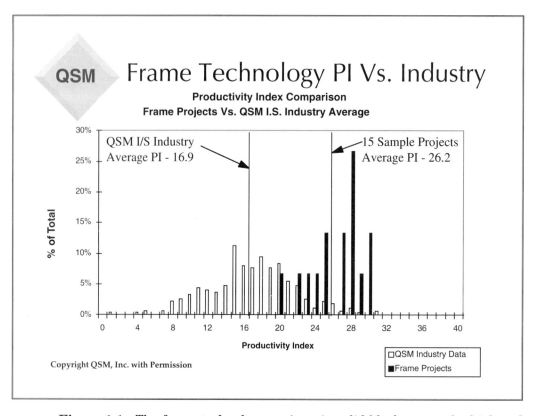

**Figure 1-1.** The frame-technology projects in solid black are at the high end of this productivity scale, compared to QSM's database of projects, shown in open bars. The height of the open bars add up to 100% of QSM's database; similarly, the black bar heights account for 100% of the 15 frame-technology projects.

The first point is that the process-productivity index represents a relationship between system size, time (from the start of detailed design to the end of acceptance testing), and effort (person-months expended during that time). In fact, that relationship turns out to be influenced much more by the project's schedule than by the effort expended. Schedule and effort are the two practical metrics with which managers are most concerned. It is useful to have an index that reflects both of these factors.

You can view the index as a measure of overall throughput. That is, it reflects the tools, methodology, management style, staff competence, and other factors that characterize the information-technology organization's ability to produce systems. If these factors don't change, then the

- ESLOC = effective source lines of code
  (no blanks/comments)
- time = detailed design to user acceptance, incl.
- effort = staff months
- B = ESLOC related skills factor (0.16 - 0.39 )

$$PI = \log_{1.272} \left[ \frac{ESLOC}{time^{4/3} * (effort / B)^{1/3}} \right] - 26.6$$

**Figure 1-2.** The QSM software equation shows that the relationship between project size, development time, and effort determines a productivity value that QSM calls the *process-productivity index.*

productivity index can be used to predict the time and effort of future projects done by that organization. On the other hand, improvements to any of these factors, say the tools, should improve the shop's productivity index.

The second point is that the index compounds process-productivity just like time compounds interest. More precisely, each increase (or decrease) of one in the index means the process productivity goes up (or down) by 27.2%, compounded. Were your bank to pay you 27.2%, compounded annually on your savings account, you would be very happy. Well, we shall soon see the kind of financial dividends in software development that such a rate can pay!

Now, the average process-productivity index of the QSM information-systems database is 16.9, as shown in Figure 1-1. The average productivity index of the frame-technology projects is 26.2. What does a difference of 9.3 (26.2 - 16.9) index values mean?

Here is where the power of compound interest shows itself. An increase of 9.3 index units compounded at 27.2% per unit, means the same people working on a project for the same length of time would produce over nine times $(1.272^{9.3} = 9.4)$ more functionality, compared to QSM's project database.[2]

---

[2] Moreover, the database projects may be superior to the software industry in general; organizations have to reach a certain level of maturity before they begin reporting data to QSM's database.

## Bottom Line Results

You may not be comfortable trying to think in terms of process productivity. You may be accustomed to thinking in terms of development time and effort. So let's get back to the bottom line. QSM's methods enable them to show the gain in process productivity also in terms of development time and effort.

There are two primary ways that higher productivity indexes contribute to the bottom line: systems that produce benefits sooner (early time-to-market) and systems that cost less to build. Figure 1-3 shows that the average reduction in time-to-market was 70%. QSM's report goes on to note that to achieve the observed 70% time compression by "brute staffing alone ... is statistically impossible, based on the latest industry data." The average size project carried out at the industry-average process productivity would take 18 months. At the study average, it took 5.3 months.

**Figure 1-3.** This management metric compares the time projects consume, from detailed design through acceptance testing, which correlates with time-to-market.

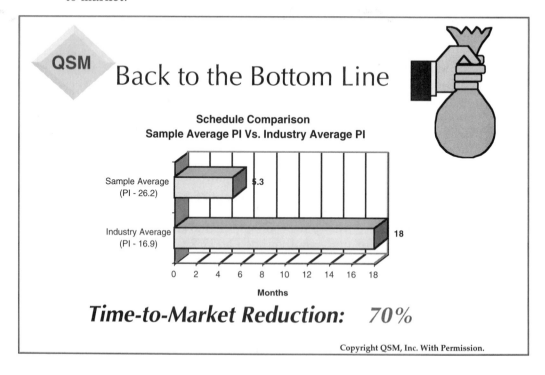

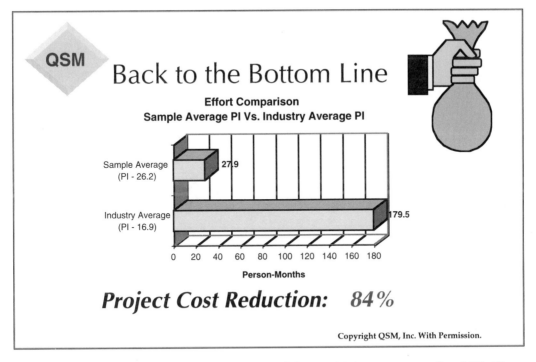

**Figure 1-4.** Effort would be reduced from 179.5 person-months–84%. Since effort is the dominant factor in software cost, cost is reduced by a like amount.

Suppose a system contributes $200,000 per month to the bottom line. Then delivering it 12 months sooner will increase the bottom line by $2.4 million.[3]

Figure 1-4 indicates an 84% reduction in effort or cost. Quoting again from QSM's report, "The effort expenditure [on the average-sized project] is reduced by approximately 152 person-months, using a fully burdened labor rate of just over $9,000 per person-month."

These bottom-line results are surely very good news for the software industry. Why can I attribute them to reuse? Because the 15 projects were diverse in both size and application type. About the only thing they had in common was the underlying technology of reuse and the set of reusable components from which they started.

---

[3] In practice, the benefit is even higher because the system is also 12 months less out of date in relation to the ever-changing needs of the business.

# Reuse:
# What Is It?

## CHAPTER 2

*As if his whole vocation*
*were endless imitation.*

William Wordsworth, 1807

W hat do we mean by the word "reuse?" Many people confuse reuse with use. They each have distinct and important roles to play in software engineering. But let us start with a rather prosaic example. When you eat a meal, you obviously use the dishes and cutlery. But are you reusing them? Well, you have certainly used them before, washed them, and are ready to use them again. But these successive uses are reuse only in a trivial sense.

When you invoke a program from a menu on a computer screen, you are certainly using it. But are you reusing it? Because there is no difference in usage each time you use the program, the notion of reuse as multiple use "as is" is not helpful. Similarly, when object A sends a message to object B, A is using the services of B, but not reusing it in any significant sense.

## Use at Run Time

What it comes down to is that use is really a run-time concept. Run time is the time during which a computer executes software modules.[1] Construction time is the time during which a programmer or a computer

---

[1]By extension, an interpreter or a compiler-linker-computer trio can also be considered to "execute" a module.

constructs the executable or interpretable module. Therefore, construction time precedes run time, as shown in Figure 2-1. As we shall soon see, reuse in other than the simple sense of "use" is a construction-time concept.

At run time, we think in terms of invoking programs, subroutines, and objects, meaning using them on an "as-is" basis. We want to maximize their usability. That means paying attention to the properties of usability—functionality, efficiency, ease-of-use—and to the interactions among these properties. There are trade-offs to be made among them. For example, the more dynamic binding (functionality) we have at run time, the less performance (efficiency).

*Binding* is the process of assigning values to appropriate variables in a module. When done at run time, this process provides the ability to vary the module's behavior. This variability, in turn, determines functionality

**Figure 2-1.** At construction time you can change the things that remain fixed at run time.

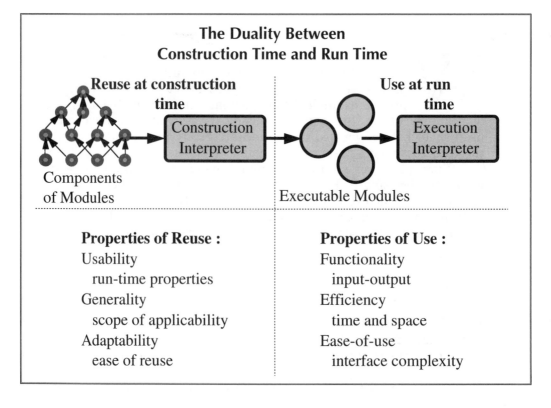

and ease-of-use. On the one hand, run-time binding provides variability at the expense of performance, and excessive variability can actually impair ease-of-use. On the other hand, we shall see that the binding of variables at construction time provides a mode of flexibility that is essentially unavailable at run time.

## Reuse at Construction Time

To resume our culinary example, suppose you need to transform your tablespoon into a teaspoon. In the physical world, such changes are literally hard to do. In the software world, however, making these kinds of changes is not only easy, it is natural. That is why in software engineering we reserve the term *reusable* for components that can be adapted to make them *usable*. By doing this, we make a conceptual leap from same to similar, yielding a major increase in the scope of what can be reused.

Changes of this scope have to be made at construction time. At run time, executables may be dynamic and flexible but, in essence, they are fixed. During execution their logic doesn't change; their data structures do not change. Indeed, this invariance must be the case or systems would not be well defined and outputs would not be repeatable.

This simple observation allows us to define construction time more precisely: those times when we can vary the data structures and methods that we choose to hold fixed at run time. Associating reuse with construction time and use with run time is crucial to addressing the issue of software development and how frame technology supports it. Indeed, it's the duality between run time and construction time that's important to appreciate.

Just as usability has three key run-time properties, reusability has three key construction-time properties: generality, adaptability, and, of course, usability (at run time). By generality, I mean in how many contexts or situations a part can be reused. By adaptability, I refer to a part's ease-of-reuse–how much work must be done to adapt it for use in each context.

Like use, reuse has its trade-offs, such as complexity. On the one hand, for example, a primitive reuse technique is to make a copy and modify it. This leads to one version becoming two, two becoming three, and so on. Soon you drown in a sea of look-alikes, taking longer to find the one you need than to write yet another version. On the other hand, if you keep only one version, each time you modify it, you give yourself retrofit nightmares, running hard just to stay compatible. Both reuse techniques, copy-and-modify and modify-and-retrofit, lack generality, causing complexities that severely limit their effectiveness.

To sum up, for software engineering purposes, *reuse is the process of adapting a generalized component to various contexts of use.*

## Enabling Reuse: Frame Technology

The fundamental challenge with which we must come to grips is what I call "same as, except." That is, this problem is the same as that one, except. . . . No doubt you have often found yourself explaining a new problem in terms of an old one. In any walk of life, if we lack the ability to take a model that works in one situation and adapt it to work in a new one, we reduce ourselves to trial and error.

In the software world, the frustration has always been that the exceptions are unpredictable and consequently difficult to plan for. Indeed, they are driven by independent agents of change. In business, competition pushes you to innovate products or services; new laws and regulations compel a continual stream of changes in operating procedures and record keeping. In addition, there are changes in computer technology, as when the world moved from dumb terminals to graphic user interfaces (GUI), or from mainframes to client/server systems. All these changes intersect in the software.

Historically, programmers have had little recourse, in the face of these unpredictable changes, except to reach into the source code and do whatever it takes. This need to "patch" what would otherwise be common code has always been the Achilles' heel of reuse. Once patched, it has become too specialized to be reused in other contexts. Moreover, as patches pile on patches, the original, relatively coherent code degrades; we lose control over its complexity. It becomes harder and harder to reuse within its own context. Ultimately, we arrive at the antithesis of software—brittleware.

But what if, instead of associating reuse with "sameness" (use as is), we switch to "similarness"? Well, similarities imply differences—they are really two sides of the same coin. Aha! If reuse mechanisms could handle differences, they would, by the same token, also be handling similarities. It is this "Aha" that underlies frame technology.

In essence frame technology is not new—it is the process of assembling products from their parts, as in Figure 2-2. If you have ever bought a desk—or a child's toy—to assemble at home, you will have seen a parts-explosion diagram (Figure 2-3) that shows you how things go together. Some of the parts will be unique to the particular product. Others, such as nuts and bolts, will be common to many products. Still others will be much the same as parts for similar toys, but will have been modified (same as,

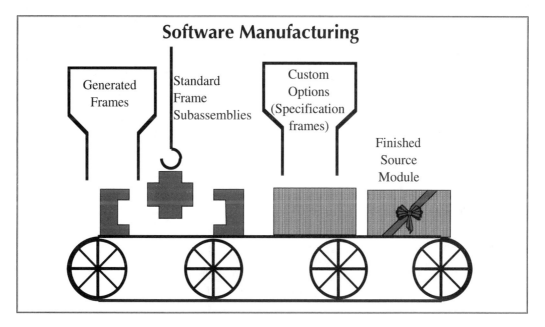

**Figure 2-2.** A software module is assembled from adaptable frame components.

except) to suit the particular toy. Frame technology is the "same as" this manufacturing analogy "except" that frames are adapted by other frames during assembly, rather than simply reused as is.

An adaptable frame is not a specific part, as the parts of any physical product are. It is generic, meaning that it contains variables—frame variables, not to be confused with run-time variables—that enable it to give rise to an indefinitely large number of specific parts.

What is inside a frame? Two kinds of information. One is the kind that you find in all software: program commands and program variables. The other is frame commands and frame variables. Here comes duality again. Whereas program commands manipulate data at run time by acting on program variables, frame commands manipulate frames at construction time by acting on frame variables. The net is that frames can adapt, and be adapted by, other frames.

Frame commands implement the concept: "same as, except." Generally the commands enable one frame to select any of the properties it needs from other frames; to delete properties that it does not need; to add new properties; to modify existing ones; to take a property and iterate it with variations on each iteration; or to make a generalized property specific to one instance.

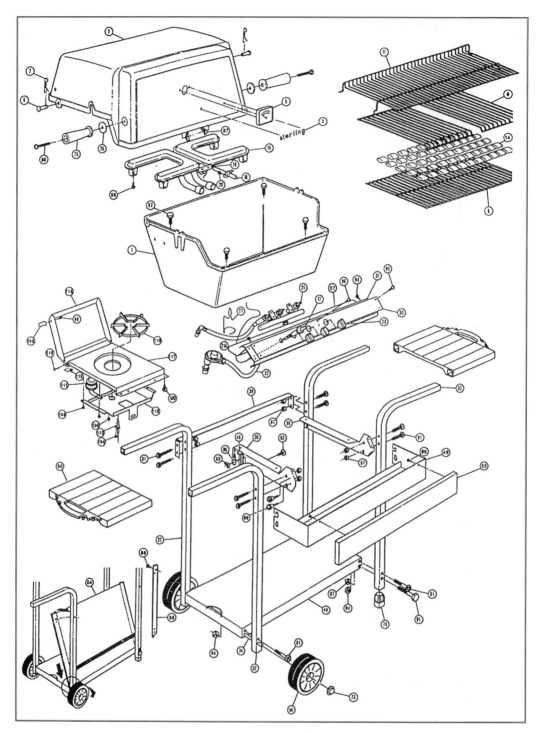

**Figure 2-3.** Example of a parts explosion diagram from a do-it-yourself kit.

## Software Source Module

Figure 2-4 is a "parts-explosion diagram" showing how to assemble a software source module from software parts. The entire diagram represents the "module." Each circle represents a frame. Each frame is a model or standard solution for some problem domain. The frame commands allow each frame to adapt any frame below it. Conversely, each frame can be adapted by any frame above it.

Frames are organized into layers, an architecture which isolates different sources of change. Figure 2-4 illustrates a four-layer architecture. Frames in the bottom layer are the most reusable. They handle input and output—databases, screens, reports, network protocols, operating systems, and so on. Such frames are reused in just about every executable program. Because they need know nothing about the particular application in which they are reused, they are relatively context free. Being independent of the application context (though they may be sensitive to the

**Figure 2-4.** This structure of frames is comparable to a parts-explosion diagram of a physical product. Putting the frames together results in a custom software source module that can be compiled and linked. Actual frame hierarchies may have any number of layers.

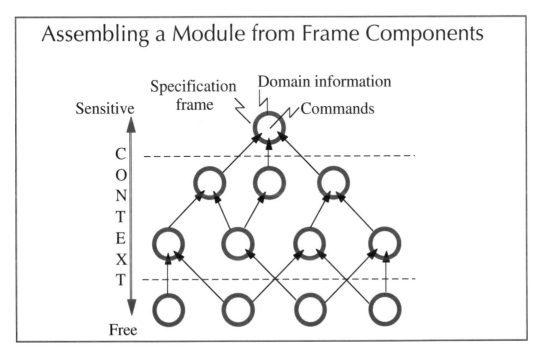

machine context), they can be standardized and supplied by component vendors. Experience indicates that these frames account for 70 to 80% of the reuse occurring in business systems.

The layer adjacent to the bottom contains frames that are reusable in applications within one organization, but not necessarily outside it. These are the frames that handle corporate standards, such as screen and report formats, security log-ons, error detection and recovery, help screens, interfaces between systems—enterprise-wide standards.

The next layer up contains frames relevant to a particular application area. As we shall see in Part II, banking might have frames for interest calculations and check processing. Manufacturing might have frames for inventory control and order processing. The possibility of reuse at this level is less because these functions are not relevant outside their own area.

As we ascend from the bottom to the top of a hierarchy, the frames become more context sensitive, that is, they become more dependent upon the application in which they are reused. The middle layers account for 15 to 25% of the reuse.

The top layer contains a single frame: the specification frame. It specifies the module's main subassemblies, how to adapt them for this module, and any other custom details. It is the only frame the developer creates to define the entire module. In mature environments, where midlevel frame layers are available, the specification frame typically contains less than 5% of the module's details. The specification frame, of course, is context specific. That is, it is not reused except in this one module.

## Design Templates

Application developers usually do not, and normally should not have to, know the various components that comprise their modules. In business environments, there are only six to a dozen fundamentally different types of programs they ever build—data entry, batch update, inquiries, screen handling, menus, report generation. After a few more, you run out. Each type corresponds to a generic specification frame called a design template.

To build a program, you simply have to know which type it is. If it is a report program, you start with the report template. It "knows" (contains references to) all the necessary report frames. Filling in a template is basically a "fill in the blanks" exercise. You see a list of typical customizing parameters and helpful explanations regarding when and how to override their default values. The application development process using templates is illustrated in Figure 2-5.

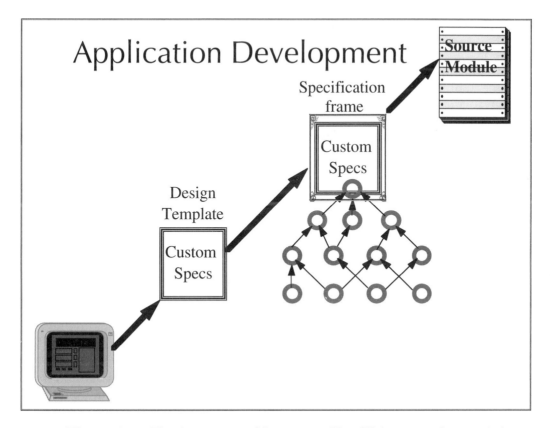

**Figure 2-5.** The frame assembly process. You fill in a template, creating a specification frame. The frame processor assembles a custom source module from the specified frame hierarchy. The result may be input to a compiler.

## Processing a Frame Hierarchy

A mechanism called the *frame processor* reads frames and carries out frame commands. The frame processor starts with a specification frame and works its way down the hierarchy, emitting a custom source module (e.g., a program) in accordance with the commands contained in the frames. From this point on, you compile and link the source and test the executable just as you always have. Thus the compile-link process is simply extended to assemble-compile-link, an automatable process.

All subsequent changes to the program go into the specification frame, not the program itself. In this way, the specification frame localizes throughout the life-cycle what is unique to this one program.

## Adaptable Reuse Is a Gateway

Frame technology provides the means to resolve many issues directly affecting the economics of software, as summarized in Table 2-1.

**Table 2-1. A Wish List of Outstanding Software Engineering Issues**

| | |
|---|---|
| Productivity | Complexity reduction |
| Quality | Open architecture |
| Adaptability | Easy maintenance |
| Performance and Tunability | Retrofit protection |
| Portability | Renovating legacy systems |
| Standards | Customizing purchased packages |
| Complexity hiding | Business reengineering |

- **Productivity.** The QSM research study reported (in Chapter 1) order-of-magnitude gains in process productivity. This level of gain corresponds nicely with our experience that reuse routinely reaches 90%. In fact, mature users, that is, organizations that have their own frame architectures, achieve better than 95% reuse.

- **Quality.** You can afford to invest more functionality, generality, and robustness in a frame than in single-use code because you can amortize the extra investment over many reuses. Moreover, frames experience more testing, hence exhibit fewer defects, than nonreused software. Frames are treated as valuable corporate assets.

- **Adaptability.** I need not belabor adaptability because I have defined reuse in terms of adaptable components. Still, I might emphasize another point. An adaptable component eliminates the need to have numerous look-alike versions. This greatly reduces the size of the component library and hence the associated engineering complexity. Frame libraries typically contain a couple hundred frames, not thousands.

- **Performance.** The duality between construction time and run time eliminates the normal trade-offs between adaptability and performance. If you need a general-purpose solution for most situations whereas others permit optimized versions, you can frame them all as selectable options at construction time. In this way, you fine-tune functionality, ease-of-use, and efficiency, while retaining adaptability.

- **Portability.** This goal is just a special case of reuse where the frame architecture isolates into a separate layer all environmental dependencies, that is, the operating system, the database platforms, and so on. The business rule frame layer is independent of the environment layers. You can target many environments with the same specification frame just by setting a software switch.

- **Standards.** A reusable component is a de facto standard, a textbook solution to a class of programming problems. But standards in the software industry have always suffered from the square-peg-in-the-round-hole effect. By that I mean a standard may be relevant, but there is usually some subtlety that doesn't fit the new situation. People often encounter more pain trying to work around rigid standards than such standards are worth. In contrast, frame technology makes it simple to inherit the relevant 90% and override locally the 10% that doesn't fit. It allows you to package software standards as paths of least resistance to desired solutions.

- **Complexity hiding.** Obviously, you shouldn't have to be an expert in how something works in order to reuse it. When you do have a need to know about GUI APIs or network protocols or database handling, or whatever, the frame hierarchy (parts-explosion diagram) provides a route map to the relevant details.

- **Complexity reduction.** In addition to the point about avoiding look-alike versions, here are three more examples of how good frame engineering reduces complexity.

    1. Separate frames isolate details affected by different sources of change. You have a single point of control for each type of change, rather than having them intermixed.

    2. The kind of context-sensitive information that is necessary to modify a collection of software structures (e.g., subroutines, macros, classes) so they mesh smoothly, is usually fragmented implicitly within and among specialized versions of those structures. Each frame, on the other hand, localizes this context information, making it explicit and manageable.

**3.** Rather than adding complexity by having extra logic to undo the effects of unwanted component "features" and side effects, frames directly adapt or delete whatever is necessary.

- **Open architecture.** You don't want to paint yourself into a technological corner that makes it difficult to accommodate new technologies. When multimedia, pen computing, or neural networks can offer your business a real advantage, you want to be able to integrate them with your existing systems. You don't want to rewrite everything just to add something new. Frame technology can be used to glue new and existing technologies together, automating the interface details. Your application developers can remain focused on business issues, rather than detouring, possibly for years, into the complexities of the new order.

- **Easy maintenance.** Why maintain 100% of a program when only 5% of it is unique? All that you actually have to maintain is the 5 to 15% of the details that are application-specific. And, rather than looking for the needle that needs changing in the haystack of other details, you need only look in the specification frame. Everything that differentiates this program from all others is collected in one place, the specification frame.

- **Retrofit protection.** What happens when your business or your technologies change in ways that should be reflected in your reused components? The good news is that you can make arbitrary changes to the reusable components that are invisible to your existing systems. In other words, you can avoid retrofitting simply for the sake of compatibility.

  This strategy works because you don't actually destroy any information in the frame you are modifying. You simply carry old and new versions side by side as selectable options within the frame. In effect, this technique provides an audit trail in the frame of how it evolved to its current form. Existing programs automatically select whichever version was current when they were defined. Similarly, new programs select the current version.

  This capability doesn't mean you are never going to retrofit. It does mean that you have a single control point for managing the retrofits of all impacted programs. And you can schedule them to suit business needs. When the user has a business case—and a budget— for making a modification to an existing system, you can also implement the retrofit at little or no extra cost. This approach to independently evolving applications and their reusable components is a crucial one-two punch at the maintenance problem, which some estimate is consuming 80% of programming resources.

- **Renovating legacy systems.** You may have millions of dollars invested in core systems. They still work, but you have little documentation to help you manage all the changes of the last decade or two. All your existing source programs are already de facto specification frames. When maintaining your "hot spots," you can whittle away at them, replacing chunks of in-line code with references to standard frames, thereby shrinking the size and complexity of the legacy code. Reusable "chunks" may be salvaged, that is, cleaned up and parameterized to make them into reusable frames.

- **Customizing software packages.** Provided you acquire the package's source code, it is straightforward to "frame" the source modules so you can isolate your customizations in specification frames. Then, each time a package vendor sends you a new release, you reframe and reapply your customizations relatively painlessly.

- **Reengineering.** This rubric covers various methods to fundamentally improve the way an organization works. Common to them is the effort to see the huge amounts of commonality that could underpin superficially different business processes. The "same as, except" mentality aids this kind of pattern recognition. Then, with frame technology, you capture these patterns in adaptable form. This approach gives you control over the dynamic balance between the standards that unify your business and the diversities essential to a thriving enterprise.

# How Reuse Changes Software Development

## CHAPTER 3

> *The country needs and, unless I mistake its temper,*
> *the country demands bold, persistent experimentation.*
> *It is common sense to take a method and try it. If it fails,*
> *admit it frankly and try another.*
>
> Franklin Delano Roosevelt, 1932

Reuse technology is a necessary but far from sufficient element of effective reuse. In my experience technology gets us at best a quarter of the way. The other three quarters involve processes and people, for after all, reusing other people's software requires trusting and sharing, the quintessentials of cooperation among groups. This chapter focuses on process, why the conventional software development process has let us down so badly, and what a components-based approach can do about it.

We have a deeply ingrained habit of thought. We treat software as a kind of hardware, something we can engineer as if it were a physical thing. It is a natural prejudice, reflecting centuries of human experience making everything from chariots to space shuttles.

We should not be too hard on ourselves. When a new paradigm emerges, the best we can do is to understand it in terms of existing paradigms. When cars were invented, our great-grandfathers called them "horseless carriages," and worried that cars would scare the horses. But after 20 years or so, people realized that cars had properties that transcended carriages. They came to appreciate that it was time to drop that obsolete metaphor and understand cars on their own terms.

25

## Software Is Not a Kind of Hardware

Sadly, after more than 40 years of software practice, the hardware metaphor remains entrenched. You can see it in our jargon. It is riddled with hardware oxymorons.

For example, we distinguish between a system's *logical design* and its *physical design*. In practice, "logical" means high level, not logical in the dictionary sense. To be sure, we build computers from AND, NAND, OR, and NOR gates—logic elements by design. The software that runs this hardware does not have to follow any such rules of logic. Indeed, we can even have virtual realities that emulate rules that are inconsistent with each other. (In Washington and other world capitals, we have legislators who are quite expert in the art of formulating inconsistent rules.) In the software realm, designs can be logical, but they need not be. Nor are designs "physical." All designs are abstract.

Brad Cox coined the oxymoron *software chips*, arguing we ought to package software into immutable objects, like integrated circuits. Indeed, we can always burn software into silicon and be done with it, speeding up our systems nicely and offering some protection from piracy. But most software changes too often for that. The very reason we call it software is to emphasize its malleability.

My favorite oxymoron is *software maintenance*. Our industry latched onto this term because people implicitly want to believe that systems that match their specifications perfectly are perfect. Thereafter, they should need only "grease and oil" maintenance. In practice, as we know only too well, to keep most software systems running like new would be sheer folly.

This hope for perfect systems underlies the once-pervasive development approach known as the waterfall methodology. The process was aptly named because, ideally, like going over Niagara Falls in a barrel, it's a one-way trip to the next level. Figure 3-1 shows the cascading process: Gather requirements. Analyze them to establish a firm specification. Design a system to satisfy the specification. Build the system. Test it. And, when documented, we are done on time and within budget. The customer will then use this system happily forever after. What an idyllic scene!

In spite of conventional engineering's own problems with cost and schedule overruns, we borrowed this process uncritically. Although we now know its many punishing shortfalls (pardon the puns) many shops continue to live with them:

- Analysis paralysis, a disease that bloats static models into too much irrelevant detail, and "stale bakes" the system (out of date before it is built).

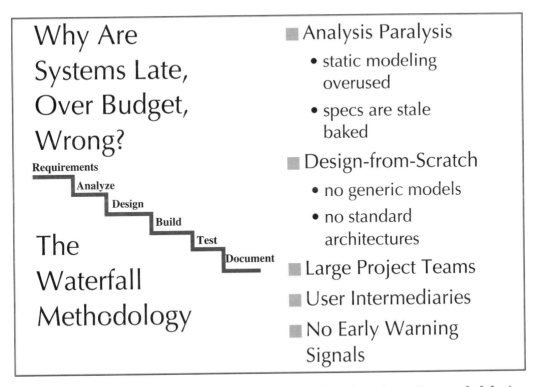

**Figure 3-1.** The waterfall model assumes that the information needed during software development cascades in one direction: from high levels to low levels. It is a far cry from reality in most shops.

- Design-from-scratch—no generic models, no standard architectures. Would you be first to cross a bridge whose engineer announced he had just designed it from scratch? Conventional engineers do not call this situation engineering. They call it research.

- Large project teams—the proverbial Mongolian hordes. This approach is not only expensive but it ignores Fred Brooks' infamous "Mythical Man Month" law: Adding bodies to a late software project makes it later.[1][3]

- Intermediaries—people who, presuming to translate between real users and systems people, end up being noise in the channel.

[1]Quantitative Software Management's process productivity equation quantifies the same conclusion. It shows that a team's production volume varies only as the cube root of the team's size—all else being equal, a team of 16 produces only twice as much as a team of 2! (i.e., $\sqrt[3]{16/2}$ = twice the output).

- No early warning signals—by the time we learn of serious requirements and design flaws, we have sunk so much time and money into the system that we end up forcing it into production anyway.

It's no wonder systems are usually late, over budget, and not what users need.

## Software Is the Same as Hardware Except. . .

Methodologists are promoting many alternatives to the waterfall, such as Boehm's spiral model [4], and Martin's RAD (rapid application development) [5] methodology. But many shops still embrace one variant of the waterfall or another. After more than 40 years of trying, the question is: why do we keep punishing ourselves this way?

We must stop designing software systems as if they were cars or TV sets. Figure 3-2 lists two obvious differences which, when combined, have profound implications for software development. The top half of the figure compares the nature of the constraints on systems. By definition, physical systems satisfy the laws of physics. These laws are:

- **Precise.** We write them in mathematical equations. They enable us to predict the properties of systems, including their constructability, with relative confidence.

- **Well known.** They are taught from high school on.

- **Objective.** They are independent of stakeholder bias.

- **Unbreakable.** Last and most important, nature compels us to go slower than light and obey gravity, no matter how much we wish otherwise.

Software could not be more different. Software is quite literally a figment of our imaginations. At best, we constrain it with a set of requirements that are:

- **Fuzzy.** They are some combination of hand waving and ambiguous statements, often incomplete, inconsistent, and hiding numerous implicit assumptions.

- **Poorly understood.** The law of unintended side-effects lurks just under the surface—subtle interactions among processes—due to the way they are implemented, that compromise, even destroy, a system's usability.

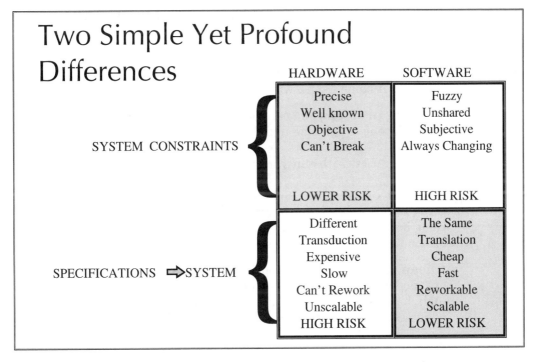

**Figure 3-2.** Software is the same as hardware, except. . . .

- **Subjective.** Each stakeholder has a different opinion about what the system could or should be like.

- **Unstable.** Even if all stakeholders share a common understanding of the requirements today, ask them again in a week or two.

   The bottom half of Figure 3-2 compares the transition from design to implementation. Designs are abstract, physical systems are not. This obvious difference creates difficult manufacturing problems:

- **A transduction problem.** A transduction converts something from one form to another, in our case, from symbols and diagrams to their analogues in the physical world. A nuclear power station is vastly more complicated than its blueprints. That complication entails serious unavoidable risks.

- **An expense problem.** Depending on the type of materials, small amounts can be very costly, not to mention the cost of factory facilities and capital equipment.

- **A time problem.** Because parts have mass, they take time to assemble.

- **A rework problem.** If you make a design error—e.g., a part designed to the wrong shape—you may have to scrap the result (and probably the mold it came from), with all the time and money that entails.

- **A scaling problem.** You cannot take the wind tunnel model of an F18 and inflate it to full size to fight in a war.

Again, the situation with software couldn't be more different:

- **Translation.** Because software and its designs are both abstract, going from the latter to the former can be a translation, much easier than a transduction. Translations are also far more amenable to automation than transductions.

- **Cheap.** Compared to conventional manufacturing, the capital costs are modest, and there are no materials to buy. True, labor costs are high, but they would be much lower if systems were assembled from adaptable parts, using the techniques described below.

- **Fast.** Software parts weigh virtually nothing; consequently, they can be assembled literally at lightning speeds.

- **Reworkable.** You can correct design errors by modifying the resulting source code. Even better, the time and cost of reassembling modules from modified designs is small enough to be an effective way to refine and test designs.

- **Scalable.** A table with a thousand elements becomes a table with a million by adding three zeroes to its declaration. While not perfectly scalable, software is orders of magnitude more scalable than hardware.

Figure 3-2 shows that the strengths and risks of software and hardware are in opposite corners. As long as we treat software as a kind of hardware, we will continue to ignore software's strengths and manage for the wrong risks. We need a development process that uses those strengths to offset the real risks.

The waterfall is most likely to work when the project delta—the gap between the properties of the desired system and those of its "off-the-shelf" components—is small, predictable, and stable. Because software has historically been designed from scratch, not from proven, relevant, reusable components, high deltas have been the norm. While conventional engineering can easily suffer from volatile requirements, its relatively stable, unbreakable physical constraints tend to lower deltas and improve their predictability, compared to software engineering.

We are in the business of building well-defined solutions to ill-defined problems. The problems are important and endlessly fascinating—predicting the weather, stock markets, your customers, diagnosing ailments, recognizing speech and images, on and on. Even well-defined problems, say calculating interest or sine functions, have ill-defined boundary conditions.[2]

Tackling ill-defined problems is relatively infeasible in hardware, which exists in the physical world of four dimensions, as compared to software. Software, rooted in the infinite dimensional space of thought stuff, presents huge opportunities and equally huge risks. It's more than easy to find good solutions to the wrong problems. Even if we like our solutions today, the problems still remain ill defined and unstable with time. Being ill defined, however, is not something from which we should recoil. It is the nature of the beast. As long as we treat software as a kind of hardware, we remain in denial. It is time to tame the beast on its own terms.

## Iterative Design Refinement

There are two keys to taming an ill-defined problem. One is to reuse proven components to create an approximate solution quickly and cheaply enough that we can use it to refine our understanding of the problem. The other key is to design components to be adaptive, so we can refine ever better approximations from previous ones. Put the two keys together and we have the elements of a process called iterative design refinement (IDR).

While most people think of reuse across systems, IDR also involves reuse across the life of a single system—reuse across time. The "same as, except" concept of reuse is fundamental to IDR, a form of rapid application development supplanting the outmoded waterfall model. If the reality of requirements is that they are never complete, why not use a quick and inexpensive approximation as a lens with which to highlight the areas needing refinement?

As users, analysts, and developers all learn more, they can incorporate refinements by means of exception-handling frames. Such frames are project specific (e.g., specification frames). Because the underlying frames customized by the project-specific frames don't actually change, you need

---

[2]Such as choosing calculation precision, input and output formats, what errors to detect, and how to handle them.

not retrofit other systems that also reuse the underlying frames. Remember, it's not the lower frames in the hierarchy that change, it's the source code assembled and emitted by the frame processor that changes.

You can visualize iterative design refinement in Figure 3-3. What you see are three reuse-intensive iterative processes, the wheels, driving each other via three feedback loops. The three processes are business analysis and design; part design and development; and application design and development. Each process, while constrained by the other two, is decoupled and iterates in parallel. The number of times each wheel cycles depends on the size and complexity of the project, as IDR scales from minor enhancements to major new developments.

## Exception-Driven Business Analysis

Business analysis entails scoping the design from the 50,000-foot level, where those figments of our imagination dwell, down to something called the *function-point boundary*. This is a level of detail just sufficient to resolve the existence of the various subject databases, objects to manipulate them, and interfaces among them and to the outside world.[3] The analysts are not designing the details of the function points, they are resolving their existence and inter-relationships.

Analysts prioritize the requirements to get the most essential ones working first. "Most essential" can mean the 20% of the system that delivers 80% of the business benefit, or the key components that are prerequisites to building the rest of the system. In aeronautical engineering, for instance, if the plane won't fly, the cabin's interior design hardly matters. So, engineers design and test the air foil first. The same considerations apply to software engineering. For example, if the system must deliver 100 transactions per second, peak load, you design and test an architecture that can support that rate first.

From this global analysis, we determine the project's scope and estimate time and effort. We use these parameters to time-box the work, perhaps also dividing the project into parallel subprojects. The inputs to this analysis are not only the application requirements, but also two others.

One input is the architecture, or framework, available for reuse prior to beginning the analysis. These models reduce what the analysts need to think about in this wheel. Take the analogy of civil engineers designing a

---

[3]This boundary is based on the function-point concept developed by Albrecht [6]. Function points are inputs, outputs, inquiries, master files, and interfaces. Analysts can identify function points (also total them, weighted by complexity) toward the end of requirements' definition.

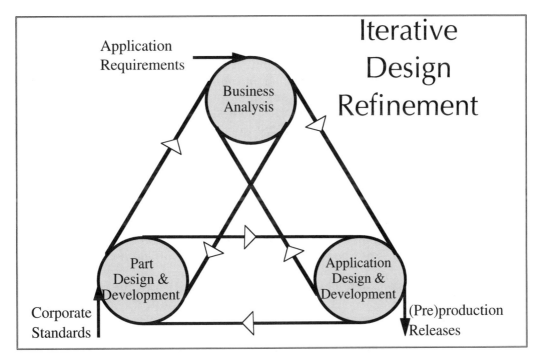

**Figure 3-3.** Iterative design refinement is a RAD approach to software development involving three reuse-intensive, cyclic processes that drive each other through three feedback loops. IDR is scalable. If a project's deltas are small, then IDR scales down to the waterfall approach.

bridge. They would start with a cantilever architecture or a suspension-bridge architecture. Then, considering the geology of the abutments, the needed length of span, and the like, they would alter the model to fit. Taking advantage of proven architectures minimizes risk and maximizes compatibility with available components.

The other input is feedback from existing versions of the system under development. Feedback from existing versions enables all stakeholders to assess how near or far the system is from delivering desired benefits and undesired side effects. With these two process inputs, analysts need focus only on unique requirements and refine them based on the currently working version.

Working models are sharp points of reference, which we can use to clarify the delta to the next version of our system. Estimating cost, schedule time, and risk in terms of deltas is more reliable than estimating from scratch.

## Preproduction and Postproduction Releases

The application design and development process assembles working systems from the organization's architecture of generic components. These parts are tailored and constrained, of course, by the function-point boundary information and feedback supplied by analysts and users. Developers design the details of those function points, such as windows, reports, files, and system interfaces. Notice that there are no external inputs to this process. It is driven completely by the other two processes, including resolution of analysis and design issues as they arise.

Developers build a working system as a series of preproduction releases, or, simply, prereleases. I avoid the word "prototype" because it has become almost pejorative in the industry, being associated with "quick and dirty," "throwaway," and "empty shell." A prerelease is a functional slice through the system, assembled rapidly from standard, high quality parts; it's just that a pre-release, by itself, may be insufficient to put into production.

The design-and-development wheel usually revolves two or three times per prerelease. The first iteration builds and tests new executables. The second one refines them, based on the stakeholder feedback from the first build. After two or three iterations, the prerelease should achieve production quality. At this point, it becomes stable and is consolidated, including testing, with prior prereleases, and is used to test subsequent ones.

Prereleases are time-boxed to manage requirements inflation. Requirements inflation, also called requirements turbulence, refers to a hallmark of ill-defined problems—the more we see, the more we want. Time-boxing means focusing on what you can deliver within a given budget and time frame. Time-boxing reinforces the prerelease prioritization rule—deliver the most critical parts first.

What happens after the system goes into production? The iterative design refinement process continues right along. Preproduction releases become postproduction releases.

## Part Design and Development

Part design and development manages the organization's reusable software assets. The need for corporate standards, application-specific parts, and generic, adaptable business rules all drive and constrain this process. These driving factors should lead to robust, well-engineered parts. Over time, as the return on investment (ROI) in the parts becomes evident, they undergo an iterative maturation process. Those parts with the potential to be incorporated into a standard architecture reach still higher levels of reusability.

Set up the reuse infrastructure as an internal profit center. It is in the business of producing and servicing products: reusable components. Projects, in effect, rent these components from the profit center. The rent comes out of the savings generated by reuse, so both the projects and the profit center benefit. If we don't treat the reuse infrastructure as a profit center, people will see it as a cost center—overhead to chop when budgets are squeezed. Conversely, the profit center approach requires managers to measure the benefits of reuse for all to see, and to use those measurements to further improve levels of reuse.

## What Iterative Design Refinement Avoids

1. "Analysis paralysis." Once the function-point boundary is reached, analysts focus on the most critical details, leaving the rest until later. Meanwhile, your working models guide your analysis with feedback that no amount of static modeling can provide.

2. Late, over-budget projects. By working on the most critical parts first, and by time-boxing the deliverables, we avoid gilding the lily—pardon me, system—we put early- and late-blooming requirements into their proper cost–benefit perspectives.

3. Massive tail-end testing that typically piles up in the waterfall. We integration-test each new prerelease with all previous ones. This process more evenly distributes the testing. And because the most critical parts are tested early and retested throughout the project, the chance diminishes that a nasty surprise will show up late in the game.

4. Unnecessary risk. Tackling ill-defined problems can never be risk free, but we do avoid freezing requirements prematurely. We do have, in early working deliverables, a powerful probe to tell us where the rails are before we get so far off track that the wasted time and money cause our project to crash.

## What Iterative Design Refinement Provides

1. Early working deliverables. Stakeholders can see early tangible progress, which sustains their enthusiasm and your credibility.

2. User understandability. Users have great difficulty comprehending entity relationship diagrams, data flow diagrams, logic structure charts, and the like. But show them a working version of the system, allow them to sit down and test drive it, and we have given them a

way of communicating with us that is highly effective—"I want a system like this except. . . ."

3. Reduced time-to-market. This benefit is inherent in building systems from adaptable components. As the QSM auditors wrote in their report, projects in their study delivered systems on average in 70% less time than comparable projects in their database.

4. Maximized bang for buck. Rather than building a system to a set of stale specifications, the iterative design refinement approach says, in effect, "Given a fixed schedule and a fixed budget, what is the very best system we can build?" We can't know the answer to this question until we actually build the system, but we are doling out funding in small increments, sustaining our momentum based on tangible evidence of working prereleases.

# Gear Your Organization for Reuse

## CHAPTER 4

> *One of the greatest pains to human nature*
> *is the pain of a new idea.*
>
> Walter Bagehot, 1869

E arlier chapters have indicated that reuse is ubiquitous in engineering and much needed in software engineering. The technology of adaptable frames embodies a principle on which we can build effective reuse techniques. I have suggested the changes in software development practices that moving to reuse necessitates and supports. All these elements are already in place.

There are two more elements to treat. To get the full benefits of reuse implies changing the infrastructure of the organization and the culture of its people. Infrastructure and culture set the ultimate limits on reuse in-the-large.

## Reuse Maturity Levels

Based on fifteen years of studying and working with organizations that practice reuse to varying degrees, I find they fall into five levels of maturity, as Table 4-1 shows. Between these levels are barriers, especially from Level Two to Level Three, that are not easily surmounted. As with most

**Table 4-1. Organizational Reuse Maturity**

| Level | Name | Typical Reuse | Typical PI |
|-------|------|---------------|------------|
| 0 | Ad hoc | 0%–40% | 13–20 |
| 1 | Latent | 40%–80% | 20–24 |
| 2 | Project | 80%–90% | 24–29 |
| 3 | Systemic | 90%–95% | 29–33 |
| 4 | Cultural | 95%–99% | 33–36 |

Typical Reuse represents reused-lines divided by total-lines (of source code, not counting blanks, comments, and code used as is). The productivity index, representing process productivity, advances sharply with the level.

things worth having, no pain, no gain. At Level Four, the gain is two orders of magnitude, almost defying belief.[1]

**Level Zero—Ad hoc.** This level provides a point of reference. As most organizations are unaware of the benefits of reuse, their PIs (process productivity indexes) currently center around QSM's industry norm of 16.9. With ad hoc reuse, individual programmers typically copy and modify source modules, usually their own.

**Level One—Latent.** These organizations, while they use frame technology, don't write their own reusable frames, other than simple data definition frames. In spite of their relative lack of interest, they do get 70 to 80% reuse from vendor-supplied frame sets. And they enjoy PIs well above the industry norm.

**Level Two—Project.** Most organizations using frame technology are at Level Two. In fact, all but one of the participants in the QSM study were at this level. Project level reuse means project developers write frames to be reused within the scope of their projects. Those projects achieve very desirable results—80 to 90% reuse and PIs from 24 to 29. But reuse is not systemic. Incompatible tools, components, and skill sets continue to coexist—so-called islands of technology. There is neither an inventory of mature, corporate standard parts, nor an infrastructure for fostering them. Level Two reuse is not self-sustaining.

[1]The reuse maturity model is not to be confused with the Software Engineering Institute's (SEI) capability maturity model. While the two models are correlated, they group organizations according to different criteria. Chapter 24 lets you assess your organization's reuse maturity.

**Level Three—Systemic.** Reuse becomes institutionalized across an Information System (IS) organization having multiple project areas within its span of control. At least 40% of developers are routinely designing systems based on a common-component architecture. Forty percent seems to be a threshold beyond which resistance crumbles and there is a rapid shift to the reuse paradigm.

Systemic reuse is characterized by having a defined (in the SEI capability maturity model sense) process to produce and support standard components. These components are robust and mature, and constitute a technical architecture for designing and building systems.The people who design and manage frames are called frame engineers. They have a separate, highly esteemed career path.

Developers are portable—because they share a common vocabulary, they can readily move between different application areas. With these characteristics, process productivity is in the low 30s, and reusable frames account for 90 to 95% of the functionality.

You might wonder why anyone would worry about going from 90 to 95% reuse—5% sounds quite marginal. Turn your view upside down, and you are going from 10% of the work to 5%. You just doubled your productivity!

With the Information Systems function achieving Level Three, the surrounding enterprise cannot sustain the pace and volume of change unless it also undergoes a fundamental attitudinal and behavioral shift. Level Three organizations typically foster incremental improvements to existing processes (as in Total Quality Management). Level Four organizations foster the invention of new processes and infrastructure (as in Business Process Reengineering). For Information Systems, this shift entails reengineering core systems accordingly. And a systemic reuse systems organization acquires the means to revamp core systems without putting the enterprise out of business. With ever more functionality being captured in technical and business architectures, the time, cost, and risk of overhauling outmoded systems becomes ever more acceptable.

**Level Four—Cultural.** The distinguishing feature of a Level Four organization is the "do better with less" attitude that the entire enterprise reflects. For example, they use metrics comprehensively to forecast each new opportunity's return on investment. Then they do whatever it takes to get that ROI!

Unlike Level Three, cultural reuse makes no distinction between frame engineer and application developer. Moreover, the entire IS group is quite compact, and often centralized. (They have gone from portable people to portable SWAT teams—James Martin's name for

Skilled with Advanced Tools.) The focus has shifted from development to orderly evolution. With so much reusable functionality available off-the-shelf, most user requirements are small "deltas" from what already exists.

Cultural reuse is associated with enormous productivity. Remember that the process productivity index reflects an exponential scale. Every three index numbers amount to doubling process productivity. Thus, Level Four organizations are as far beyond Level Two as Level Two is beyond Level Zero. That is a big jump. Because relatively few organizations can achieve PI levels of 33 to 36, they can dominate their competitors with nimbleness and sophistication.

Level Two is not hard to reach. And, for selected projects, enjoying 70% reductions in time-to-market and 84% reductions in costs is certainly not shabby. But trying to move beyond Level Two may be like hitting a brick wall.

## Barriers to Systemic and Cultural Reuse

The phrase "best practice" is facile and popular these days. My point is that you cannot get to best practice by simply knowing what it is. Getting there requires overcoming the barriers, level by level. Consider the hurdles between project and systemic reuse, let alone best practice (cultural reuse). There are at least five types: conceptual, technological, managerial, infrastructural, and cultural.

### Conceptual Barriers

There are many myths and misconceptions about reuse that cause it to fail. Some serious ones are:

- Confusing reuse with use-as-is. Not perceiving the "same as, except" nature of reuse prevents people from capturing in component architectures the tremendous amounts of similarity that exist across organizations.

- Confusing assemblers with generators. Code generators shrink-wrap their data structures and algorithms at the factory—one size fits all. Fighting with clumsy and inefficient generators has given productivity tools a bad reputation. Letting you control every assembled line of code was a prime objective of frame technology.

- Believing reuse requires big investments up front. It's not only unnecessary but wrong to try to perfect reusable components before reusing them in real systems. Reuse can and should pay for itself as it goes.

- Believing diverse lines of business embody few commonalities. We share 97.5% of our genes with chimpanzees; sheep and cows share 89%![2] Operating units that appear to be quite diverse can still overlap their cores by 90% or more. (Much more challenging is to induce quasi-independent business units to share common components with each other.)

- Designing software as a kind of hardware, thus building systems late, over budget, and misfitting current needs. We must use software's exquisite adaptability and self-modeling ability to keep our well-defined solutions suitably close to our ill-defined problems. In other words, reuse across time—the process of iterative design refinement.

## Technological Barriers

- Organizations often lack common standards, common components, and a common set of tools for reusing them. The absence of systemic reuse correlates, in large organizations, with the "one of everything" syndrome—technology islands. Imagine if every state in the United States had a different railway gauge or drove on different sides of the road, or had its own time zone.

  In the name of keeping abreast of latest developments, companies pay a heavy price beyond simple incompatibility: lost productivity, increased complexity, duplicated features, overlapping systems, and, to support all this, duplicated staff, management, and overheads. An organization is far better off to insist on a common infrastructure and on tools that may not be "best in class," but are compatible and adequate, than to indulge their gadgeteers in bleeding-edge technologies. By all means keep abreast. But when it comes to infrastructure, incompatible tools and standards are the thin edges of nonreusable wedges.

- Brittle, obsolete systems. Today's great new systems are tomorrow's euphemistically termed "legacy systems." The trick is to get out of the resource-sucking, maintenance tar pit and stay out. The pit may lack life buoys and winches, but tools and techniques do exist for the arduous task of finding components worth salvaging and of reconditioning them to be adaptable and reusable.

---

[2]Ledyard Stebbins, *Darwin to DNA, Molecules to Humanity*, W.H. Freeman and Company, San Francisco, 1982, pp 129.

- Missing or incomplete and inflexible architectures. Our industry has had decades of experience designing run-time architectures. Client-server, distributed processing, and object-oriented environments exemplify modern run-time architectural styles. But what of construction time? What about equipping ourselves to deal with changes—customizations, interfaces, enhancements—to our run-time executables? At construction time we need component architectures that are adaptive. This approach is natural to reuse. Its absence, conversely, is a barrier.

- Metrics. Reuse has a major contribution to make to many bottom-line objectives and is easy to measure, to boot. Tom DeMarco's famous truism "You can't control what you can't measure" is no truer than the fact that few IS organizations quantify quality, productivity, and flexibility. Fewer still explicitly use what they do measure to improve processes. With today's tools for measuring objectively and unobtrusively, excuses for not doing so have worn thin.

## Managerial Barriers

Everybody wants improvement, but:

- There is too little consensus on common tools and standards. Project managers, in particular, are paid to complete their projects on time and on budget. In serving this mandate, a project manager resists anything she perceives as jeopardizing her critical path, such as standards that might get in her way, or off-the-shelf components that she does not trust. (If the components are not well supported she is probably right to resist!) The net result: the greater good of the organization suffers.

- Major risks go uncontrolled. Examples: We set requirements in ignorance of what designs and components are available off the shelf. Result—we miss opportunities to reuse and hence to avoid construction work; we increase duplication and hence downstream support costs. We automate yesterday's view of the business, not what it will need tomorrow. We write code any which way, its future adaptability be damned. We expend excessive efforts designing and implementing highly normalized relational models, and ignore performance questions until it's too late to save the project. I could go on.

- Decisions focus on technology trends rather than business criteria. By its nature, reuse technology is infrastructural, not directly in the face of customers and end-users. This implies that the ability to interconnect people and systems, induce commonality, enforce standards, and promote stability are the dominant business criteria in choosing reuse technology. Trendy, "flavor of the month" technologies need not apply.

- Managers represent the established order. I do not mean to be too harsh. They are responsible for getting the day-to-day work done, and monumental change can upset the apple cart.

## Infrastructural Barriers

- The mother of all barriers is project team size. The communication burden among team members grows exponentially with size. Because systems are tightly coupled—a single misplaced period can cause arbitrary changes in behavior—precise communication among developers is essential. But developers, being human, are loosely coupled, communicating in ambiguous natural languages, such as English. The ideal team size is one. Beyond three or four, a team suffers diminishing, even negative, returns.

  In my experience, small teams are successful at tackling large projects because they adapt the available frame architectures. At Automated Financial Systems (AFS), for example, one person built an 800,000-line system in 8 months. At Noma Industries and other companies, one-person teams are the norm. In the above shops, two- and three-man teams are formed when the problem requires a lot of reusable frame writing.

- Monopolistic Information Systems departments. When an organization's users form a captive market for its IS department, even the best of intentions degenerate into monopolistic practices—too expensive and unresponsive, self-perpetuating—a barrier to innovation.

- Obsolete processes. The waterfall methodology and user intermediaries, as I explained in the last chapter.

- Obsolete supporting infrastructure. For example, when technology automates tasks on software development's critical path, previously noncritical tasks become critical. To take an example, suppose a gap in requirements normally takes stakeholders two weeks to clarify—analyze, discuss, build consensus, get necessary approvals, and give developers a go-ahead. No problem. There is plenty of work to keep developers busy. But with automated software construction, a requirements gap can put developers into a thumb-twiddling mode in a matter of hours.

**Table 4-2.  Political Cultural Barriers. How many barriers apply to your organization?**

| Change-Resistant | Hay Pay Plan | Cowboy Mentality |
|---|---|---|
| Fear of tests/measures | Peer rivalry | Gadgeteers |
| Incompetence | Lack of commitment | Plagiarism is bad |
| Entrenched apathy | Fear of failure | "All is unique" |
| Fear of the unknown | Arcane = job protection | Taboo to speak out |

## Cultural Barriers

People have written at length on organizations' and individuals' resistance to change. Table 4-2 is a cultural mosaic of attitudes that I have seen in various organizations. Most are self-explanatory except perhaps for a couple.

Hay Pay Plan. Hay is a consulting firm that provides management salary surveys and compensation plans that, while in principle take contribution into account, in practice, compensate executives based on head count (number of staff reporting to them). Under such a plan, small is not beautiful.

Cowboy mentality. By this, I mean the pervasive inattention to professionalism—programmers who cut corners, code obscurely, generalize poorly, document badly, ignore efficiency issues, and so on. Reusability is predicated on people who possess the opposite of these characteristics. The good news is reuse technology makes professionalism easier to practice.

Cultural barriers are hardly changeable overnight. As I said earlier, don't despair if your organization is not ready to achieve systemic or cultural reuse (Level Three or Four). The benefits of project reuse are considerable and quite accessible.

## Business Effectiveness Through Systemic Reuse

Like someone who wants to take up jogging, we need a vision of our future selves that is sufficiently strong to sustain the aches and pains of getting there. Possible visions include some combination of the following goals.

- Major reduction in time-to-market
- Treatment of IS as strategic enabler
- Major reductions in information systems size and cost
- Reengineering the business

## Is Your Business Case Plausible?

In order to convince yourself and your organization to undertake the paradigm shift that is systemic reuse, you need a sound business case, backed by a credible roll-out plan. The following questions should help you write a business case.

1. What are your enterprise's de facto "spans of control"—limits of cooperative behavior? If two managers who should be cooperating don't normally talk to each other, or talk but don't trust each other, they exist in two different de facto spans of control—no matter what the organization chart says.

   Systemic reuse can be successful only within a given span of control, say an IS group devoted to one department or line of business. If individual project teams are the largest units across which you can induce cooperative behavior, you are stuck at reuse maturity Level Two.

   If you plan to enlarge one span, be prepared to curtail others. Such power shifts may require a combination of carrots and sticks: decision making may have to become less consensus-oriented; people's self-interests may have to be "readjusted" toward the greater good of the organization.

2. For a given span, what are your milestones? How much of each goal can you achieve and by when? Quantifying your goals forces objectivity and, of course, the use of metrics. It also drives the urgency and aggressiveness with which you must make changes.

3. For each milestone, what percents of manager and staff time can be reallocated, or, failing that, must be temporarily added? The issue here is that everyone is already very busy keeping things going day-to-day. Certainly, the business must keep running down the road, even as it changes its tires. But nothing will happen unless management allocates enough resources to kickstart the plan. One way to alleviate risk is to "stagger-start" functional groupings within the span of control—a SWAT team works intensively with one group long enough to get them started on the rollout plan, then moves on to another group.

   This question tests whether the organization really believes enough in the vision to disrupt its well-established behavior patterns. Until reuse frees up sufficient internal capacity, you may require external management resources who are expert in the new ways.

**4.** Of the various roll-out plan details (described in the next section), which are the most problematic for your organization? How do you plan to achieve them and what are the costs?

**5.** When should the anticipated returns-on-investment pay for the costs of change? Are the ROIs adequate for the risks involved? If not, consider increasing the span of control, and/or the goals and pace of the roll-out.

**6.** What are the risks? Can they be managed, or do they appear to jeopardize critical aspects of the business? If so, consider a smaller scale effort which can be accelerated in the context of a better understanding of what it takes to move ahead.

## The Elements of Your Roll-Out Plan

The milestones of your business case set the pace of your roll-out plan. The way to write the plan is to work backward from your milestone dates to figure out how aggressively you "ramp up." This calculation may turn up some surprises that will cause you to revise your answers to the above questions. We might call this "iterative plan refinement."

No matter how aggressive your plan may be, it will encompass the following elements, discussed below.

—Involve senior executives

—Educate/Train/Coach

—Roll out projects

—Move to a hybrid organization

—Create a new career path: Frame Engineers

—Create a frame engineering department

—Evolve system and business architectures

—Measure and reward

*Involve senior executives.* They are the only element in the organization with the clout to overcome the barriers to change. They form a Reuse Steering Committee, with representation from user departments, information systems, and an ex officio reuse expert. They set policies that induce behavior and attitude changes. They also monitor and guide progress, and remove barriers. The buck stops here.

Beyond clout and strong support, senior management has to project the vision of the new organization and what it will mean to be employed there. As I said, this vision has to be strong enough in everyone's mind to make the pain well worth bearing. And executives should be perceived to be sharing in that pain. Unless their own careers are seen to be at risk, the rest of the organization will cynically hunker down until the storm blows over. You may have already seen this phenomenon a few times.

*Educate/train/coach* staff and managers (including those who manage users). Educate everyone to overcome conceptual barriers, inspire vision, and imbue the "do better with less" attitude; train generalists both to know the business and to assemble systems from reusable components; coach novices (by experts) how to apply theory to practice. Schedule courses to precede practical application just-in-time. This is all common sense. But in reality the education and coaching elements are often not well synchronized, putting roll-outs at serious risk.

*Roll out projects*, medium sized with high reuse potential. Initial projects should not be "betting the bank," but they should be real—laboratory experiments bring out the tire kickers who tell you all the reasons this new-fangled idea won't work in your environment. Real projects with tight deadlines clarify the mind and focus people on what really matters. Moreover, from real projects emerge realistic components.

Seed projects with at least one competent person per four novices. This seeding will ensure frames get written and properly reused, and novices receive proper skills transfer. The sooner you can achieve self-sustaining reuse—at least 40% of resources practicing reuse routinely—the better.

*Move to a hybrid organization.* A centralized infrastructure is required to support reuse across multiple projects and departments. On the one hand, it is centralized because it is where your corporate standards are defined and your common parts are managed. It is where your software staff is recruited, trained, and allocated to various projects. It is where their performance is evaluated. On the other hand, software projects are decentralized, so developers can immerse themselves in the business problems their skills are trying to solve. This immersion includes the frame engineers. They should not work centrally because of the ivory tower effect—designing elegant frames that don't cut it on the shop floor. By doing their work as members of project SWAT teams, frame engineers can ensure that the corporate standards are observed locally, work shoulder to shoulder with the reusers of their frames, and coach novices.

Frame engineers form the glue that binds the hybrid organization together. While allocated to a project, their salaries are paid from that project's budget. But their solid-line accountability is back to the central infrastructure, with dotted-line accountability to the project manager. Experience has taught me this lesson. Let me explain it.

The project-centric power structure, traditional in information systems departments, must be readjusted to ensure that the greater good of the enterprise is properly balanced with project imperatives. Project managers must agree up front that their own interests are best served when the frame engineers are not pressured into other duties, such as doing Johnny's work because Johnny is not pulling his weight. Yes, priorities often have to be juggled. But the solid line is there to stop expedience from becoming habitual.

*Create a new career path: frame engineers.* Frame engineers are to developers as developers are to end-users. They are a small group of people, who are known to be highly proficient programmers with a flair for generalizing solutions well. Why not give them a career path that maximizes their value to the organization? Rather than rewarding such people with Peter Principle promotions into management, provide them with equivalent salaries and highly respected roles as frame engineers. Those roles not only include developing standard frameworks but also: acting as consultants to project managers and coaches to novices, managing the corporation's reusable assets, defining system standards and software architectures, and ensuring corporate frames are properly deployed and reused.

*Create a frame engineering department.* Here are a few of its functions:

— Define standards for frames, systems, development processes, reuse metrics, measurement, reporting, and process improvements.
— Mature frames, catalogue them, and ensure their effective deployment in various projects.
— Manage the evolution of the standard frame set.
— Manage the careers of frame engineers.
— Contract frame engineers to projects.

One way to help the frame engineering department manager act as a counterweight to project managers is to make frame engineering a profit center. With a good return on investment, he gains support from senior management. He has a strong incentive to insist that his frame engineers tend to frame business, unless a project manager can make a convincing case that there is more profit to be made pulling a project out of the hole. Even then, the frame engineering department manager will reevaluate the equation every Monday morning.

*Evolve system and business architectures.* As described under technological barriers, these layered frameworks provide a common infrastructure for your systems. They make interfaces and platforms transparent; they embody corporate standards. They make possible the combination of high-speed development and high quality—faster, cheaper, better. They also make possible the cost-effective replacement of obsolete systems. There is a process (described in Chapters 19 and 20) to design, write, test, and mature these architectures, but it may take two or three years to complete. So the plan must provide milestones and resources for this process.

*Measure and reward.* Measure to improve processes, not staff. You first need to know your starting point—a baseline. Then to calculate your ROIs, you baseline-compare each reuse-based project's time-to-market, cost, and user satisfaction. Again, a baseline of component reuse frequencies will enable you to spot anomalies, prove benefits, and suggest which frames justify further investments.

Based on real benefits, reward people for their reuse efforts, psychologically and/or materially. Vision gets reuse rolling, but incentives keep it going until it becomes self-sustaining.

## It Has Been Done

There are only a few cultural-reuse organizations (Level Four). One is large, over $10 billion a year in revenue. They insist on anonymity to protect their competitive edge. It is a business operating in nearly every country in the world. They sailed through the last recession with record sales and profits. (One of their tactics is to buy weak sisters that they can vertically integrate with their business, eviscerate the existing information systems, and put in their own standard frame-based systems.)

How many software developers do you think they have? Typical for their revenues would be a department of several thousand. Their number blows my mind: 40 people. That's worldwide. And they use no outside contractors. They have hundreds of systems serving all these far-flung units. Yet with these 40 people they process over 28,000 requests for changes and enhancements per year, as well as absorbing new subsidiaries. Now you can understand why they chose anonymity.

Many organizations would be happy to reduce their information systems staff from 3,000 to 2,400, a 20% cut. That is the level you read about in downsizing stories. Getting down to 40 is something else. It involves fundamental changes, also known as a *paradigm shift.*

Of course, these 40 are not your average developers. They are all excellent frame engineers. They don't need the centralized-decentralized hybrid of Level Three. They are all in one room! Time and again they told me, "We can do what we do because we are so small."

It took only three of them, for example, to implement a network of VAXes that supports their entire European operations. My point is that in any large enterprise, there are at least 40 people of their caliber. Support them with good reuse technology and infrastructure, surround them with a company culture that rewards doing better with less, and diligently measures every ROI—then 40 top people are all they need!

Going from thousands to 40 is arduous and may not be desirable in many circumstances. Still, we now have a grasp of the magnitude of the effect that is possible. Set your goals to be appropriate to your circumstances and progress from there.

# An Advanced Form of Object Orientation

## CHAPTER 5

> *Use harms and even destroys beauty. The noblest*
> *function of an object is to be contemplated.*
>
> Miguel de Unamuno, 1914

A new paradigm typically requires the passage of a generation before it is widely adopted. During most of that period the paradigm is ignored or resisted. Object orientation dates from the early 1970s, perhaps even a few years before. It has only become well known in the last few years. Conferences on the subject are well attended. Books sell well. But evidence accumulates that the paradigm, as implemented in languages like C++ and Smalltalk,[1] is not meeting people's expectations. This chapter, which may be skipped by readers unfamiliar with OO, explains why, and what can be done about it.

Object orientation is not a set of languages. It is a set of ideas for implementing systems as collections of objects. Objects are executable modules that behave like semi-autonomous agents. For example, a business system would likely model each customer as a distinct object. Thus all customer objects would have similar functions, but each customer object would have unique data. Objects enforce *encapsulation*, meaning an object's data can be read and written only by that object's functions.

---

[1]It is dangerous to make sweeping statements about concepts that have implementations in over 60 different object-oriented languages. Experienced programmers, with sufficient insight, desire, and discipline, can circumvent the issues discussed in this chapter. But in practice, as the evidence shows, few do.

Objects can be highly interactive, invoking each other's functions to obtain and update information from each other.

A critical facet of software engineering involves optimizing the properties of "usability" (functionality, ease-of-use, and efficiency). The object-orientation paradigm, including emerging interchange standards such as CORBA, is a major step forward. Why? Because it greatly multiplies the run-time "use" of objects. Objects are an excellent way to model complex, dynamic behaviors.

But, as I explained in Chapter 2, multiple use should not be confused with reuse. Use and reuse are dual concepts, involving complimentary mechanisms. Frames and objects are such complimentary mechanisms, the former operating at construction time, the latter at run-time. As we shall see, OOs primary support for reuse—class inheritance—has serious weaknesses. To enable "reuse" to play its proper dual role, we need to eliminate those weaknesses. Doing so will simplify the analysis and design of large, complex systems, and automate the vast bulk of their construction. It will also reduce the work of evolving them to suit ever-changing needs.

Making use of the "same as, except" notion, we can observe how "classes are the same as frames, except. . . ." Incorporating these exceptions into object-oriented practices can strengthen the paradigm, putting use and reuse on an equal footing. Table 5-1 summarizes the following discussion.

## First Exception: How Frame Hierarchies Are Organized

A frame hierarchy defines how parts combine to make an object. The parts, being frames, are not themselves objects in the sense of encapsulated executables. Rather, they are data structures and/or methods that can be separately reused as components of other objects.

We draw frame hierarchies as parts-explosion diagrams, and call the relationship among components "has a," for reasons that will become apparent in the next paragraph. A higher frame is a subassembly whose components are lower level frames. In this context, a higher frame means one closer to the specification frame at the top of the hierarchy. This top is sometimes called the "root," since it is the source from which the hierarchy grows. The higher the frame, the more specific it is; the lower, the more general.

Figure 5-1 shows two ways we could model customers in an information system. In the first way, (a), each customer "has a" subassembly of three frames: identification, current status, and history. Each subassembly "has a" pair of component frames: one contains data structures, the other contains methods to manage them. The customer frame may be adapted to

**Table 5-1  Frames are the same as Classes, Except...**

| Frames | Classes |
|---|---|
| Focus is on reuse at construction-time | Focus is on run-time use (the simplest form of reuse) |
| A Frame's data and methods are not necessarily encapsulated | A Class encapsulates data and methods |
| Frames assemble into an encapsulated object by means of construction-time adaptations | Objects aggregate into an object by means of run-time links |
| Frames form hierarchies of generalized components | Classes form hierarchies of abstractions |
| Frames localize context sensitive information | Classes fragment context sensitive information |
| Frames model the domain's natural graininess | Most classes are very small—fine-grained |
| Frames adapt "same as except," freeing multiple inheritance from paradoxes | Classes inherit same as plus; hard to select, modify, or delete properties; leads to multiple inheritance paradoxes |
| A frame selects from other frames just the properties it needs | A class inherits all properties from all its ancestor classes |
| Multiple polymorphic variants can be defined within a single frame | Each polymorphic variant forces the creation of a separate class |
| It is easy to spot small differences among polymorphs | Polymorphs suffer from "sea of look alikes" syndrome |
| Typical library has hundreds of frames, accessed by a dozen or less object frameworks (templates) | Typical library has thousands of classes, accessed as a drawer full of spare parts |

various kinds of customers, such as a retail customer, and in turn adapts its more general components. For example, the identification frame could be adapted to identify customers, suppliers, employees, and so forth.

In contrast, a conventional object-oriented class hierarchy expresses abstraction relationships, not component relationships. This relationship is called "is a." In part (b) of Figure 5- 1, for example, you have a retail customer, which "is a" kind of customer, which "is a" kind of external agent, and so on. But a retail customer is not a component of a customer nor vice

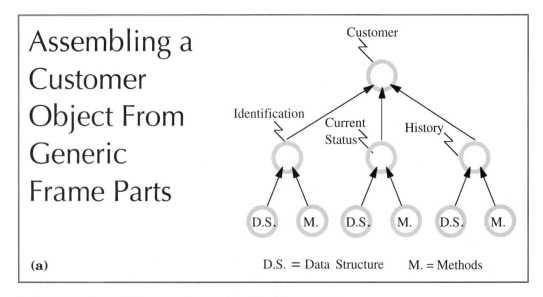

## Assembling a Customer Object From Generic Frame Parts

(a)

D.S. = Data Structure        M. = Methods

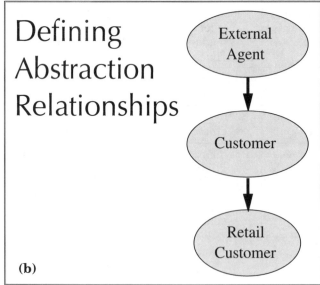

## Defining Abstraction Relationships

(b)

**Figure 5-1.** This diagram partitions a customer-information domain in two different ways. Part (a) shows a division into generic components. These components could be adapted to suppliers and employees; part (b) shows a division into abstractions. A residential customer is not a component of a customer nor vice versa.

versa. In the object-oriented hierarchy, a higher class is more general than a lower class, the reverse of a frame hierarchy.

How, then, does conventional object orientation express the "has a" relationship? It does so at run time. Components are objects; they connect by passing messages (or invoking each other) while they execute. This message passing has important corollaries:

1. A component must be an encapsulation, not a partial object—a naked data structure, for example.
2. The inheritance mechanism cannot implement "has a" relationships.
3. An aggregated object, one composed of objects, cannot localize its own context-sensitive information. Such information, which explains how the various sub-classed component objects "fit" together, is fragmented among them.

Why should we care how objects are defined? We naturally define things in terms of their most stable characteristics. Most component relationships are structurally invariant—is your head detachable at run time? Of course not. The relationship between you and your head remains invariant throughout your life!

It may come as a bit of a shock, but abstractions are less stable than component relationships. Why? Because there are many more ways to generalize something than to divide it into pieces. While we ceaselessly refine our generalizations, the real world blithely ignores them all; it just is. Therefore, structural invariance can and should play a major role in the explicit definitions of macroscopic (composite) objects at construction time. Conversely, forcing all component relationships to be defined only at run time seriously impedes proper domain analysis and design, as the rest of this chapter shows.

Causing abstractions and components to be treated as two separate hierarchies (rather than one) creates a "double meshing" (a partitioning of the partitioning) of the domain. This double meshing creates a modeling dilemma (how to ensure that the two hierarchies mesh properly), and a discontinuity between analysis and design. That is, the macroscopic objects that analysts resolve from the domain do not smoothly decompose into the microscopic classes that designers need to invent for the objects. Coad, Yourdon, and many others have complained about this discontinuity.

## Second Exception: Unify Abstraction and Component Relationships

If frame hierarchies express "has a" relationships, how do they express abstractions? Well, frames can be generic. That is, each generic frame consists of logic and data structures, parameterized to be adapted by other frames. A generic frame can give rise to an unlimited number of specialized parts, as part (a) in Figure 5-1 shows for customers. Specialization is, of course, what subclasses also do.

A major difference between frames and classes is that you don't have to derive a separate (polymorphic) subclass for each specialized part. A subassembly frame typically specializes multiple parts (from generic component frames). In this way, related specializations—all the context-sensitive details—are explicitly localized in one frame, rather than being lost among multiple (polymorphic) subclasses. By so doing, we capture both abstraction-specialization and component-subcomponent relationships in a single hierarchy. In other words, we unify the "is a" and "has a" relationships at construction time. That unification, in turn, simplifies the analysis and design of complex domains.

In a nutshell, "parts-oriented" analysis and design goes like this:

1. Take a first cut at the principal objects in a domain, their main states, and how they interact.
2. Resolve them into archetypal components by comparing their structural and functional similarities to each other and to existing subassemblies.
3. For components that don't already exist, design frames by applying simple reuse principles (e.g., A and B belong in the same frame if every known context that reuses one also reuses the other).

That's basically it; you are now ready to assemble a prerelease version of the system, use it to test your analysis and design, then iterate on the details. One aspect of this simplification is that frames express the various degrees of graininess that are directly meaningful in the domain. Some frames may be huge, others tiny, and anything in between. That is not the case with conventional classes. Most have only one or two properties each. As a result, developers cannot express macroscopic structures in single classes. That is the discontinuity problem—the lack of a way to combine abstraction relationships with component relationships among macroscopic classes.

A related problem is the nature of inheritance in object-oriented languages. It leads us to make classes very small, and that is the subject of the third exception.

## Third Exception: Adapt Rather than Inherit

Conventional inheritance mechanisms are too weak to handle the numerous small tweaks necessary, especially to data structures, to deal properly with multiple and repeated inheritance. Examples include the following:

1. Unless a method can be inherited as-is, you must redundantly recode its unchanged parts (or fragment the method). Unfortunately, the smaller the difference, the larger the redundancy within which it gets buried.

**2.** Modifying inherited data structures is discouraged.

**3.** Classes normally inherit everything; they inherit every property from every ancestor class. As Scott Guthrey put it, "You get the whole gorilla even if you only need a banana."[7]

To avoid the problems caused by weak inheritance, object-oriented designers are taught to derive tiny subclasses, one or two small properties each. As a result, they drown in a sea of (polymorphic) look-alikes.[2] As Tom DeMarco remarked, "Libraries with 30,000 objects are virtually useless." In contrast, typical reusable frame libraries contain about 200 frames. As a result, you need far fewer frames to span a given domain. The complexity of the domain representation goes down and reuse per frame goes up. The ultimate bottom line is, as QSM reported in its study in Chapter 1, it works.

## A Visit to the Object-Oriented

In the fall of 1994, Computer Science Corporation invited me to speak to its Object-Oriented Action Group in Boston. The group consists of corporate information officers and other managers from companies trying to build systems using C++ and Smalltalk.

I was a bit apprehensive about this "opportunity." Would I be dodging tomatoes? Would their eyes glaze over? Or would they simply dismiss me as irrelevant? I sat through a whole day of speakers, listening to one after another echo the lack of significant reuse from their efforts to date. I was surprised by this unanimity. I had not thought that people so committed to object orientation would admit that they were not achieving one of object orientation's fundamental claims, reuse.

Then I gave my talk, much like what you have read in these first few chapters. After it, Dr. Nicholas Vitalari, a Computer Science Corporation vice president and executive director of CSC Summit, told the audience:

> "You have just seen the future. You have seen where object orientation must go if it is to survive. It has to move toward a manufacturing paradigm for constructing objects. Mr. Bassett has shown us a new epistemology for object-oriented information domains."

The audience gasped, asking what "epistemology" meant.

> "It is a way of understanding how to represent the information in a domain," Vitalari responded.

---

[2]A generation ago, the redundancy dilemma in example 1 above caused people with subroutine libraries, the then-popular reuse strategy, to drown similarly.

People came up to talk with me afterward, saying things like: "You've just discussed the dirty little secrets that everyone wants to ignore." One said: "You are about 10 years ahead of us." Another asked: "Can we fix what we are doing, or do we have to start all over again?" Again, I was surprised by their candor.

More samplings:

- A 1995 survey to determine the "state of OO" [2], polled 72 members of the Connecticut Object Oriented Users Group. Having analyzed the results, the surveyors concluded: "the 'satisfaction index' with OO seems to be mediocre at best with the majority of respondents giving it a '2' on a scale of 1 to 5" [8].

- A tutorial at an object-oriented symposium in October 1995 cited QSM's Productivity Index (PI) in the 18 to 20 range as evidence of object oriented's success [9]. You may recall from Chapter 1 that QSM is the metrics company having an extensive industry database of software project measurements. As shown in Figure 1-1, the industry average PI is 16.9; frame project PIs averaged 26.2, with all 15 projects above the range considered a success at this OO symposium.

- More generally, OO conference presenters seem satisfied with 40 to 50% reuse (or is that multiple use?). Such PIs and reuse levels would alarm frame technologists.

To sum up, frames are not meant to replace objects; rather they are complimentary. A frame is in essence an adaptive, generic class, adaptive in the way it highlights changes to the smallest details of component frames. Generic in the way it defines an archetypal example, parameterized to give rise to an unlimited number of small or large variations. By bringing "has a" and "is a" relationships together at construction time, and by strengthening the inheritance mechanism to deal with "same as, except" reuse, object orientation might yet fulfill its promise to inherit the earth.

# Reuse Underlies the Practice of Engineering

## CHAPTER 6

*Software lacks the institutionalized mechanisms of a mature engineering discipline for recording and disseminating demonstrably good designs and ways to choose among design alternatives.*

Mary Shaw

*S*oftware engineering became a popular term due to a 1968 NATO workshop by that name [10]. Software has had a precocious childhood and a turbulent adolescence. Long on ivory tower ideas and religious wars, it has been short on general principles of proven practicality. There is a great need to set this hand-waving discipline on solid foundations. One of these foundations is the ability to reuse solidly designed components and subassemblies. This capability to reuse is an established routine in older branches of engineering, such as electrical and aeronautical engineering.

Signs of nascent maturity in software engineering include:

1. The interest in object-oriented design and programming, where new classes inherit capabilities from existing classes.

2. The continuing expansion of frame technology, the principal interest of Part II.

3. The growth in interest in domain analysis, which breaks down software domains into reusable components, discussed further in Chapter 14.

## What Is Engineering?

Before proceeding with a detailed study of frame technology, we need to set the software engineering stage. Just what is engineering? By answering this question, we will appreciate, on the one hand, that long-standing engineering principles do underlie the development of software.

Shaw provides an excellent model, using civil and chemical engineering as examples, of the germination of any engineering discipline. She shows how current software practice has evolved from a craft to a commercialization stage, and why it is not yet professional engineering [11].

### Definition of Engineering

Shaw's working definition of engineering is:

> The disciplined application of scientific knowledge to resolve conflicting constraints and requirements for problems of immediate practical significance.

"Definitions of engineering," she continues, "share some common clauses:

**Creating cost-effective solutions. . .** Engineering is not just about solving problems; it is about solving problems with economical use of all resources, including money.

**To practical problems. . .** Engineering deals with practical problems whose solutions matter to people outside the engineering domain—the customers.

**By applying scientific knowledge. . .** Engineering solves problems in a particular way: by applying science, mathematics, and design analysis.

**To building things. . .** Engineering emphasizes the solutions, which are usually tangible artifacts.

**In the service of mankind.** Engineering not only serves the immediate customer, but it also develops technology and expertise that supports the society."

Let us apply some aspects of this definition more specifically to software engineering.

## Use of Resources

"Engineering makes economical use of all resources, including money."

Enabled by sound principles of electronic engineering, computer technology has sustained for decades an exponential growth in cost-effective power and capacity. Much software piggybacks on that growth by sweeping inefficiencies "under the hardware rug." Some computer manufacturers' operating systems reflect this attitude as do many commercial packages. Yet, even the most conceivably fast machines would be prostrated for billions of years by such straightforward problems as playing a perfect game of chess. Preeminent concern for time and space efficiency is not only a professional attitude, it's integral to cost effectiveness. In short, software engineering has a way to go in economizing the use of computing resources.

## Service to Society

"Engineering not only serves the immediate customer, it also develops technology and expertise that supports the society."

This principle is an important aspect of reuse in engineering. Software practice has been singularly backward in sharing solutions to problems that avoid reinvention of similar wheels. Given that information is the stock-in-trade of software, this irony illustrates that effective mechanisms for sharing have yet to become standard in software. Our cultural aversion to plagiarism, also known as the "not invented here" syndrome, is deeply ingrained. Sharing solutions, or reuse, thus, is not only a technical issue, but also a cultural one.

Indeed, most computer science course assignments implicitly shun reuse. Students write programs from scratch, then throw them away. How much more interesting and appropriate projects would be if we required students also to extend, adapt, and/or improve model solutions (developed by their teachers and their peers and selected for their pedagogic value).

## Conflict Resolution

"Resolve conflicting constraints" is a fundamental component of Shaw's definition, yet current software practice often ignores it. Software systems, for example, often force end-users to act unnaturally:

- Poor or nonexistent exception handling,
- Inconsistencies among user interfaces,
- Information shown out of proper context,
- Slow response times,
- Redundant data entry.

And when software developers resolve conflicts and inconsistencies, they use mostly ad hoc techniques—the "any which way" that typifies a preengineering craft.

Current wisdom, in fact, implicitly denies that the systemization of conflict resolution is important! Three examples illustrate this:

1. Database normalization is a theory that helps us to define data tables that are independent of each other and of the processes that operate upon them [12]. As an analysis and modeling technique, the theory is valuable.

   Well-tuned database implementations, however, are always "denormalized," made to reflect the context-sensitive nature of reality. Yet denormalization somehow remains less respectable than normalization. Recently, a very large project to build a complex customer information system failed, due in no small part to an attempt to implement the databases in fifth-normal form—even the parts of phone numbers were segmented into separate tables.

2. Integrated CASE technologies foundered because conflict resolution was ignored. They insisted on developing systems by starting with the view from "50,000 feet," then descending to (executable) ground level by adding layer upon layer of detail. Each layer had to be strictly consistent with all higher layers, even though higher layers are but idealizations of reality. Were conflict resolution systematized in these tools, the 5 to 20% of exceptions would be highlighted and would automatically add, modify, or delete the idealized rules as necessary.

3. The use-as-is view of reusability, discussed in the last chapter, implicitly assumes that incompatibilities between modules never arise. Because the assumption is false, the complexity resulting from our ad hoc ways of coping has grown into a major headache.

That computers epitomize the ultimate in logical, repeatable behavior is another major bias toward consistency. But our bias toward zero inconsistency severely limits the sophistication of software systems. The reason is that our capacity for complexity is used up achieving perfect consistency. Building a part that is consistent with every possible situation that exists or may come up is far more demanding than building a good approximation that can be easily tailored, if needed.

In reality, inconsistency is common and perfectly normal, scientific and cultural biases notwithstanding. In succeeding chapters, we shall see how frame technology systematizes inconsistency handling.

## Sharing Solutions

Shaw emphasizes that engineering critically depends on developing and sharing a reusable corpus. On the one hand:

> "Engineering shares prior solutions rather than relying on virtuoso problem solving";

> "Most engineering disciplines capture, organize, and share design knowledge."

On the other hand, she characterizes current software practice differently:

> "Knowledge about techniques that work is not shared effectively with later projects, nor is there a large body of development knowledge organized for ready reference";

> "Current notations for software designs are not adequate for the task of both recording and communicating";

> "Software in most application domains is treated more often as original than routine."

In Shaw's evolutionary model of engineering practice, the maturation of a supporting science is the last critical step necessary to enable professional engineering. In civil engineering, a combination of statics and materials science matured by 1850; in chemical engineering, atomic theory was combined with the science of large-scale chemical processes around 1890.

In Shaw's model, current software practice is "in some cases craft and in some cases commercial practice." Characteristic of the commercial stage of evolution are practices such as "life-cycle models, routine methodologies, cost estimation techniques, documentation frameworks, configuration-management tools, quality-assurance techniques, and other techniques for standardizing production activities."

Shaw's characterization of engineering fits an emerging software engineering discipline, including her observation: "Engineering emphasizes the solutions, which are usually tangible artifacts."

In the case of software, tangibility is not an issue, given that software solutions are always manifested through hardware interpreters, which are tangible. Software itself, of course, is "soft." It is that intangible softness that is the source of essential differences between software engineering and traditional engineering. We require a modeling schema and a supporting theory, effective in "the packaging of [practical models] for operational use." I hope to show that frame technology is such a schema.

## Software Engineering: A Definition

In light of the foregoing, there should be no surprises in the following definition of software engineering:

The application of formal[1] methods in the cost-effective development (analysis, design, construction and evolution) of cost-effective software systems.

The definition's double emphasis on cost-effectiveness is long overdue in a 40-plus-year-old industry where techno-speak still baffles business concerns. The first "cost-effective" aims at delivering systems when people need them, at prices they can afford. The second one reflects the need for the delivered systems to deliver real benefits.

The definition also echoes the duality of construction time and run time. Each enables the other. Construction obviously enables execution. And execution feeds back to construction in order to guide the evolution of subsequent versions. This process is called *iterative design refinement*, the subject of Part III.

## Is Software a Synonym for Programs?

The very word software needs discussion. The usage of this word is still a matter of some controversy. It originated as a colloquialism, an appealing synonym that distinguishes computer hardware from programs. Yet pioneer Edsger Dykstra does not use the word. For him software is not soft; programs should have formal proofs of correctness.

In current usage, programs are representations of fixed (not necessarily terminating), algorithms, distinct from subroutines, objects, macros, and so forth. But that is not the key distinction. Programs can be implemented in computer hardware or firmware or software; they can be stored on tape, disk, paper, RAM, ROM, or, for that matter, clay tablets.

The subtle but important distinction here is that software should be soft. When it is burned into ROM or inscribed on clay tablets, it has lost an essential property: trivial modifiability.

It is the very softness of software that provides incredible and dangerous power. To offset this danger, most commercial software, most pro-

---

[1]"Formal" is used in the dictionary sense of a logical or systematic series of steps, not in the restricted sense of "formal methods" as one of the methodologies of software development.

gramming languages, and even some hardware architectures, actually prohibit self-modifying software.

## Validity

But we do apply this power of easy modifiability as we try to satisfy ever-changing real-world needs. Is it not common for requirements to be wrong? That is why proofs of correctness are a distraction when it comes to the more important question of validity—whether or not a software system aptly models the real world.

Detecting requirements errors is not amenable via proofs; rather, it is a never-ending series of judgment calls, involving problem analysis, design, and end-user feedback. This process is where most of a software engineer's time and efforts are spent, and rightly so.

The ability to build robust systems to a given set of specifications should be taken for granted.[2] In fact, techniques exist for preventing and catching errors, both at construction time and at run time. But no combination of proofs can demonstrate system validity.

## Circumstances Change

Even if we could agree that a program was both true and valid, it would not remain so for very long. Because both the reality in which software operates and our perceptions of that reality change unpredictably, software has a unique role in the way we deal with such change. Software's nature is to be soft, to keep up with changing circumstances. To expect a new proof of correctness every time a system changes is silly.

Thus, software development has more to do with engineering than with theorems. No civil engineer can offer a proof that a bridge or a building cannot fall down. Overstress them and they fall. Complex software systems are similarly vulnerable. Engineering is a discipline for designing and building complex structures. It is applicable not only in the traditional fields, but also in software. Engineering disciplines are not infallible. It is not practical to prove software correct every time circumstances require change, but engineered systems do operate cost-effectively within their tolerance limits.

---

[2]Robust certainly does not mean error-free. In "The risks of software," Littlewood and Strigini cite Edward N. Adams's finding that the mean time to failure for over one-third of the defects in well-debugged software systems is more than 5,000 years! In other words, robust systems continue to operate because most of the remaining defects occur on a scale of tens to hundreds of years [13].

## Getting There from Here

As we approach the end of Part I, I can put flesh on the bare bones of this chapter by looking at one company's early experience in advancing from where most IS departments are to a successful reuse culture. It is a topic, "Managing the Transition," to which I devote much more space in Part IV. Meanwhile, I rely on Mark Twain, who once said: "Few things are harder to put up with than the annoyance of a good example."

I shall call the company involved the Great Trust of Canada. The events to be described took place in the latter half of the 1980s. At that time, we had fully developed frame technology, but did not yet appreciate some of the finer points of its application.

At the time, Great Trust had 4,500 employees in several hundred branches. Every employee was a hands-on user of software systems. The company had 230 people in IS development and 130 in operations. Of the 230 IS people, about 90 were analysts and 100 were programmers. The software people also supported a sister company in the real estate business with more than 300 branches.

I estimate that this organization achieved systemic reuse maturity (Level Three). It had no user intermediaries. It dedicated fewer than five people to so-called maintenance. It had centralized the management of its frames. When its frame engineers worked on a project, they were solid-line responsible to central frame management with dotted-line accountability to decentralized project team managers.

Some extracts from the company's internal "User Guide for Computer Automated Programming" indicate how this central group operated. Called Systems Development Productivity, it had a mandate to "automate the automaters." It supported the project teams, provided common reusable shells, identified opportunities for reuse, and worked on project teams building application frames and corporate frames, as required. It also provided in-house training.

The Systems Development Productivity group defined the standards that were incorporated into the company's architecture. The Guide goes on to say that frames are "best suited for larger projects." Further, it expects that "additional productivity gains will be achieved as our repository of reusable frames grows." Moreover, "the systems specification level (SPC) DECREASES THE AMOUNT OF MAINTAINABLE CODE FROM 100% TO 10-30% [capitals in original]." The Guide adds, **"This concept of 'reusable' programs is extremely important as we move from a 'job-shop' mode to an 'assembly-line' mode** [bold in original]."

### Trust System

The Trust system was a mission-critical application, the largest in the organization. It was a CICS on-line mainframe system. It was built in 1987–1988 by a team who had no prior exposure to on-line work. They had been batch-systems programmers. They were pioneers in two important ways:

1. They used an iterative RAD (rapid application development) methodology before we had worked out fully the concepts of iterative design refinement (which we take up in Part III).
2. They understood the importance of construction-time architectures in an era when the concept was virtually unknown.

In three months, they designed and built a sophisticated six-layer frame architecture to prepare the ground for the Trust system. Figure 6-1 illustrates the six-layer architectural pyramid. The bottom four layers are

**Figure 6-1.** Architecture enforces design standards; layers promote design reuse.

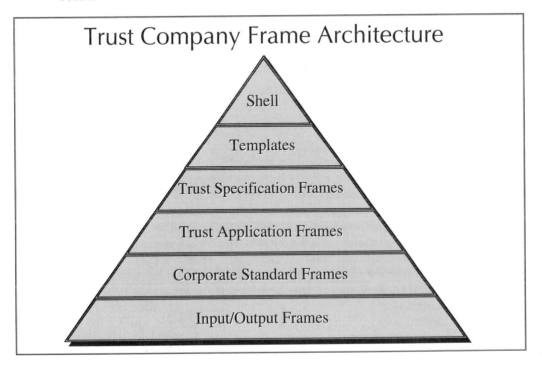

typical of what many organizations use today (quotations are from Great Trust):

1. I/O frames (acquired from Netron) are at the base.
2. Corporate-standard frames ("written to ensure maximum portability [i.e.,] that hardware code incompatibilities are isolated").
3. Trust application frames (that "can also be used to hide detailed technical and business logic from the developer").
4. Specification frames.
5. At the fifth layer are templates, which predefine types of executables.
6. At the apex of the pyramid is something they call a "shell."

Without a shell, a developer would fill in one template per specification frame (defining a single executable module). A shell predefines a complete subsystem. In other words, filling in a shell causes all the necessary templates to be filled in to define a subsystem of executables. So, the first cut subsystem can be built and tested immediately. Then, based on user feedback, programmers tailor the SPCs, and the RAD process iterates.

The Trust system consisted of over a thousand executables, constructed from about 965 frames. That is a very large number. Today, we would design such an architecture to have less than half as many frames by combining related functions and ensuring they were appropriately generic.

The team, seven developers and two frame engineers, achieved enormous productivity—over 300 programs finished in two months! This kind of speed creates its own problems, to the point where the team wondered out loud, "Is shell development too quick?"

## Lessons Learned

For example, users, unused to extreme responsiveness, became excited and began demanding silly things. As a result, the project suffered from "runaway requirements."

Another lesson the team learned was that, rather than build the architecture in advance, they should have co-evolved it with the Trust system. Many pragmatic issues arose during Trust system iterations that the architecture could not have anticipated. These issues made it necessary to rework frames in ways that would otherwise have been unnecessary. In particular, because of the architecture's prematurity, the group had generalized some frames in ways that were inappropriate, causing them to perform poorly. This experience is one of the reasons why iterative design refinement stresses that components should co-evolve with the systems that use them.

Still, for 1987, building a large Trust system so quickly was a remarkable achievement. In hindsight, the experience stressed to me that one of the strong benefits of the layered architecture approach was its ability to define and enforce consistent design standards. Strong standards not only eliminated many system integration bugs; it enabled the team to reuse the architecture in other systems by simply replacing the Trust application frame layer.

By reparameterizing their shells and recustomizing the automatically created specs, the team went on to build quite different systems very rapidly, functionally speaking. For example, one person, with no prior CICS or mainframe experience, built a CICS front-end for their "security access rules" in three months. He developed, on a workbench personal computer, 74 application-layer frames, used a shell to build the system, tested it on the PC, then ported it to the company's mainframes.

Using frames, the Great Trust of Canada made substantial progress toward solving the perennial problems of software development: too many requirements fluctuations, too many developers, too long a period of development, too many projects awaiting development work, too many defects.

With this example in mind, we proceed to a more thorough consideration of the principles and practices underlying them—a reuse approach to software engineering.

# PART 2

# FRAMES ENABLE REUSE

In all walks of life, people much prefer to start with a solution they know works and modify it to suit the current problem, rather than start from scratch. It comes as no surprise that people prefer this with software, too. Indeed, the star programmers are the ones with the best filing systems.

Paradoxically, the more "soft"ware is modified, the "harder" it seems to get. This is because the modification process is typically a haphazard, error-prone, very slow,

71

manual editing activity. The cumulative results are far more complex—read late, expensive, faulty, inefficient, inflexible, functionally impoverished—than they ought to be. This situation is commonly referred to as the "software crisis."

The good news is software can be engineered to be truly "soft." That is, people can start with high quality existing solution components, define the changes necessary to accommodate different circumstances, then mold those components into new solutions automatically. And do it again and again, both across systems and across the life of a single system.

The concept of "use-as-is" is but one of many deeply ingrained habits of thought that cause misunderstandings of software's essential properties. This particular attitude implies that a software component, if it is to be reused, ought to be used as is. In this part, I begin by challenging this assumption and other implicit assumptions about the nature of software.

As I said before, it is the very "softness" of software that provides both incredible and dangerous power. To tame and harness this softness requires formalizing the simple, universal, "same as, except" problem-solving paradigm: namely, this problem is the same as that one, except. . . . The act of formalization leads straight to frames. Frames and frameworks, therefore, are the focus of this part.

Frame technology assembles custom software from adaptable frame components quickly and inexpensively. The technology is independent of language and problem domain, and hence is suited to the construction of all kinds of software.

Analysis and design benefit strongly from the presence of frameworks. A framework is a set of frames with a layered architecture that isolates different sources of change. They allow complex systems to be designed, built, and evolved as small differences, called deltas, from high-level models.

The technology of frames is simple to understand from first principles. It is also the "same as, except" numerous other programming ideas and mechanisms, and is often confused with them. These ideas and mechanisms include: macros, subroutines, copy-and-modify, skeletons, generators, programming languages, structured programming, artificial intelligence frames, and, of course, object-oriented classes. After grasping frames from first principles, I find the comparison to other ideas sheds considerable light on how to better engineer software for reuse.

Part II then gets into the fascinating questions of how to analyze an information domain, what archetypes are and why they are the best way to bridge from ill-defined problems to well-defined solutions. From archetypical patterns, how do we design the best software parts with which to build our solutions? From many years of practical experience have come empirical answers to these questions. I conclude Part II by illustrating some of the answers in a detailed case study taken from a real project.

# Use Is to Reuse as Run Time Is to Construction Time

O ver the last four decades, the world has witnessed the dawn of the information age. Illuminating this dawn is a brilliant new light: *software*. Software is pure essence of mind, suitably formalized to command and control society's engines of automation: computers. It is the very "softness" of software that sets it apart. It enables computers to model both reality and fantasy with equal ease and arbitrary precision. It can be rapidly altered as needs and perceptions change. With its unlimited potential for useful representation and easy adaptability, software is the ultimate modeling medium.

In industrially advanced countries today, some 60% of the work force have jobs that involve information. The value of these countries' computer software and hardware, including the work needed to run computer systems within organizations, is almost a tenth of their gross national products [14]. In the United States, the National Research Council has estimated inhouse development at $150–$200 billion [15].

Capers Jones estimates there are 1,750,000 professional software personnel in the United States and perhaps 12,000,000 in the entire world. In addition to the professionals, he estimates 10,000,000 end-users in the

United States and 30,000,000 in the world who do some programming [16]. The point of these numbers is that software dominates the costs of information.

## Overcoming the Malaise

For all its vibrant growth, there is a chronic malaise in the industry: poor productivity and quality, software that is hard to modify and hard to move from one type of computer to another. Because of our failure to grasp the nature of software, productivity and quality improve very slowly. For example, the predominant opinion is that software productivity improves only in the range of 5% per year. In comparison, computer processing power and capacity advance at about 25% per year. As an outcome of the slow growth in software development capability, five-year backlogs for new applications and two-year backlogs for modifications are commonplace.

Moreover, software production is still largely a cottage industry. We unconsciously reveal this mentality when we refer to ourselves as "shops" and "software houses." It is ironic that software, the very powerhouse that drives automation, is itself still largely a handmade commodity. The basic reason is clear enough: the industry is young. There is still a high rate of technological change—in computers, the networks that interconnect them, and the languages and techniques for designing and constructing software systems.

As I already mentioned, as with all new paradigms, there has been an initial period of healthy confusion. Software's "craft" phase has been an exciting half-century of brash precocity, experimentation, fads, buzzwords, religious wars—an on-going turmoil. Recently, there have been signs that software practice is beginning to mature, to acquire the substance and rigor that are the hallmarks of an engineering discipline. Emerging from this pandemonium are principles that can lead us out of the wilderness.

## Principle of Reuse

Fundamental to all mature engineering disciplines is the principle of reuse. These disciplines take the concept so much for granted that it is not even part of their jargon! Indeed, it is basic to all problem solving. However, the nature of reuse and its role in software engineering is more subtle than in the "hard" engineering disciplines. For example, the "software IC" metaphor implicitly suggests reusable components are fixed-function modules, an analogy with integrated-circuit chip engineering . This metaphor confuses run-time use with construction-time reuse, a confusion with serious implications for software engineering.[17]

Reuse is not a matter of stringing callable load modules together in different combinations. Reuse has to be more general because we must be able to change the properties—data attributes and logic—that are held fixed during execution. Since such modifications cannot occur during the execution of software modules, reuse is fundamentally a construction-time concept. All run-time properties derive from it.

Once we better understand the nature of reusability and properly formalize it, that understanding will catalyze the transformation of our craft into a true engineering profession. Such a maturation will have far-reaching effects on the chronic ills of current practice.

## The World Is NOT Made Out of Lego Blocks!

One might argue: "What's the big deal? We have been reusing software since the first stored-program computer, half a century ago. People reuse object modules every time they invoke them. Programmers copy existing source-code when writing 'new' programs. What's so hard to understand about reusability?"

### Identical/Nonidentical

When thinking about reusability, it is natural to look for what is the same about a group of things. One frame and a few subassemblies span many models of Chevrolets, Pontiacs, and Oldsmobiles. When engineering a group of physical products, one strives to maximize the number of identical parts they share. Obviously, the fewer and more alike the components, the simpler the resulting products are to manufacture and the more reliable they are to operate.

In the physical world, the source of most of our intuitions, even "sameness" is a hard problem. Until Henry Ford, we didn't know how to mass produce identical copies of complex things, let alone nonidentical copies. It has taken most of this century (with an aggressive push from Japan) to achieve mass production techniques that can tailor each unit of production to a customer's custom specifications.

Unlike the concrete world, in the abstract world of software, "sameness" is trivial. The software world makes identical copies of the most sophisticated systems in almost no time at almost no cost. Moreover, whenever we execute or interpret any module (e.g., a program, a subroutine, a method) we reuse it as-is, trivial as this kind of reuse is. This "Lego Block" concept of reuse has been ingrained in us since the earliest days of computing—and why not! We can design a black-box software module, analogous to a physical mechanism, to exhibit any behavior we desire at run time.

## Too Many Parts

Still, if we had enough such parts to build whatever we want, would this be effective reuse? No. There would be just too many parts for their reuse to be practical.

The argument is reductio ad absurdum: In theory, to assemble all software—in fact, all information—just two parts are sufficient: 0 and 1. Indeed, the entire world as we know it is made from two kinds of elementary particles, electrons and quarks. Nevertheless, when we contemplate building a bridge, we don't start with electrons and quarks as the building blocks.

Similarly, starting with individual bits, or even larger aggregations than bits, is not effective in building information systems:

1. The gulf separating the properties of bits from the properties of the things we want to build is just too vast. We want the properties of our constructs to be readily predictable from those of their components. The components and the resulting constructs should be close enough for our minds to bridge the gap.
2. The time and complexity of assembling vast numbers of very tiny individual parts are overwhelming.

We can greatly reduce time and complexity by: ($a$) creating parts that are reusable assemblies of other parts, and ($b$) constructing a variety of different results from a small number of generic part  by modifying those parts. The results are the same,  except for their  differences.

Corollary: The generic parts reused in ($b$) are not use-as-is!

No one today thinks of binary bits as reusable software components, but in the pioneering days of the computer age we had no choice. Machine languages were all we had: the first generation programming languages (1GLs). Because sizable binary programs were far too difficult to write and to modify correctly, people soon invented higher level languages:  the so-called $n$GLs, where $n = 2, 3, 4, 5$.

Assembly languages (2GLs),
Fortran, Cobol, Lisp (3GLs),
Focus, Mantis, Oracle (4GLs),
Prolog (5GL).

Each increase in $n$ was accompanied by the same hyperbole: "self-programming computers have arrived!" Even decades ago, when the pioneers first invented 2GLs, they gave them overstated names, such as IBM 1401 Autocoder.

In the early days, people also invented "code generators" such as RPG (report program generator). More recently, computer-aided systems engineering (CASE) tools and object-oriented languages have emerged. These languages employ the Lego Block strategy. They contain various statement types: IF statements, assignment statements, and so on. Each statement type is a reusable, black-box component (its properties are immutable). By putting such parts together in different combinations, programmers can write an infinite number of possible programs. Although using the statements of an $n$GL is essentially similar to reusing object-oriented program subroutines or objects, there are interesting differences, depending on $n$.

## Level of Graininess

On the one hand, for n ≤ 3, a programmer can tune an $n$GL program for performance and for compliance with complex requirements. But, because the graininess of the statements (reused components) is small, she will be distracted by too much detail. The myriad details obscure a clear perception of what a program does. It is like building a skyscraper entirely with bricks and mortar instead of prefabricated forms.

On the other hand, the "$n > 3$" languages (including subroutine libraries, code generators, and CASE tools), allow a programmer to express abstractions that describe the problem domain directly. Their graininess can be too large. This situation is analogous to building a wall without being able to cut its bricks or use mortar. The resulting program is hard to tune for adequate performance, or for subtle dependencies and conflicting constraints.

Especially for software, engineering complex systems entirely from macroscopic black boxes is no more desirable than engineering them entirely from microscopic ones.

> **Effective software reuse involves components of all size scales, down to bits.**

There is no level of graininess below which software constructs never have to go, other than the bit. A single bit can change the fate of the world! This is not to say that tiny parts should be prevalent. Having to discriminate among thousands of tiny parts will cause developers to drown in a sea of look-alikes. Having relevant large parts ameliorates this problem as long as they are easily tuned to the needs of their surrounding contexts. This tuning involves small parts, and so the circle goes.

## Need for Construction-Time Variability

The world is too full of conflicting constraints and subtle dependencies for immutable parts to fully anticipate all the circumstances with which they will have to cope. Moreover, the world changes quickly and unpredictably. For these reasons, use-as-is components, no matter how well thought-out and flexible, are an insufficient organizing principle for the complexities of software engineering.

Given the insufficiency of the Lego approach, why is it perennially popular, manifesting itself in so many guises over the history of our craft? The shallow answer is simplicity. Any problem domain can be artificially simplified or temporarily held static to allow the strategy to work for a while. At a deeper level, inappropriate physical and mathematical metaphors shape our intuitions about software. Moreover, there has been little appreciation of the fundamental role that context-sensitivity plays in software reuse.

> **Effective reuse involves construction-time variability that is sensitive to differing contexts of use.**

Much of what follows is devoted to the necessity of this principle.

## The Construction-Time Run-Time Duality

Use-as-is is a very important property of executables. It is also the simplest possible notion of reuse. If the shoe fits, wear it, goes the old saying. Beneath most software issues, however, lie too many ill-fitting shoes.

Sacrificing performance for flexibility is very common. Unnecessary execution-time penalties accrue when binding parameters to values that never change during execution. Such unnecessary sacrifices are symptomatic of software engineering's immaturity. Construction and execution serve different purposes, and hence are guided by separate principles.

> **Principles of operation concern *usability*—functionality, efficiency, and ease-of-use—of executable modules.**

> **Principles of construction concern *reusability*—usability, generality, and adaptability—of components of executable modules.**

To understand these principles, we require clear definitions of some basic terminology (listed in Table 7-1).

**Table 7-1    Terminology Necessary to Understand Construction-Time / Run-Time Duality**

Module
Interpreter
Semantics
Execution
Run time
Usability
Construction interpreter
Construction time
Construction semantics
Component
Parameters
Reusability

## Module

Whether it takes the form of object code, source code, graphic diagrams, or any other form, a module is a group of symbols—a piece of text and/or data—that can be consistently referenced as a unit. Other than this definition, a module has no meaning by itself—no intrinsic semantics.

## Interpreter

Whether it takes the form of a computer, another module (which has its own interpreter), a human being, or any other form, an interpreter is an agent capable of interacting with modules, using a set of fixed rules. It too has no intrinsic semantics other than this definition.

## Semantics

Semantics is the behavior (e.g., the output) resulting from a given interpreter interpreting a given module. It is important to realize that meaning, or semantics, does not reside in either modules or interpreters. It resides in the interaction between them. Change one or the other and the semantics could change dramatically. Semantics also has time-and-space aspects. That is, two interpreters of the same module may produce functionally equivalent behavior, but in the process consume vastly different amounts of time and/or space.

## Execution

Strictly speaking, execution is the direct interpretation of a given (binary) module by a given (binary) computer. In this book, when a module can be interpreted by a compiler-linker-computer trio, or by any *functionally equivalent* interpreter, it also will be said to be *executable*.

## Run Time

This is the time during which a module is executed. Because it is customary for many different modules to be executed by the same interpreter, we customarily ascribe semantics to executable modules. While we can discuss the properties of a program or the attributes of data as if they were inherent in the modules that represent them, this practice is a dangerous shorthand. Meaning is in the eye of the interpreter. When people and computers both read a formal definition, their interpretations are often significantly different!

We describe the behavior of an execution as a sequence of *states*. At each moment in time, we consider the execution's *state* as the values of everything that can change during execution. These are the values of all the module's and interpreter's variables, including inputs and outputs (if any). Why variables? Things that remain constant during execution have no behavior; they cannot be used to distinguish between two behaviors of the same module. (Again, if we always use the same interpreter, we can restrict attention to the *states* of the module being executed.)

## Usability

A module's usability depends on: its *functionality* (execution semantics), its *efficiency* (time and memory consumption), and its *ease-of-use* (interface complexity).

At run time, the states that a module can and cannot have limit the ways the module can be *used*. The usefulness of a payroll program, for example, critically depends on functionality—correct sequences of states among many variables having to do with incomes and deductions. Efficiency—the time required to go from beginning states to end states, and the size of the memory required—also limits the ways a module can be used. Finally, usability obviously depends on ease-of-use. How easily can a module's various users (both human and other modules) obtain its functionality?

The study of execution semantics has dominated computer science from the beginning. The present writing focuses on construction semantics in the belief that software engineering is the offspring of both computer science and conventional engineering. Just as automotive engineering deals with vital issues beyond how cars are driven, software engineering involves key issues beyond software use. Thus we approach construction by formally distinguishing reuse from use.

Reuse deals with variability that cannot be part of a module's execution semantics. We are talking about varying properties that are usually static at run time, such as: program logic, the attributes of data structures, constants, the number and types of subroutine arguments, and on and on. Yes, in principle, any of these properties could vary during a module's execution. But if no properties of a module were invariant, it wouldn't be well defined. Nor could its outputs be trusted. The fact that, from time to time, we do need to modify properties that remain fixed during execution is why reuse involves a different type of variability.

We are talking about the construction of modules. When a module is (re)constructed, what varies is the form, content, and *interrelationships* of its components. A programmer constructs a program by writing certain programming language statements in a certain order. A code generator does much the same thing. Construction semantics can also be provided through automated construction interpreters.

## Construction Interpreter

Informally, construction time is the time during which run-time invariant properties of executable modules can be varied. An agent that carries out such variations—a programmer, component assembler, code generator, compiler—could be called a construction interpreter.

Providing an automated construction interpreter to complement existing automated execution interpreters establishes a duality between the two kinds of variability. And the terms *construction time* and *run time* can be interleaved without confusion, as might be exemplified in artificial intelligence applications. However, we don't need AI to tap the power of this duality.

## Construction Time

Construction time is the run time of a construction interpreter whose execution results in executable modules.

## Component

A component is a module that is interpreted by a construction interpreter. Confusion over the word "component" arises because executable modules are linked into larger aggregates. Thus programs and Dynamically Linked Libraries (DLLs) become components of a system; object-oriented's objects become components of "aggregated objects." While linking executables is an important aspect of execution semantics, it is treated by other authors extensively. I focus on mechanisms that alter the form and content of modules, things linkers never do. So for us, a component is always a part of an executable module.

Components are read-only inputs to the construction interpreter, just as executable modules are read-only inputs to the execution interpreter. In both cases, it's the outputs that vary, depending on the inputs.

## Construction Semantics

If we settle on one construction interpreter and one execution interpreter, then we can ascribe construction semantics to components, which, for their invariant portions, includes execution semantics. Reusability deals with varying the form, content, and interrelationships of components in order to construct executables.

## Parameters

Just as run-time variables are essential to automated use, construction-time variables, called *parameters*, are essential to automated reuse. The existence of dual sets of parameters permits independent optimization of dual properties:

1. Execution modules can be designed to optimize usability (trading off functionality with performance and ease-of-use), and

2. construction modules can be designed to optimize reusability (trading off usability with generality and adaptability).

## Reusability

As the dual of usability, we can characterize reusability as follows:

> **A component's reusability depends on: its *usability* (construction semantics) its *generality* (scope of applicability) and its *adaptability* (ease-of-reuse).**

At construction time, we seek to construct modules that are usable (as defined for usability). This is the dual of modules at run time being functional. What is the construction-time dual of efficiency? Well, similar modules should have common components. This fact suggests a construction efficiency goal: to be able to build the most modules from the fewest components. That goal makes generality the dual of efficiency. Finally, adaptability—how easily a component's various reusers (other components and software engineers) can apply it to each context of use—is clearly the dual of ease-of-use.

Reusable components, whose parameters are bound at construction time, yield usable modules, whose variables may or may not be bound at run time. This decision should depend only on usability considerations, sacrificing neither generality nor adaptability.

The parallel with biology is more than coincidental: Construction-time DNA yields run-time organisms; DNA and its organism are two different representations of the same thing. This duality serves two complementary purposes. DNA facilitates modifying organism properties; organisms facilitate executing them, as-is. The same can and should be true of software, for the same reason.

The concepts introduced in this chapter are interrelated. As I introduced in Chapter 2, Figure 7-1 visualizes the relationship of these concepts. Exploring the implications of one construction interpreter, frame technology, is the essence of the rest of Part II.

**Figure 7-1.** Generality and adaptability can be optimized independently of usability.

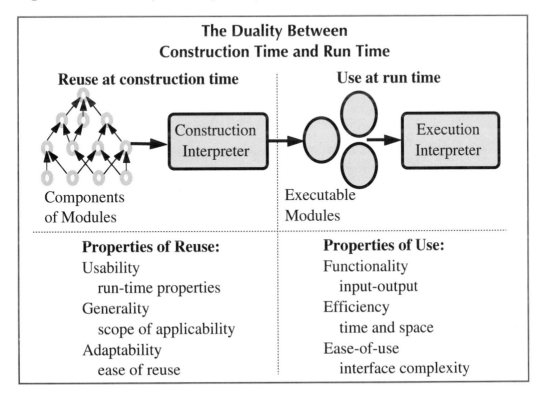

# An Introduction to Frame Technology

## CHAPTER 8

> *No rule is so general, which admits*
> *not some exception.*
>
> Robert Burton, 1621

T he previous chapter set the stage for frame concepts. This chapter introduces frames through the concepts that led me to them: copy-and-modify, same-as-except, and software parts.

These parts can be understood from four different perspectives. For software manufacturers they are bills of materials and subassemblies; for analysts they are archetypes and deltas; for designers they are domain experts and design models; and for mathematicians they are lattice elements and resemble fractals.

## Copy-and-Modify

Even without automated tools, good programmers reuse software. When called upon to write a new program, they look for a similar one, then copy and modify it. By renaming, adding, modifying, deleting, and rearranging various details, they create the new program. Productivity studies show that the star programmers are the ones with the best filing systems.

Copy-and-modify works because many pieces carry forward with little change. Considering the time that has already been expended to debug the subtleties in those pieces, much new effort can be avoided. People naturally prefer to reuse things that work than to start from scratch.

Although a step in the right direction, copy-and-modify fails to realize the full potential of software reuse. It also creates gratuitous complexity:

1. Which modules get reused is ad hoc. There is no systematic way of knowing what is available. Major reuse opportunities are lost.
2. Because the modules were not designed to be reused, it often takes more work to ascertain which chunks of text are relevant and edit them than to write them from scratch.
3. Programmers typically edit character by character, all the time trying to be fastidious about grammar and punctuation. This work is error-prone technical drudgery.
4. Copying creates redundancy, causing our systems to become unwieldy and complex. Over time each copy experiences random evolutionary drift, adding further unnecessary complexity. Worse, should we change the original and want it reflected in all its customized clones, we are condemned to modify them, one by one, manually.
5. Worst of all, we lose control over which details make each module unique and which are common among modules. The unique details are scattered in various nooks and crannies, indistinguishable from surrounding text. Even though two modules may, in reality, be 95% the same, programmers who "copy and modify" have to treat them as if they have nothing in common. This reality, more than any other reason, accounts for the alarming statistic that 70 to 80% of software effort is dedicated to so-called maintenance.

Copy-and-modify is the most basic and by far the most common form of reuse. While effective in the hands of virtuoso programmers, as a routine engineering discipline it leaves much to be desired. Frame technology was born out of these frustrations.

## Same-as-Except

In everyday life, an effective way to describe something unfamiliar is to start with something familiar, then describe the differences. A convertible is a car with a removable roof. Answering "what" and "how" questions in this manner is so familiar to us that we are seldom consciously aware of it. It's called same-as-except: $X$ is the same as $Y$, except. . . .

Perhaps without thinking of it that way, we naturally specify software requirements by exception:

"I want a file management system with the following:

- Automatic key assignment when records are created;
- Instead of actually deleting records, rewrite them with deletion flags that I can later undelete;
- When scrolling through the file, display sequence numbers in bold for all records with deletion flags; etc."

We do this to reduce complexity. Complexity should be proportional to novelty, not the size of the system (e.g., lines of code).

***Effective reuse highlights novelty—makes exceptions easy to see and control—while hiding what is routinely the same.***

Copy-and-modify is obviously a form of same-as-except. The basic problem is that copying does not hide and modifying does not highlight. Factoring exceptions from sameness formalizes and quantifies the notion of similarity,[1] as opposed to the notion of sameness.

With this background on reuse, we can now proceed directly to frames.

## Frames Are Software Parts

The frame concept has been defined and used in many ways. Marvin Minsky, for example, pioneered its application to artificial intelligence [18]. Intuitively, a frame, such as a picture frame or a car frame or even a frame of mind, is a generic structure that can give rise to a variety of specific instances. Thus, a sufficiently flexible car frame could give rise to Lincolns and Cadillacs, sedans and convertibles. Software frames are inherently more flexible than the physical kind because properties can be deleted as easily as added.

Even genes have framelike properties. They are strings of text, which when copied and modified, give rise to unique organisms. Each cell has a complete copy, but selects only certain regions of its DNA strands for protein synthesis, depending on cell type. Moreover, extraordinary diversity arises from small genetic differences—mutations to single letters (nucleotide base-pairs) in DNA texts. Nature evolves incredibly complex species this way.

From our discussion of copy-and-modify, the lesson for (software) engineering is to satisfy a maximum diversity of requirements with a minimum quantity of components.

---

[1]A module's similarity to another module can be measured as the size of the differences divided by the size of the common parts.

Before getting more formal in the next chapter, here are four general ways to understand frames.

## Perspective 1.  Software Manufacturing:  A frame is both an adaptable component and a bill of materials

Ordinary bills of materials, say for manufacturing TV sets, simply itemize components (chassis, bezel, controls, power supply, etc.) to be used on an as-is basis. Moreover, such a bill is not a component; it is a piece of paper. Frames are not only components in their own right, but they itemize their sub-components and contain commands for adapting those subcomponents. Figure 8-1 lists the contents of a typical frame.

A frame is a bill of materials that tells how to (sub)assemble (part of) a module from itself (as one of the components) and its sub-bills (component frames). Frame commands assemble and adapt, meaning that they add, modify, select, iterate, instance, and delete frame details during module assembly. While it is a form of copy-and-modify, it avoids all the problems discussed earlier.

**Generic frames have parameter defaults.**  What does Figure 8-1 mean when it uses the adjective generic? Any data definition, method, or frame command can have embedded parameters. As you may recall, for us parameters are construction-time variables. As such, they are set to default values by a given frame and overridden by any frame that reuses it. Defaults can be nested, and can range in graininess from null to the entire frame. This default-override mechanism enables the properties of a frame to be altered by other frames. This is what it means to say a frame is generic—it can give rise to an unlimited number of specific instances. ("Instance" can also be used as a verb, meaning "to take something generic and make it specific.")

**Figure 8-1.**  A typical frame contains these elements.

```
Frame name and short description.
Default generic-parameter settings for this frame.
Default component details:
     Generic data types (zero or more);
     Generic function types (zero or more).
Default subassembly references (zero or more):
     Frame X and commands to adapt X and its subassembly;
     Frame Y and commands to adapt Y and its subassembly;
     and so on, naming subassemblies by their topmost frames.
```

Frames rely heavily on the use of default values. All frame details, even its name, can be defined as frame parameter defaults. Defaults endow a frame with its reuse potential. When frame *A* reuses subassemblies *B* and *C*, as shown in Figure 8-2, *A* can override any defaults in frames *B* through *F*. But *A* only overrides what it needs for its context. By so doing, each frame localizes all information relevant to its context.

Figure 8-1 shows the two kinds of information a frame contains:

1. *Default generic data types and function types,* which are instanced and assembled into the module unless overridden by another frame. In Figure 8-2, frame *B* can be overridden by frame *A*. Frame *D* can be overridden by both *A* and *B*.

2. *Frame commands,* which specify how default definitions in subassembly frames are to be instanced, selected, extended, modified, deleted, and/or iterated. (These commands can themselves be default-overridden from other frames, just like the data and function types.) The next chapter goes into the details.

As you might expect, just as mechanical parts are shown in parts-explosion diagrams, so frames are organized into hierarchies or trees of subassemblies as Figure 8-2 illustrates. (Technically, frames form mathematical lattices, as explained at the end of the chapter.)

**Specification frame.**  The root of an entire tree (assembly) is its *SPeCification* frame, or SPC for short. It is a module's master bill of materials, specifying its major subassemblies (subtrees), and any details unique to this module. Assembly begins with the SPC and proceeds down the tree, as shown in Figure 8-2. Each frame, including the SPC, being the root of its own (sub)tree, can *adapt* any frame in its (sub)tree.

This raises an interesting question: what happens when two or more frames on the same path to the SPC want to adapt the same underlying frame? (In the diagram, suppose *A* and *B* both adapt *E*.). If they try to set the same parameter to different values, the frame closest to the SPC wins. (In the diagram, *A* would win; it is the SPC.) It wins because it is in a position to take into account things that are invisible to frames deeper down in the tree. In other words, global overrides local. (*B* and *C* would never conflict over *E,* as two separate versions of *E* are produced.)

An SPC contains all and only the information unique to one assembled module. Just like other frames, it sets parameters to adapt various features of its components and adds in its own expertise. Unlike other

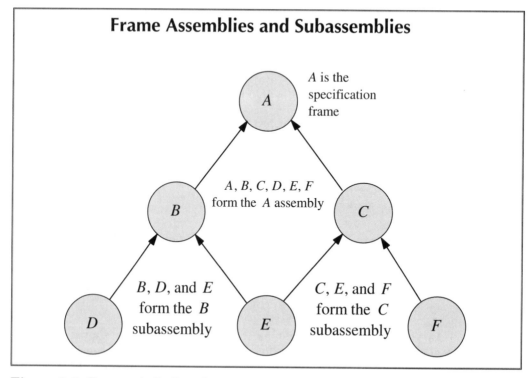

## Frame Assemblies and Subassemblies

$A$ is the specification frame

$A, B, C, D, E, F$ form the $A$ assembly

$B, D$, and $E$ form the $B$ subassembly

$C, E$, and $F$ form the $C$ subassembly

**Figure 8-2.** Frames $A, B, C,$ and so on are pictured as a parts-explosion diagram with the specification frame at the "root" (top). The arrows show how the parts go together. $B$ adapts $E$ differently than $C$ does.

frames, it is not normally reused and hence lacks parameters for being adapted by other frames.

There is a one-to-one correspondence between SPCs and constructed modules. Thus, programmers think of SPCs as programs (or objects, sub-routines, documentation, etc., depending on the environment). An SPC is both a blueprint for assembling a module and the one place where all the details that distinguish it from every other module can be kept.

***Important note:*** frames are read-only inputs to the frame processor. Frame adaptation is really shorthand for saying: at program construction-time, the frame processor parses the frames, performs the embedded frame commands, and emits a text module according to those commands. This is how we copy-and-modify while keeping our custom details isolated and our common components available for reuse. We eat our cake and still have it, so to speak.

Of course, prior to module assembly, some agent must see to it that the necessary frames are in the appropriate read-only libraries. This agent may be a human frame engineer, a software tool capable of generating frames from other information, such as data dictionaries and system models, or a combination of people and tools.

Now let's switch perspectives.

## Perspective 2. Domain Analysis: A frame is a domain archetype (plus deltas)

Two simple ideas, archetypes and deltas, will help us connect frames to analysis.

**Archetype.** "The original pattern, or model, from which all other things of the same kind are made; prototype."

*[Webster's New World Dictionary]*

**Delta.** A small difference between two things.

*[from mathematics]*

Surprisingly, a relatively few archetypes characterize or span almost any given domain of practical importance.[2] All useful instances then arise as deltas from these few archetypes. This fact has been exploited to great effect in many diverse domains, from communications theory to manufacturing.

Analyze the bird domain and you find six or seven archetypical birds will, with small deltas, give rise to all birds, including those that don't fly. They should also be able to give rise to hybrids. The mythical griffin (Figure 8-3), for example, should be derivable from bird and beast archetypes by, among other changes, deleting unwanted details from each component (Figure 8-4). A griffin is less than the sum of its (generic) parts.

Frames represent archetypes because each contains an archetypical example of an information domain or category. Frames also embody a strong notion of delta. A frame isolates all the differences between the specific forms of the parts it needs and the generic forms defined by the component frames in its subtree.

In Figure 8-1, the commands to adapt the subassembly frames are the deltas. The strength of this embodiment lies in the complexity reduction it achieves. All the context-sensitive information needed to make generic

---

[2] Cognitive psychologists would not be surprised. They know that people organize their knowledge into domains containing at most six or seven categories (subdomains) each. When a domain's complexity exceeds this limit, we form new (sub)domains having their own (sub)categories. (We probably limit ourselves to six or seven nesting levels too, but that is already enough to store many hundreds of thousands of different categories and the relationships among them.) So it is not the domains that have any intrinsic validity, but rather how our minds superimpose order on the world.

**Figure 8-3.** The mythical griffin is the result of the ancients making an imaginative combination of the eagle and the lion.

parts specific to the context of one frame's domain is explicit and localized. This avoids the need to clutter your component libraries with specific variants, and informs you of exactly why those variants exist and exactly what was done to make them mesh smoothly.

To build software, we must define data and functions. The software archetypes, then, are data types and function types, suitable for framing (i.e., potentially reusable). Encapsulations of these component archetypes, in turn, are defined by "wrapper" frames, higher level frames (including SPCs) that package data type frames with function type frames. In the

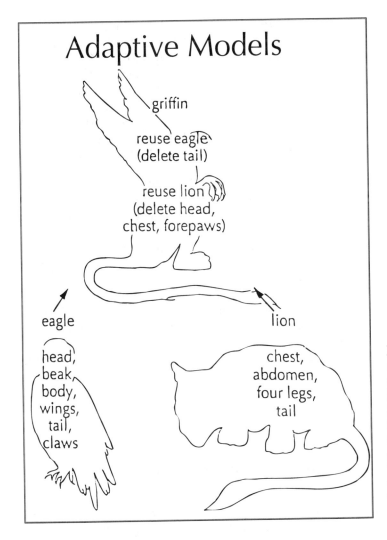

## Adaptive Models

griffin

reuse eagle
(delete tail)

reuse lion
(delete head,
chest, forepaws)

eagle

lion

head,
beak,
body,
wings,
tail,
claws

chest,
abdomen,
four legs,
tail

**Figure 8-4.** The ancients took the chest, abdomen, legs, and tail from the lion, and the head, wings, claws, etc., from the eagle, but had to delete the lion's head and the eagle's tail. Thus, making a new entity is not only additive, but also frequently subtractive.

business world, for example, inventory, customer, order, and supplier are familiar *data types*; and data entry, file updates, and inquiries are but a few of the common *function types*. Such types, when formally framed, are adaptable to unlimited specific executables.

Data-entry, for example, refers to a large category of modules that share a common set of properties, such as buffers and protocols for window controls and error handling. These properties can be embodied in standard, reusable data-entry frames. Each data-entry module, requiring a specific graphical user interface and specific methods associated with the

GUI's controls, can be specified in other frames that adapt the standard ones. In this way, any module can be constructed from a relatively few standard frames, each characterizing the archetype of an infinite category of specific components. As Figure 8-1 shows, a standard frame may contain zero or more data types and function types, parameterized for adaptation.

**Business reengineering.**  Frames emphasize the symmetry between similarities and differences. But to exploit reuse effectively, we need to understand how to strike a new balance between commonality and diversity.

On the one hand, we can obtain diverse behaviors from surprisingly small deltas. Scratch the surface of an apparently custom system and you find 90% of it can be shared with the rest of your business. On the other hand, the archetypes—common standards—need to be agreed upon. Unless each business unit appreciates how small the deltas can be (hence how large their common interests really are), each will set their own local standards, incompatible with the rest.

It takes trust, cooperation, and hard work to improve the greater good. Learning to share and work together, especially after years of "doing your own thing," is not a technology issue. It is cultural and political. And I have the scars on my back to prove it!

One way to convince people is to show them how easy it is to override the standards, deriving local standards from the more generic ones. If the deltas to the standards reach a level where a new standard would yield smaller deltas, then it is time to consider a change to the standard. Frame technology encourages and supports this evolutionary process. The rest is, as they say, an exercise left to the reader.

## Perspective 3.  Systems Design: A frame is a domain expert, a design model

We can think of a frame as specializing in a particular domain, a category of similar problems. It is a domain expert[3] containing one or more design models, collectively spanning its domain. But experts rely on other experts to help them. So it is with frames. They form hierarchies, corresponding to their subdomain—that is, component—relationships.

If the least reused frames are SPCs, it stands to reason that the most reused frames are at the opposite ends of frame trees from the roots (SPCs), forming the trees' "leaves." Reuse correlates inversely with context-sensitivity. What are the most context-free subdomains? In business domains, they involve input and output, the external environments of sys-

---

[3]Frame domain experts are not to be confused with AI's expert systems.

tems. Thus, the most reused domain experts are frames that handle generic database schemas, screens, reports, network protocols, other systems, operating systems, and so on. Figure 8-5 illustrates how you might design a layered architecture with frames.

**Architecture-related frames.**  In the middle levels of Figure 8-5 each frame models specialized domain knowledge that is less generic, more specific, than the frames it adapts. For example, the layer of frames just above the "system architecture" layer (I/O) is usually a "technical architecture." This term refers to environment-specific models for interfacing with users and other systems, standard log-on security checking, standard data-view constructors, etc. Those frames, in turn, rely on the input/output frames that are standard across organizations. Higher layers may embody "application" architectures or design models. One layer may be standard for the enterprise; a higher layer may be standard to a particular business unit and/or application domain.

The reason for layering these architectural models is to isolate sources of change, to minimize their impact on the other layers. Client-server environments, for example, may have a layer that isolates the API (application program interface) calls from the client and server layers. The layer will be designed as separate executables if they execute in separate

**Figure 8-5.**  Construction-time architectures are isolated into layers. The layers may be further subdivided. By layering, we minimize the impact of changes, including switching between monolithic and distributed-processing architectures at run time.

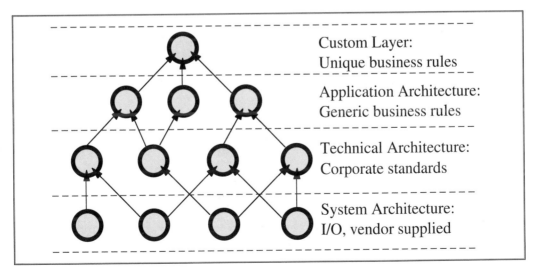

Custom Layer:
Unique business rules

Application Architecture:
Generic business rules

Technical Architecture:
Corporate standards

System Architecture:
I/O, vendor supplied

computers. Change isolation is the key to keeping maintenance costs low. Figure 8-6 is reproduced here with the kind permission of Barclays Bank. It is a simplified view of their construction architecture for managing customer cases, from inquiry through approvals to final disposition.If the system requires a distributed-processing run-time architecture, simply align the various layer boundaries with the desired distribution. The subassemblies in any distributed layer can be encapsulated as callable executables having their own SPCs. You may also design the frames to permit hybrid monolithic and distributed run-time architectures.

**Unify development with maintenance.** Specifying software as deltas to what exists unifies the techniques employed in new development with those employed in "maintenance." That is, new development specifies deltas to existing frames, in the same way maintenance specifies deltas to the frames used to construct the existing system, using exactly the same techniques.

Until now, without a way to keep models and their customizations (archetypes and deltas) isolated from each other, programmers felt they had to resort to ad hoc patches, programming "any which way." But by "framing" a module—parameterizing its logic and data structures as reassignable defaults—programmers can control unpredictable and apparently random changes (deltas) systematically. We shall see how this approach converts ad hoc programming into disciplined engineering.

**Figure 8-6.** Generic case application framework. With permission of Barclaycard.

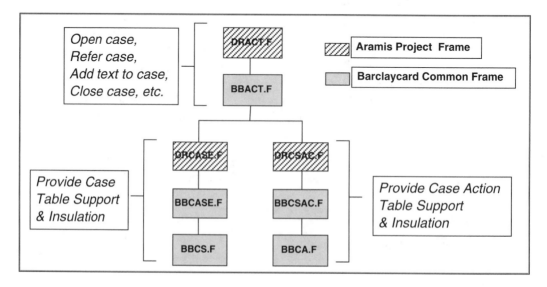

## Perspective 4.  For the Mathematically Inclined: Frames form lattices and resemble fractals

Frame-tree paths extending down from specification frames lead to progressively more heavily reused frames. In Figure 8-2, $A$ reuses $B$ and $C$, $B$ reuses $D$ and $E$, and $C$ reuses $E$ and $F$. In general, if $X$ reuses $Y$, then $Y$ is as reusable as $X$, or more so.

*Proof:*  whenever $X$ is reused, so is $Y$; but $Y$ might also be reused in some other subassembly $Z$, without $X$.

Frame reuse always implies the potential to adapt, and vice versa. These verbs conform to the mathematical notion of a partial ordering. Denoting "reuses" and "adapts" by "$\geq$" allows us to express their partial ordering properties:

Reflective:       $X \geq X$              for all $X$

Transitive:       $X \geq Y$ and $Y \geq Z$       $=> X \geq Z$

Nonsymmetric:  $X \geq Y$ and $Y \geq X$       $<=> X = Y$

Several interesting consequences flow from partial orderings. One is that frames form lattices and are thus characterizable with modern algebraic methods and theorems.

Another is that the ability of frames to both adapt and be adapted by other frames implies that components and composition operators are not essentially different. This unification of operators with operands underlies why frames handle context-sensitivity well. If an algebra of context-sensitivity lurks here, I speculate it would greatly increase our understanding of complex systems.

Finally, the self-similarity of fractals, at different levels of granularity, is reminiscent of frames' self-similar organization into trees of subtrees. (Lattices become trees by replicating elements that have more than one parent.) Could fractal geometry help us better analyze information domains?

# Frames Work

To sum up the discussion, each frame is both a component and the "boss" of its own subassembly. Being the boss means it can preempt any part of any subordinate's default solution. That is, the boss prevails over all subordinate frames in assigning values to frame parameters. Of course, the boss has bosses too, with the boss of an entire hierarchy being its SPC.

A frame processor assembles a frame hierarchy into a complete and specific module, such as a custom source program. Frames may produce text modules in any language(s), including English. All software can be constructed from frames because ordinary text files are trivial (use-as-is) frames. Adaptable frames enable most complexity to be hidden, making sophisticated systems easier to design and, particularly important, easier to adapt to changing needs.

Sound principles of analysis and design depend on sound principles of construction. Frames aid domain analysis by formalizing archetypical examples of each component of the domain (category). We explore this subject in Chapter 14. Frames aid design by embodying proven design models, engineered to be adapted to the specifics of a given system. By factoring the models into layers that isolate different sources of change, as Figure 8-5 illustrates, systems can be designed to be portable and easy to evolve (maintain). Chapter 16 goes into details.

Frames seem to be related to the mathematics of lattices and fractals, subjects awaiting further study.

But theory and rhetoric aside, in practice, frames actually work. They are being used to simplify the design and automate the construction and evolution of complex business systems, as the QSM study described in Chapter 1 attests. And frames are not limited to business systems. They can formalize reusable solution components in any problem domain and in any language.

# The Main Frame Commands

## CHAPTER 9

> *Humpty Dumpty sat on a wall;*
> *Humpty Dumpty had a great fall;*
> *All the king's horses and all the king's men*
> *Couldn't put Humpty Dumpty together again.*
>
> Mother Goose

Frame commands play two roles: operationally, they automate the copy-and-modify editing that programmers used to do by hand; conceptually, they provide a precise vocabulary for articulating software engineering issues. This chapter defines frames from a formal, operational point of view. This view gives us the vocabulary we will need to discuss the engineering concepts.

Before explaining the main commands, we need a wee bit more terminology:

A frame's ancestors are all frames above that frame on the path to and including the specification frame. Ancestor frames are also called *adaptor frames*, as any of a frame's ancestors may adapt it.

A frame's *descendents* are any frames below it in a frame hierarchy, where the SPC frame is always at the top.

A *parent* is an immediate ancestor.

A *child* is an immediate descendant.

*Siblings* are children with a common parent. Figure 9-1 illustrates these terms.

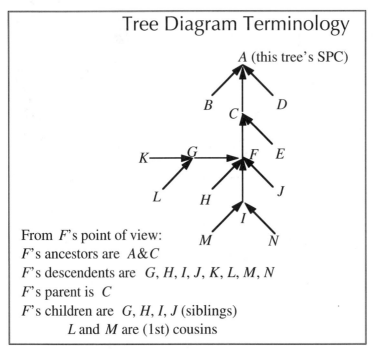

From *F*'s point of view:

*F*'s ancestors are  *A*&*C*

*F*'s descendents are  *G, H, I, J, K, L, M, N*

*F*'s parent is  *C*

*F*'s children are  *G, H, I, J* (siblings)

   *L* and *M* are (1st) cousins

**Figure 9-1.** By analogy to a family tree, the frames in a frame hierarchy may be referred to similarly.

A *frame* is a module, stored simply as a text file. Each frame should be independent of its adaptor frames. If a child has more than one parent, as shown several times in Figure 8-5, each parent can adapt that child independently; each parent in effect gets a separate copy to adapt. (In this way lattices are processed as trees, as shown in Figure 8-2.)

*Frame-name* is the name of the file that stores the frame.

*Frame-text* refers to a group of one or more lines contained within a frame. Frame-text is either a *frame command*, or *generic-text*. Generic-text may contain embedded parameters.

## Variables and Expressions

A *var* is a parameter, a frame variable whose values are assigned by frame commands and referenced from within frame-text. A *var* name can be composed of capital letters, digits, underscores, and/or dollar signs. All other symbols act to terminate the name. *Var* values are arbitrary symbol strings.

An expression may be a string delimited by quotes or apostrophes. An expression may also be an integer (delimited by spaces), or an arithmetic expression delimited by parentheses.

*;var*  A semicolon prefixed to a *var* is a reference to the current value of *var*. *Var*s may be defined as null (zero length strings). You can also test to see if a *var* is defined or not. If *var* is defined, *;var* causes *var*'s value to be substituted in place of *;var*. Such references can occur at any character position in frame-text, including command names, frame-names, break-names, and *var* names. Concatenated references such as *;A;B* are substituted from right to left; that is, *;B* then *;A*. If a value becomes part of (or is itself) another *var*'s reference, substitution continues until no semicolons are left. For example: suppose we have three *var* Names, each with a value as follows:

| *Var* Names:  | I | SWITCH1 | ON  |
|---------------|---|---------|-----|
| *Var* Values: | 1 | ON      | OFF |

Then "ON" will be substituted for ";SWITCH;I" and "OFF" will be substituted for ";;SWITCH;I."

## The Frame Processor

The frame processor emits an output file of ordinary text (text devoid of frame commands and *;var*s) from a tree of input frames. Figure 9-2 shows the path the processor takes through the frames in a hierarchy. The processor interprets each frame as a sequence of lines, starting with the first line of (usually) a specification frame. Each line is broken down and interpreted in four steps:

1. Replace all *;var* references with their values; and if any values are references, replace them too, until no *;var* references remain.

2. If the first symbol on the line resulting from step 1 is a period, the line is (part of) a frame command to be interpreted as in steps 3 and 4; otherwise emit the line resulting from step 1.

3. Parse the frame command into a list of tokens. A token is any symbol string that is delimited by spaces (and/or the ends of the line), or by

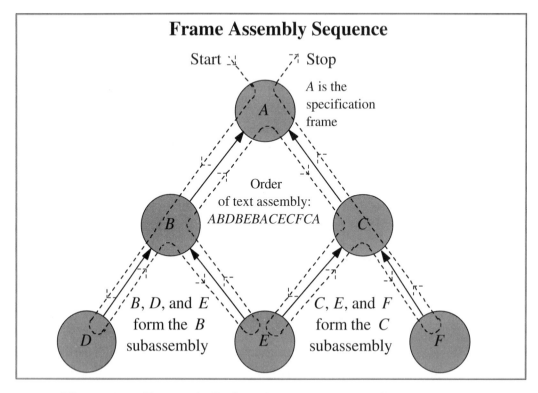

**Figure 9-2.** Frames *A*, *B*, *C*, and so on are pictured as a vertical structure with the specification frame at the "root" (top). The dashed lines show the order in which the frame processor assembles the frames.

quotes ("), or by apostrophes ('). Delimiters are not normally considered to be parts of tokens, but can be specially embedded.

**4.** Perform the Java command.

**For an animated Java simulation of the frame processor operating on the examples in this chapter, please visit Netron's web site http://www.netron.com and select "Paul Bassett on reuse."**

## Main Commands

Frame syntax is not a fullblown programming language. It is deliberately simplified in order to focus on the issues to do with adapting solutions expressed in other (programming) languages.

There are only five main commands, listed in Table 9-1. Other specialized commands exist, but are not essential to a first understanding of the technology.

**Table 9-1  The Main Frame Commands**

.BREAK (pronounced dot break)
.COPY/INSERT
.REPLACE
.SELECT
.WHILE

## Reading Frame Command Explanations

[ ] surrounds an optional token;

{,,} means choose one token from the enclosed list of tokens separated by commas;

. . . (ellipsis) means zero or more repetitions of the preceding token;

italicized names refer to tokens and other syntactic variables;

% and all text to the right of the percent symbol is a frame comment about the construction process which is not emitted.

### .BREAK *break-name*
### [*frame-text*]
### .END-BREAK [*break-name*]

BREAK declares *break-name* to be a parameter within a frame whose optional default value is frame-text. This default is processed into ordinary text unless some ancestor frame's INSERT overrides the default (see the COPY command). The following is a simple frame:

```
.%Frame Humpty
This is a Humpty Dumpty archetype.
.BREAK Egg
Humpty Dumpty sat on a wall.
Humpty Dumpty had a great fall.
.END-BREAK Egg
Poor Humpty died.
.%End frame
```

Processing Humpty yields:

---

This is a Humpty Dumpty archetype.
Humpty Dumpty sat on a wall.
Humpty Dumpty had a great fall.
Poor Humpty died.

---

BREAKs create named blocks of default frame-text. Each BREAK
END-BREAK pair brackets an overrideable property of the frame, such as
generic data types and function types. BREAKs may be nested but not otherwise overlapped. To force a property to be part of the constructed module, simply leave it outside all BREAK brackets.

BREAKs enable frames to be adapted in unanticipated ways. The
COPY/INSERT command, described next, accomplishes such adaptations.

**.COPY** *frame-name* **[SAMELEVEL] [NOCAP]**
**[.INSERT[{-BEFORE,-AFTER}]** *break-name*
 [*frame-text*]
]. . .
**.END-COPY** [*frame-name*]

COPY/INSERT suspends processing of the current frame until the tree,
rooted in (the child frame called) frame-name, has been fully processed.
The INSERTs are used to prefix, suffix, and/or override the break-name's
default frame-text. The INSERTs can act on BREAKs located anywhere in
the tree rooted in frame-name. Here is a simple example:

---

.%Frame to demonstrate .COPY/INSERT
.COPY Humpty
.   INSERT-AFTER Egg
All the king's horses and all the king's men
Could not put Humpty together again.
.END-COPY Humpty
.%End frame

---

Processing the above frame yields:

---

This is a Humpty Dumpty archetype.
Humpty Dumpty sat on a wall.
Humpty Dumpty had a great fall.
All the king's horses and all the king's men
Could not put Humpty together again.
Poor Humpty died.

---

It is important that a frame be able to adapt any of its descendent frames, not just its children. Frames designed to be "free of each other's contexts" may clash. As the "boss" of its tree, a frame has the power to resolve conflicts among descendent cousins.

Frame-text can be inserted -BEFORE or -AFTER or instead of (i.e., to override) the default frame-text associated with break-name. Note that an INSERT's frame-text is processed, not in the context of its defining frame, but in the context where the frame-text is inserted. This means the values of *vars* embedded in the INSERTed frame-text can depend on assignments (see REPLACE below) made in intermediate frames (in the chain down to and including the frame where the BREAK is defined). To delete a BREAK's default simply INSERT null frame-text, as in:

```
.COPY X
.  INSERT A %Override A's default frame-text with nothing.
.END-COPY
```

Should two or more ancestors try to override the same BREAK, the one closest to the SPC has priority. That is, the lower ancestors' INSERTs to that BREAK are ignored. This reflects the principle that context-sensitivity overrides context freedom, with ultimate authority residing in the SPC.

SAMELEVEL means the scope of COPYed frame's commands is the subtree rooted in the COPYing frame (rather than rooted in the COPYed frame). For example, if frame $A$ contains ".COPY B SAMELEVEL", then any and all REPLACEs inside $B$ have the same scope as (if they had been REPLACEd inside) $A$. Thus a frame that sets parameters can be reused by other frames.

NOCAP stops the frame processor from processing frame commands. The COPYed frame (tree) will be emitted as ordinary text; that is, you can use frames to assemble frames, or preassemble large subassemblies and simply embed them in the module being assembled.

### .R[EPLACE] *var* [SAMELEVEL] BY [*expression*]

REPLACE conditionally evaluates the expression and assigns the result to the variable *var*. "Conditionally" means if an ancestor frame has already REPLACEd this variable, then the current REPLACE is ignored; the ancestor's assignment takes precedence. REPLACE emits nothing; instead it may cause the frame processor to add or change a variable in the internal variables table that it keeps during the assembly process.

Here is a simple REPLACE example:

```
.%Frame to demonstrate .REPLACE
.R KING BY queen
.COPY Humpty
. INSERT-AFTER Egg
All the ;KING's horses and all the ;KING's men
Could not put Humpty together again.
.END-COPY Humpty
.%End frame
```

It produces the following output:

```
This is a Humpty Dumpty archetype.
Humpty Dumpty sat on a wall.
Humpty Dumpty had a great fall.
All the queen's horses and all the queen's men
Could not put Humpty together again.
Poor Humpty died.
```

Frame variables are ubiquitous. Their uses include parameterizing frame commands, avoiding name clashes, and making ordinary text into generic-text. For example, data attributes, table-names, and Boolean expressions all may be generalized with *;var* references. Frame variables can be indexed by other frame variables (see the WHILE example below); frame variables can also take frame-names as values, and hence frame-tree structures are themselves variable.

The SAMELEVEL option permits information to be passed up the hierarchy. It can be used only when frame $X$ INSERTs REPLACEs into a component frame $Y$. Without this option, the *var* defined by a REPLACE becomes undefined when $Y$ finishes (exits). REPLACE SAMELEVEL delays the undefinition until $X$, the frame doing the INSERTing, finishes. Thus *var* values set in a relatively context free frame, $Y$, can be used by its customizing frame, $X$, and hence by the rest of $X$'s subtree. Context-free information like this often cannot become known to the hierarchy in any other way. Perhaps it comes from frame vendors, or from a data dictionary.

**.SELECT** *case-parameter*
**[.[OR]WHEN** [{=, <>, <, >, <=, >=}] [*case*]
  [*frame-text*]
**]** ...
**[.OTHERWISE**
  [*frame-text*]
**]**
**.END-SELECT** [*case-parameter*]

SELECT is a construction-time case statement. It contains a list of cases: (case, frame-text) pairs. SELECT compares the case-parameter token to each case using one of the six relational operators shown above (if omitted, "=" is assumed). For all true relations, the corresponding frame-texts are processed. The optional OTHERWISE clause is processed when no relations are true. Usually, case-parameter is a *;var* and *case* is a constant.

To illustrate:

```
.%Frame to demonstrate .SELECT
.R KING BY queen
.SELECT ;KING
.  WHEN queen
.     COPY Humpty
.        INSERT Egg
The ;KING sat on the throne.
The ;KING got hit by a stone.
.        END-COPY Humpty
.  WHEN jack
The ;KING of hearts took Humpty off the wall.
Humpty became the ;KING of hearts' ball.
.END-SELECT ;KING
.%End frame
```

produces:

---

This is a Humpty Dumpty archetype.
The queen sat on the throne.
The queen got hit by a stone.
Poor Humpty died.

---

SELECT and BREAK are complementary mechanisms. BREAK exists to permit adaptor frames to INSERT unpredicted variations, whereas SELECT exists to localize known variations. To SELECT the needed version, adaptor frames need only set a *var*. When inverting a matrix, for example, regular and sparse matrices require two quite different data structures. But the Gaussian elimination algorithm can be parameterized to contain the differences in various SELECTs. Special case optimizations are another typical use for selects:

```
.SELECT ;SPEED
. WHEN speedy
      souped up variation goes here
. OTHERWISE
      normal case goes here
.END-SELECT ;SPEED
```

Instead of SELECTing predefined variations, ancestor frames could explicitly INSERT each one, which is appropriate if each is unrelated and exists only in one frame. But if they are related or recur, you should have a single point of control. SELECT enables you to eliminate duplication, and/or control co-related cases, with a single REPLACE switch.

SELECT allows multiple archetypes to be packaged into one frame (tree) so that adaptor frames can treat the frame as the expert for that domain. Adaptor frames set switches to select the features they need, and customize them, if necessary. Deciding how to group features into frames is an interesting engineering issue, discussed further in Chapter 15.

Another important role for SELECT is automatic version control. As old code is superseded by new or replacement code, SELECTs, parameterized on a date related *;var* (a version control parameter), are used to ensure existing modules that reuse the frame do not need to be disturbed. Chapter 16 goes into details.

**.WHILE ;*var*  ...**
**[*frame-text*]**
**.END-WHILE[;*var*...]**

WHILE iterates the processing of its *frame-text* while all the *;var* references on the WHILE line remain defined. As soon as one becomes undefined, the WHILE loop terminates. The body of the WHILE must contain a REPLACE that, after a finite number of iterations, causes a *var* to become undefined. Consider the following example.

```
.%Frame to demonstrate .WHILE
.R FACE1 BY king
.R FACE2 BY queen
.R FACE3 BY jack
.R NUM BY 1
.WHILE ;FACE;NUM %think of NUM as indexing FACE
The ;FACE;NUM of hearts will make Humpty better.
.R NUM BY ( ;NUM + 1 )
.END-WHILE ;FACE;NUM
.%End frame
```

This frame produces:

```
The king of hearts will make Humpty better.
The queen of hearts will make Humpty better.
The jack of hearts will make Humpty better.
```

A common application of WHILE is processing input data. Most window variables will be processed in a standard way: display, prompt, read, test, store, and update. But the number of such variables (and their attributes) obviously depends on the particular window. An adaptor frame would specify specific variable attributes in (indexed) frame-variables and a window handling frame would iterate accordingly.

The five principal commands have now been introduced. Collectively, these commands provide a formal (operational) definition of frames.

Figures 9-3 through 9-7 were drawn from a Barclays Bank (UK) internal presentation on reuse, and are reproduced here with their kind permission. Figure 9-6 is an example of an actual SPC for a program to manage system tables, taken from a system to settle credit card transactions. Figure 9-7 is a simplified view of the actual frame hierarchy that the SPC adapts. The borders of the boxes illustrates the architectural layers. Programs such as the one illustrated are routinely designed, built, and tested in less than a half-day.

**Figure 9-3.** Flexible settlement requirements.

■ On-line *CICS* screen-based program

■ Maintains a parameter table

■ Requires all data changes to be
  verified by a supervisor (dual control)

■ Requires all updates to be recorded to
  the project's audit table

**Figure 9-4.** Your mission. . . .

■ Code & Unit test this program by 18:00

■ You can reuse (but NOT copy) as much
  of anyone else's code as you need.

■ BUT you are limited to 10 lines of your
  own COBOL

**Figure 9-5.** Five steps to implement. . . .

■ Paint the screen

■ Generate the SQL frame for the table

■ Copy the SPC template & customize it

■ Generate, compile & link the program

■ Unit test the program

```
************************************************************
*   This program is the property of Barclays Bank PLC.    *
************************************************************
*    System : Daily Settlement, Entity Maintenance Suite.*
*    Program : DZnnn.S                                    *
*    Version : 01.01                                      *
*    Author : Construction Team, Darwin Programme         *
*      Date : April 1995                                  *
* Function : Maintain Exception Type Parameter Table.     *
************************************************************


    .   REPLACE $VERSION        BY 02.07.00
    .   REPLACE SPC_VERSION      BY 19950510

   .COPY DZLIBS.F SAMELEVEL      % Frame library locations

   .COPY DZPSDO.F SAMELEVEL      % Standard CICS txn support
    .   REPLACE DZPSDO_CICS_ENTRY BY NO % Disable txnid start
   .END-COPY



WORKING-STORAGE SECTION.

    .   REPLACE BBSCRN_PFKEY_LINE1 BY WS-PFKEY-LINE1 %PFkeys
    01   WS-PFKEY-LINE1.
         03   FILLER      PIC X(15)   VALUE 'Enter=Process, '.
         03   FILLER      PIC X(09)   VALUE 'F1=Help, '.
         03   FILLER      PIC X(09)   VALUE 'F3=Exit  '.

    MAIN SECTION.
    MAIN-01.
         PERFORM INITIALIZATION.
         PERFORM BBMAINT-GENERATE.

    INITIALIZATION SECTION.
   .COPY DZEMAINT.F
    .   REPLACE DB2TABLENAME           BY TDWET
    .   REPLACE DZEMAINT_SQLKEY1        BY ETREF
    .   REPLACE DZEMAINT_SQLKEYPIC1     BY X(2)
    .   REPLACE DZEMAINT_KEYNAME1       BY ;DB2TABLENAME-ETREF
    .   REPLACE DZEMAINT_SQLFLD1        BY DESC
    .   REPLACE DZEMAINT_SQLFLDPIC1     BY X(25)
    .   REPLACE DZEMAINT_FLDNAME1       BY ;DB2TABLENAME-DESC
   .END-COPY
```

**Figure 9-6.** An actual Barclaycard SPC.

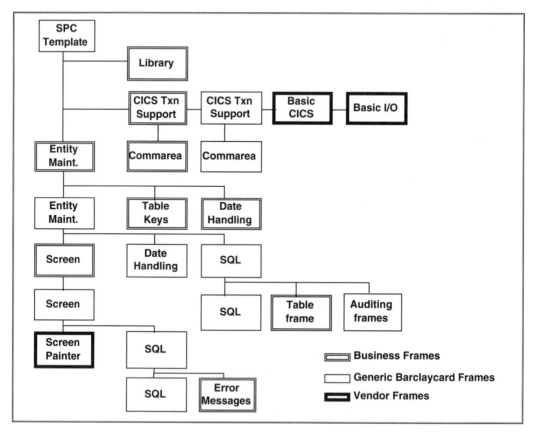

**Figure 9-7.** An actual 3-layer construction architecture designed at Barclays Bank.

# Frames: "Like, But Oh How Different!"

## CHAPTER 10

> *Frames: " Like, But Oh How Different!"*
>
> William Wordsworth, 1807

I n the effort to harness reusability, over the decades the software industry has developed many tools and techniques that could be considered framelike. Now that you have been introduced to frame concepts, you may wonder how they are "the same as, except" these other ideas. More importantly, these comparisons make fine lenses for clarifying subtle reuse issues.

In particular, in this chapter we shall examine connections with artificial intelligence, skeleton code, macros, and generators. In the next chapter we consider structured programming, programming languages, and subroutines. Then, in the following chapter we turn to object-oriented technology, a topic of importance because of the potential for improving the paradigm.

But first, people also apply framelike concepts in many nonsoftware settings. As a prelude to the primary comparisons, we consider two of these many settings: music and manufacturing.

*Reusable melodies.* How do song writers compose three-minute songs out of about 30 seconds of unique melody? A song will normally have a main theme, *T*, and a chorus, *C*, arranged in temporal patterns such as *TCTCTC*, or *TCCTCC*. Each repetition of the theme (sometimes) contains a variation in words, harmonies, instruments, et cetera. In addition to temporal patterns, there are instrumental patterns. In a symphony, each type of instrument (woodwinds, brass, strings, percussion) plays a variation on the theme. That variation is a score appropriate to that instrument's type and role.

The parallel between computing and music is striking. Musicians with instruments interpret scores, much as computers interpret programs. Composers are akin to programmers, and musical themes are framelike. Themes are reused in a "same as, except" way—different instrument, different tempo, different words. To the human ear, a "sameness" comes through, but with a difference. Let's hope frames, musical and software, produce harmonies that are both rich and enriching!

*Manufacturing-to-order.* In a dealer's showroom, in about 20 minutes you can order a car as unique as your finger prints. In principle, every car on the manufacturer's assembly line can be one-of-a-kind. How are they made in high volume and high quality at affordable costs?

When touring an auto plant, the first thing you notice is that every car on the line looks the same. Of course, you are literally looking at the frames. It is the combinatorial explosion of options that can be welded, bolted, and sprayed onto frames that result in unique cars. Because their frames are engineered for such options, it's the hundreds of millions of dollars invested in automatic assembly equipment and robot welders that provide the cost-effectiveness of modern manufacturing-to-order.

The manufacturing metaphor illustrates how software frames transcend the physical parallel in two ways.

1. Software frames have more engineering degrees of freedom. For example, it's much easier to add to than subtract from a physical frame. You cannot order a sedan without a back seat. Software frames are inherently more flexible because they can have more options than any given instance needs. Not only can the relevant options be fine-tuned (rather than used-as-is), but the irrelevant can be dropped at no cost.

2. The parts of a car are heterogeneous, meaning they require a variety of tools and processes to connect them. In contrast, frames homogenize the software assembly process. Frames package all components, custom and generic, uniformly so that a single mechanism, the frame processor, handles the entire assembly process. This homogeneity increases the ability to reuse components; it also suggests a common approach to designing feeders such as editors, analyzers, and application modeling tools.

## Frames in Artificial Intelligence

My use of frame hierarchies and default BREAKs was inspired by the "frames" and "slots" used in artificial intelligence, notably by Marvin Minsky [18].

The original motivation for frames in artificial intelligence was more descriptive than prescriptive. A typical AI problem is to enable a robot to recognize which room it is in. The robot looks for various features of "roomhood" by consulting its generic room frame. Thus, rooms usually have four walls, one or more doors, zero or more windows, furniture, and so forth. Each of the main components of a room may subdivide into a tree of frames. To describe the room it is in, the robot fills in "slots" in the frames with the specific details. The room may contain surprises, such as having five walls or no ceiling. AI frames implement the notion of "usually" with default values for the slots, as well as the ability to tailor and delete them.

This slot-filling scenario is analogous to INSERTing custom details into BREAKs. Other than syntactic details, the main difference between my frames and Minsky frames is their purposes. The purpose of Minsky frames is *analysis*: to recognize patterns, to parse complex data, to discriminate relevance from irrelevance, to choose among semantic categories. The purpose of my frames is *synthesis*: to construct the run-time modules from generic models and from specifications supplied by external agents such as analysts and systems designers. Minsky intended frames to be used at run time. My intent is reuse at construction time.

## Skeleton Code

Many experienced analysts and programmers, noticing that most programs are essentially new variations on old themes, have gone to the trouble of creating libraries of code skeletons. These skeletons may be thought of as programs with holes. You simply copy the appropriate skeleton and manually "flesh it out" with an editor. Skeletons are a step beyond the ad hoc "copy-and-modify" technique, and a step before frames.

By "framing" (i.e., parameterizing) the skeleton, and storing the edits in other frames, you automate the tedious, error-prone, character-at-a-time editing. You also avoid having to look at a skeleton's details every time.

Skeletons are not organized into hierarchies; one skeleton seldom nests with others. Single-level structures cannot support isolating different sources of change into different architectural layers.

Skeletons illustrate the problems with "embedding" as a reuse technique (as opposed to "linking"). Suppose a skeleton that has been reused in

50 programs is enhanced. If you need the enhancement in the 50 programs, the retrofit must be done manually 50 times. Had the skeleton been a frame, you would have three options:

1. As with skeletons, change it once and make the change visible only to new programs.

2. Change it once and automatically propagate it to all 50 programs. There is a good chance that the retrofit can be propagated automatically, without changing any specification frames. Even if the change does impact the SPCs, the impacts are easier to spot and adjust because they are not mixed into the nooks and crannies of 50 customized skeletons.

3. Hide the changes in a separate wrapper frame. This option preserves the original frame and offers the enhancement to new and old programs on a case-by-case basis. Chapter 16 treats wrapper frames in detail.

The retrofit problem points to an important strategy for software evolution. The more reused a component is, the more context-insensitive, and hence the slower it is likely to evolve. Frames make it easy to exploit this gradient, to group details by their contexts so that most changes do not cross context boundaries. Otherwise, because context specifics are randomly mixed with context-free details, small changes can have a global impact. I cannot stress enough the value of being able to avoid this kind of unnecessary complexity.

## Macros

A frame is a species of macro. COPY corresponds to macro invocation; REPLACE corresponds to setting macro variables. Macros have been indispensable at the assembly language level. With notable exceptions, such as Meta-Cobol, PL/I, and C, why most higher level languages have no or atrophied macro facilities mystifies me.

Copybooks are a weak form of macro found in Cobol. Kirk Hansen introduces frames to Cobol programmers at ManuLife as "copybooks on steroids." In common practice, a copybook is a module of text, often a file definition, included into source programs as-is. This practice causes a proliferation of look-alike copybooks. Even so, copybooks hide information that cannot be hidden by calling external subroutines. So they are in wide use.

Macros highlight interesting reusability issues as enumerated in the following.

## 1. Decoupled Parameter Passing

Conventional macros have a "daisy-chaining" parameter passing convention. That is, if macro $X$ invokes $Y$, and $Y$ invokes $Z$, parameters passed from $X$ to $Z$ must either pass through $Y$ or must be global to all macros.

Daisy-chaining forces macro $Y$ to be more context-sensitive, hence less reusable than it should be. If frames $X$, $Y$, $Z$ invoke each other as above, $X$ parameterizes $Z$ directly without involving $Y$.

## 2. Hierarchical Parameter Scoping

Conventional macros use a "flat" scoping. That is, all parameters are global; once one macro defines them, they can be set and reset by all others. When a macro is exited, global parameters can easily be left in random states. This makes it too easy for unrelated macros to interfere with each other destructively. Avoiding this interference in a system having many global parameters saddles each macro with managing their states. This state management is a housekeeping duty that obscures the main thrust.

Frame parameters, on the other hand, are local to the frame that first sets their values. This means they can be set and reset only within their defining frames; descendent frames can only read them. Moreover, when a defining frame exits, all its parameters become undefined; destructive interference and state-keeping details are avoided. (REPLACE SAMELEVEL is the exception that proves this rule.)

## 3. Parameter Passing by Exception

Frame-parameter passing is designed to highlight the exceptional and hide the mundane. Each parameter is passed by an individual value assignment. Only the parameters that change need to be passed. This method of passing allows frames to have hundreds of parameters, increasing their generality and adaptability. Ancestor frames typically ignore almost all of them, since their values are almost always suitably (re)set within local frames or their parents.

A frame typically initializes (using REPLACEs) to default values all the parameters it uses. Given this, there are two ways to pass a parameter: broadcast and narrowcast, as illustrated in Figure 10-1.

*Broadcast.* Frame $F$, setting a parameter, automatically overrides all descendent frame defaults for that parameter. For example, ".R GUI BY

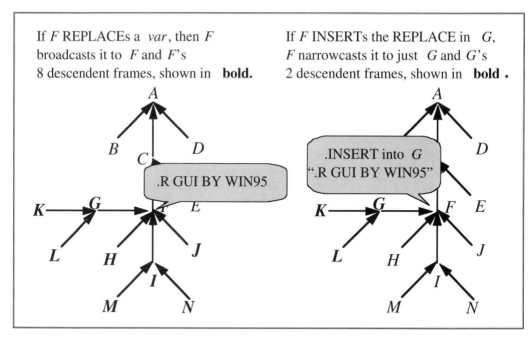

**Figure 10-1.** Frames use "broadcasting" and "narrowcasting" to explicitly control the scope of frame-parameter passing. The parameter values in two nonoverlapping contexts cannot interfere with each other. Perhaps, *GUI*, by default, handles MAC GUIs.

WIN95" causes all graphical user interface frames in *F*'s subtree to support Windows-95 instead of their normal defaults, say Presentation Manager for some and MACs for others.

*Narrowcast.* F INSERTs ".R GUI BY WIN95" into a particular subframe *G* at a BREAK subsequent to the default initialization. Now the scope of the setting is the subtree rooted in *G*, not *F*. Broad- and narrowcasting give software engineers control over cross-talk among various contexts.

ManuLife has applied this scoping power to enforce a discipline where application developers (SPC writers) never write INSERTs! In their frame architecture, a developer need only define her program's main characteristics (via broadcasting) and unique source code, if any. Lower level frames hide all the narrowcasting and other context-sensitive details. Their architecture enables application developers to avoid customizing specific components. I was surprised to learn that this degree of context separation was possible.

## 4. Unlimited Open Parameters

Macros usually employ "closed" parameters, ones that limit macro callers to a set of options predefined within the macro. In particular, macros find it hard to modify the bodies of other macros. Closed parameters have the decided virtue of simplicity. However, as is often the case, if a macro's author did not anticipate the need for a certain option, the macro's callers must work around the inflexibility, or not reuse the macro.

Work-arounds accelerate software brittleness: (a) Work-around details are spliced into the surrounding code. Such splices obscure the original code, complicating subsequent modifications and/or future macro invocations. (b) The details of a work-around often become fragmented from each other, further increasing the complexity of subsequent changes. (a) and (b) are symptoms of a deeper issue: the details are not being associated with the right context—the macro causing the work-around. (c) They add unnecessary run-time inefficiency to the solution when a work-around has to undo parts of what the macro did.

Frames support "open" parameters, INSERTs, as well as closed ones. That is, rather than work-arounds, other frames can, if necessary, directly rework—remove or replace—any parts of a frame that doní't fit the local context.

A software engineer cannot, and should not try to, anticipate every conceivable need. He simply surrounds every structure within a frame with a BREAK. (In the absurd extreme, he can eviscerate a frame's entire contents.) Reworks do not obscure an adaptor frame's structure because the syntax formally separates one from the other. Related details are not fragmented; rather they are grouped in one place within an adaptor frame—one or more contiguous INSERTs that take effect throughout the subtree. Direct modification promotes run-time efficiency because it ensures that only appropriate functionality exists at run time. Open parameters are cheap insurance against the unpredictable contingencies of reuse.

## 5. Language Richness

Programming languages often have too many ways to say the same thing. C++, APL, Meta-Cobol, and other macro hybrids are examples of languages in which we *over-specify*, (as opposed to languages in which we *under-specify*, in the sense of lacking ways to say certain things). In practice, even though such languages could be used to emulate same-as-except reuse, they are not so used because: (a) the required coding discipline would impose too heavy a burden, (b) the resulting solutions would be error prone, hard to debug, and understand, (c) the solutions would be frail—small changes often cause large effects—the opposite of the robust solutions we need, and (d) most important, language influences the way we think; those that are not conducive to same-as-except reuse inhibit people from adopting the requisite modes of thought, strategies, and tactics.

## Generators

We need to distinguish between module generation (what generators do) and module assembly (what frames do).

A generator, like a compiler, is a program that translates expressions from one language into another. For example, a GUI generator may convert a window layout (plus controls and variable attributes) into source code that, when compiled and linked, will appropriately animate end-user screens. Figure 10-2 illustrates how compilers, generators, and assemblers fit together.

Unlike compilers for general-purpose programming, a generator is an expert at writing code for a specialized problem domain. One generator might handle GUI screens, another reports, another is good for database design, another for insurance underwriting rules, and so on. A good visual representation (language) highlights the "what you see is what you get," or WYSIWYG, model of the problem. It also hides all of the consequential details, such as you would see in an equivalent C program.

The very power of generators is also their weakness. Because each generator is an expert at only a part of the overall problem, how should we cope with the missing pieces, or with side effects when fitting them together, or, for that matter, generated pieces that are inappropriate? Figure 10-3 lists four approaches.

**Figure 10-2.** A developer, using a special-purpose editor, prepares a high-level specification as input to a code generator or an assembler.

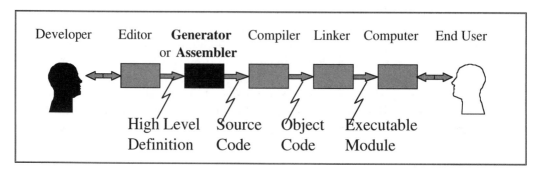

One approach keeps adding programming features to a generator (e.g., a report generator is extended to support file input/output). This approach can be a trap. In supporting such additional features, a generator may introduce unwelcome side effects into what it used to do well. Such extensions also obscure the natural notation which would otherwise remain optimized for its original raison d'etre (e.g., reports). The result evolves into a general-purpose programming language. This evolution is what happened to RPG and more recently to IBM's CSP (Cross System Product).

So-called white-box generators allow programmers to edit the generated code. This capability is problematic because it prevents regenerating the code on pain of having to re-edit every time.

Black-box generators avoid this problem by preventing such editing. Instead, they provide user exits—points within the generated code where external routines can be attached. This technique limits the customizations to additional functionality and work-arounds; you cannot change things like the sizes and attributes of the generated data structures, and you cannot modify or delete unwanted functionality. Black-box generators are little better than white ones.

**Figure 10-3.** Four strategies for overcoming the limitations of code generators.

1. Add more programming power to the language input to the generator.
2. White Box: developers directly modify the generated code.

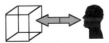

3. Black Box: developers attach methods to external exits.

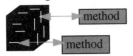

4. Gray Box: developers use SPCs to adapt generated frames.

SPC
frame

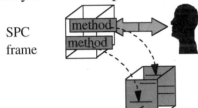

Generated frame with BREAKs for slots

What if generators were to emit frames rather than raw source code? Such frames can contain parameters and BREAKs for every data structure and method. Now you can keep novel details, ones that tailor the generator's stereotype output, in separate frames, such as specification frames. This could be called a gray-box approach since you treat the output as a black box where possible and a white box where necessary.

In fact, you can take this idea to its most effective limit: don't emit source code at all! The editor translates bi-directionally between the developer's visual representation of a solution's attributes and an SPC-like frame containing a list of REPLACEs, one per attribute. The *semantics*, the data types and function types into which all inputs for a given domain translate, exists in other, off-the-shelf, adaptable frames. These frames are now under the local control of developers and users, rather than a generator writer who does not understand your applications' contexts. The less "how to" logic that is "hard wired" into a generator's output, the more responsive to end-users' needs the result can be.

This strategy shrinks code generation to (bi-directional) translation. It translates information from a format suitable for human manipulation (i.e., WYSIWYG layouts and attributes) to an equivalent one suitable for automated assembly (i.e., frame processing).

This strategy works because independent sources of change are isolated. When changes are required, say to the layout of a report, you make them independently of changes that, say, interface the report to a novel database schema. Each source of change may be translated from different (graphical) languages into components that are assembled into custom results.

To conclude: there is much skepticism about the real utility of software tools. My guess is that inept generators are largely to blame. Too many programmers found that, after the novelty had rubbed off, so had their noses! Their grindstone had merely shifted from writing their own code to working around a generator's.

Generators that produce frames can be reused indefinitely. Programs are manufactured from an inventory of standard subassemblies and custom components, where the frame processor performs automatic fabrication. The intellectual capital assets of the company can now reside in that inventory, together with the manufacturing tools, rather than principally in the minds of craftsmen who may be here today and gone tomorrow.

# Adaptively Reusing the Tried and True

*It's quite likely that 99 percent of all the software subroutines that mankind will ever need have already been coded hundreds of times—but instead of reusing them, we persist in writing them again and again.*

Ed Yourdon

Three programming devices of long standing are subroutines, structured programming, and programming languages. We examine each for what it can teach us about adaptive reuse.

## Subroutines

People have confused frames more with subroutines than with any other construct. Are they two alternative ways to do the same thing? After all, subroutines compute results, call subroutines, and pass variables, and so do frames.

Subroutines have been around almost as long as programming itself. The idea is to allow programmers to extend a programming language's built-in functionality. Objects in object-oriented programming languages are a modern incarnation of this idea (about which we shall have much more to say in the following two chapters).

Historically and even now, people have considered external subroutines to be reusable components. Of course, subroutines were and are very useful. But people were not thinking about reuse as we now know it. The words "use" and "reuse" are not synonyms, as we have taken great pains to point out.

## Subroutines and Frames Are Duals

Subroutines (or functions or objects) are called (performed, invoked) at run time; they input and output data. Frames are not called at run time, and do not process data (in the normal sense of the word). They are invoked at construction time, process other frames, and construct source modules.

Indeed, frames construct subroutines! The idea is to define a subroutine as a generic frame (tree). Then, as each variation arises, a subroutine SPC highlights the deltas between its subroutine version and the generic frames. Remember, the deltas can add or subtract functionality in small or large increments. Moreover, changes to the generic form can be made in one place, and propagated to, or hidden from, existing variants, as required. So frames are a way to package subroutines to reduce redundancy and avoid the "sea of look-alikes" syndrome that is endemic to most subroutine libraries.

Frames are also a way to package the calling interfaces to subroutines, or more generally, to application programming interfaces (APIs). A complex API will typically have a similar calling pattern across many contexts of use. Or different APIs will be similar (because on the other side of the interface lies a sea of look-alikes). By framing the calls, the application programmer gains a simple, standard call, and all the variations are hidden and taken care of in the frame.

# Structured Programming

In the 1970s, structured programming took the computer science world by storm, a major advance in software engineering. Some form of the ideas, due to E. W. Dijkstra in the Netherlands, C. Bohm and G. Jacopini in Italy, and Harlan D. Mills in the United States, should by now be firmly entrenched in virtually every programming shop.

## Three Constructs

The essential concepts are simple. For any computable problem there is an infinite number of distinct but functionally equivalent solutions. Instead of the ad hoc methods formerly used, structured programming uses a "top-down" method of decomposing problems that results in programs composed with only three single-entry, single-exit constructs: process, if-then-else, and while (as shown in Figure 11-1). Bohm and Jacopini proved that the three constructs of structured programming are sufficient to compute any computable function. (There is an immense literature on this subject to which interested readers can refer for details.)

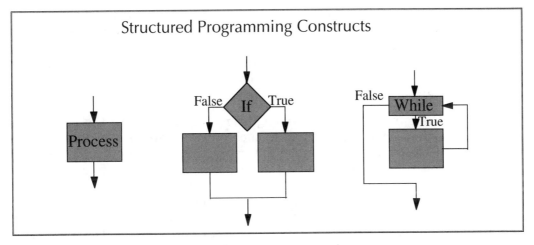

**Figure 11-1.** Any computable function can be computed by suitably concatenating and nesting these three control mechanisms.

Dijkstra, in particular, was interested in structured programming because it would simplify programs and thus facilitate proving them correct. While that goal has proved questionable, structured programming caught on because, done reasonably, it greatly facilitates problem analysis and simplifies the resulting programs.

While structured programming took a major step toward reducing the complexity of programs, it has not defused the crisis in software construction and evolution (or so-called "maintenance"). Many well-structured programs are still hard to understand, and harder still to modify reliably. The question is, why, after so much time to settle in, has structured programming not fulfilled its promise?

## Structured Programming Lacks Structure

The problem is this: even if we restrict ourselves to the rules of structured programming, we are still left with an unlimited number of ways to program a function. If programs, once proven correct, never needed alteration, we wouldn't care too much about the particular decomposition, provided the proof was tractable. (Program efficiency criteria can also be proven.) In reality, it is a rare program indeed that, once written, never changes. (And the bad news is that, once modified, a new proof is needed.)

Of the myriad ways to structure the same program, almost all are atrocious. Which aren't? Most criteria for reasonable structure focus on adaptability, not provability:

- Does the decomposition resolve into existing reusable parts?
- Are the parts sufficiently decoupled so that a change to one part does not affect many others?
- Is a part simple enough that the time needed to understand it is comparable to the time needed to change it?
- Can we easily add new parts to a module after it has been written?

These and many similar engineering questions are the criteria for what is reasonable. Yet, for most such concerns, structured programming is mute. In other words, I am in the ironic position of arguing that, far from over-constraining and limiting a programmer's creative freedom, structured programming fails to provide enough structure!

Why, in biological systems, do *phenotypes* exist at run time, and *genotypes* at construction time? Phenotypes are living organisms, analogues of executable code. Genotypes are the genes, DNA, biological frameworks for constructing phenotypes. Each structure encodes a capability lacking in the other. Being parsimonious, Nature has nevertheless found these dual structures to be fundamental to all living things. Perhaps the use-reuse duality is fundamental to structured programming as well.

## Framing Structured Code

Structured programming necessarily focuses on what is supposed to happen at run time. It simply does not address the question of reuse at construction time. We need a complementary set of criteria to help us sort the reasonable structures from the rest. Adaptability and generality are two such criteria.

Structured programming's (nested) structures naturally map into (subassembly) frames and (nested) BREAKs, allowing us to separate and generalize them into independently reusable components. Parameters within the components enable not only the original structures to arise by default, but also a host of other variations.

We have, with frames, a vocabulary for analyzing reuse. We can, with some engineering precision and objectivity, distinguish effective structures from the merely plausible. Some examples:

- One reuse metric calculates what percentage of each module's ESLOC (source lines of code minus blanks and comments) was derived from its SPC, and compares it to the system's average percent.

  Figure 11-2 is such an analysis report. For each program (and in total), its ESLOC is shown, and what percent of it came from its SPC, any generated frames, and the frame libraries. The right-hand columns split the frame libraries' percent into the percent of ESLOC

| Program Name | COBOL lines from .C | | | | All lines from .S | | | | | | Reuse Categories (see legend below) | | | | | | |
|---|---|---|---|---|---|---|---|---|---|---|---|---|---|---|---|---|---|---|
| | ESLOC | SPC | Gen | Frm | TOTAL | SLOC | CAP | Cmt | Blnk | Variance Level | 1 | 2 | 3 | 4 | 5 | 6 | 7 |
| DS300.S | 1206 | 11% | 14% | 75% | 280 | 48% | 17% | 26% | 8% | 4.0% | --- | 5% | 45% | 50% | --- | --- | --- |
| DS301.S | 5256 | 21% | 9% | 71% | 2158 | 52% | 8% | 13% | 13% | 3.5% | --- | 19% | 61% | 20% | --- | --- | --- |
| DS302.S | 4084 | 3% | 16% | 82% | 308 | 38% | 21% | 19% | 22% | 2.3% | --- | 19% | 60% | 21% | --- | --- | --- |
| DS303.S | 3266 | 8% | 18% | 74% | 582 | 46% | 23% | 18% | 13% | 1.2% | --- | 19% | 49% | 32% | --- | --- | --- |
| DS104.S | 7712 | 13% | 12% | 75% | 1610 | 74% | 9% | 8% | 10% | 15.9% | --- | 18% | 69% | 13% | --- | --- | --- |
| DS305.S | 3499 | 5% | 11% | 85% | 281 | 61% | 11% | 14% | 14% | 8.1% | --- | 19% | 57% | 24% | --- | --- | --- |
| DS306.S | 5618 | 2% | 9% | 89% | 214 | 53% | 16% | 21% | 10% | 10.8% | --- | 17% | 69% | 14% | --- | --- | --- |
| DS307.S | 7453 | 10% | 13% | 77% | 1469 | 74% | 10% | 5% | 12% | 34.2% | --- | 18% | 68% | 14% | --- | --- | --- |
| DS310.S | 7061 | 12% | 10% | 78% | 1273 | 70% | 5% | 11% | 14% | 4.1% | --- | 18% | 69% | 14% | --- | --- | --- |
| DS311.S | 8580 | 23% | 11% | 66% | 2215 | 83% | 5% | 8% | 4% | 5.9% | --- | 21% | 66% | 14% | --- | --- | --- |
| DS312.S | 7877 | 17% | 13% | 70% | 1914 | 76% | 5% | 6% | 13% | 10.1% | --- | 18% | 68% | 13% | --- | --- | --- |
| DS313.S | 6825 | 5% | 16% | 79% | 1048 | 75% | 10% | 5% | 10% | 53.1% | --- | 19% | 68% | 13% | --- | --- | --- |
| DS314.S | 6529 | 7% | 13% | 80% | 722 | 63% | 15% | 11% | 12% | 3.8% | --- | 19% | 69% | 13% | --- | --- | --- |
| DS315.S | 6927 | 5% | 14% | 81% | 634 | 57% | 26% | 6% | 11% | 2.2% | --- | 19% | 69% | 13% | --- | --- | --- |
| DS316.S | 7672 | 10% | 12% | 78% | 1517 | 50% | 7% | 22% | 21% | 1.9% | --- | 17% | 70% | 13% | --- | --- | --- |
| DS317.S | 6266 | 2% | 13% | 84% | 273 | 56% | 21% | 14% | 10% | 5.7% | --- | 19% | 68% | 13% | --- | --- | --- |
| DS318.S | 5694 | 6% | 13% | 81% | 676 | 61% | 16% | 9% | 14% | 2.6% | --- | 20% | 66% | 14% | --- | --- | --- |
| DS319.S | 6802 | 6% | 14% | 80% | 666 | 54% | 13% | 13% | 9% | 1.1% | --- | 17% | 69% | 13% | --- | --- | --- |
| DS320.S | 6120 | 6% | 10% | 84% | 567 | 58% | 13% | 13% | 7% | 1.6% | --- | 17% | 69% | 14% | --- | --- | --- |
| DS321.S | 8630 | 22% | 11% | 67% | 2170 | 77% | 11% | 4% | 8% | 13.1% | --- | 19% | 67% | 14% | --- | --- | --- |
| DS322.S | 5743 | 3% | 10% | 88% | 304 | 56% | 20% | 16% | 8% | 5.5% | --- | 17% | 68% | 14% | --- | --- | --- |
| DS323.S | 5581 | 2% | 9% | 89% | 201 | 50% | 18% | 23% | 9% | 11.2% | --- | 18% | 69% | 14% | --- | --- | --- |
| DS124.S | 6087 | 2% | 13% | 84% | 242 | 61% | 11% | 18% | 10% | 5.2% | --- | 18% | 68% | 15% | --- | --- | --- |
| DS325.S | 6638 | 3% | 15% | 82% | 534 | 68% | 17% | 7% | 7% | 45.2% | --- | 18% | 68% | 14% | --- | --- | --- |
| DS310.S | 6438 | 2% | 12% | 85% | 294 | 53% | 17% | 14% | 16% | 5.0% | --- | 17% | 70% | 14% | --- | --- | --- |
| DS332.S | 3821 | 5% | 20% | 75% | 319 | 65% | 10% | 18% | 8% | 2.3% | --- | 17% | 58% | 26% | --- | --- | --- |
| DS333.S | 3473 | 2% | 22% | 76% | 177 | 46% | 27% | 21% | 7% | 6.2% | --- | 20% | 51% | 28% | --- | --- | --- |
| DS343.S | 6059 | 4% | 13% | 83% | 447 | 57% | 20% | 8% | 14% | 0.1% | --- | 18% | 68% | 14% | --- | --- | --- |
| DS344.S | 2871 | 2% | 16% | 82% | 208 | 31% | 44% | 15% | 10% | 6.5% | 1% | 21% | 49% | 30% | --- | --- | --- |
| DS399.S | 1878 | 16% | 0% | 84% | 392 | 59% | 21% | 13% | 7% | 31.5% | --- | 13% | 57% | 30% | --- | --- | --- |
| DS410.S | 3556 | 10% | 18% | 73% | 958 | 37% | 19% | 21% | 23% | 0.7% | --- | 14% | 58% | 28% | --- | --- | --- |
| DS411.S | 4866 | 15% | 17% | 69% | 1540 | 44% | 13% | 21% | 22% | 1.5% | --- | 16% | 63% | 21% | --- | --- | --- |
| DS415.S | 1015 | 6% | 16% | 79% | 141 | 43% | 20% | 22% | 16% | 2.9% | --- | 0% | 43% | 57% | --- | --- | --- |
| TOTALS | 182203 | 9% | 13% | 79% | 26434 | 63% | 12% | 13% | 12% | | 0% | 18% | 66% | 16% | 0% | 0% | 0% |

Total files analyzed: 33

Reuse Categories

1. LOCAL DIRECTORY
2. K:\NETRON\FRAMES\
3. K:\NETRON\PVCS\CS\REF\
4. K:\NETRON\CAP\
5.
6.
7. OTHER

Figure 11-2. FRAT image of ESLOC Reuse Report printout.

that came from up to seven frame categories. The middle set of columns further analyze the contents of each SPC. Anomalies stick right out.

- A frame's adaptability is inversely related to the amount of information needed to adapt it. If frame $F$ reuses frame $G$, $G$'s adaptability to $F$'s context is inversely related to the size of the text that $F$ INSERTs into $G$.

- A frame's generality is relative to other frames in its reuse category— e.g., application frames, corporate standard, vendor supplied. We simply compare the number of times a frame is reused to the average for its category.

Figure 11-3 illustrates this. The Frame Reuse Analysis Table (FRAT) lists frames from each category and counts the number of reuses (COPYs) from the SPCs and in total. The average reuse per frame in each category is also computed for comparison purposes. Notice that the category with the most frames has the lowest average reuse. This category contains the business rules.

- Other important but subtle reuse questions include: When do a component's variations belong with it, rather than with its adaptors (SELECTs versus INSERTs)? Are the properties of a frame "genericized" appropriately (i.e., how often are various SELECTs being selected, parameter defaults being overridden, and so on)?

**Figure 11-3.** FRAT image of frame reuse counts by category.

| | FRAME NAME | SPC .COPYs | TOTAL .COPYs |
|---|---|---|---|
| REUSE CATEGORY: K:\NETRON\CAP\ | FRAME NAME | SPC .COPYs | TOTAL .COPYs |
| | ATTRB.F | 42 | 347 |
| | LINK.F | 0 | 49 |
| | CVTXN.F | 0 | 33 |
| | PSEUD.F0 | 0 | 33 |
| | PSEUD.F1 | 0 | 33 |
| | PSEUD.F2 | 0 | 33 |
| | STANDARD | 0 | 33 |
| | PFKEY.F3 | 0 | 32 |
| | WSIO.F | 0 | 32 |
| | WSIO.FC | 0 | 32 |
| | WSIO.FP | 0 | 32 |
| | WSIO.FS | 0 | 32 |
| | SDATE.F | 0 | 31 |
| | VDATE.F | 0 | 31 |
| | ATTRB.F1 | 0 | 6 |

```
REUSE TOTAL        FRAMES:      15    SPC:    42           789

.COPYs FROM K:\NETRON\CAP\                         789
----------------------------------------------------- = ------- =   52.600
DIFFERENT FRAMES FROM K:\NETRON\CAP\                15
```

```
REUSE CATEGORY:   K:\NETRON\FRAMES\
                                  FRAME NAME    SPC .COPYs    TOTAL .COPYs

                                  SQLFL.F             0            2066
                                  SQLWR.F            31             600
                                  SQLKE.F             0             594
                                  TSQUE.F             6             236
                                  TSQUE.F1            0             235
                                  BBCONF.F            0              33
                                  CSLIBS.F           33              33
                                  SQLCU.F             0               8

REUSE TOTAL          FRAMES:        8    SPC:    70            3805

.COPYs FROM K:\NETRON\FRAMES\                          3805
-------------------------------------------------- = ------- =  475.625
DIFFERENT FRAMES FROM K:\NETRON\FRAMES\                  8


                                  FRAME NAME    SPC .COPYs    TOTAL .COPYs


REUSE CATEGORY:   K:\NETRON\PVCS\CS\REF\
                                  FRAME NAME    SPC .COPYs    TOTAL .COPYs

                                  BBPOPLK.            0             138
                                  SQLD1.F             0              38
                                  BCSMI.FR            1              34
                                  BBPSDO.F           33              33
                                  BNCOM.FR            0              33
                                  BBSCRN.F            2              32
                                  BBWSIO.F            0              32
                                  SQLER.F             0              32
                                  BBDATE.F            1              31
                                  BCSECURE            1              31
                                  TCSCASE.            0              31
                                  TCSMLU.F            0              31
                                  TCSQRTY.            0              31
                                  TCSSPSP.            0              31
                                  BBSCRNSV            0              30
                                  TCSSPL.F            0              30
                                  BBNAV.F             1              29
                                  BCSCOMMS            0              29
                                  BNFLOW.F            0              29
                                  TCSSN.FR            0              29
                                  BBQTYPE.            0              28
                                  BCINIT.F            0              28
                                  BCQTPROG            0              28
                                  TCSCN.FR            1              28
                                  TCSCSAC.            0              27
                                  BBMXSQNO            0              26
                                  BCCSAC.F            1              26
                                  TCSCABA.            0              26
                                  BCCABA.F            0              25
                                  BCCATX.F            0              25
                                  BCPROCCA            0              25
                                  TCSCATX.            0              25
                                  TCSCCA.F            0              25
                                  BBGRPATT            0              24
                                  BCNXTCS.            0              23
                                  BCSTWKCS            0              23
                                  TCSDEPT.            0              23
                                  BBCDT.F             1              22
                                  BBACTION            0              21
                                  BBREFER.            0              21
                                  TCSAC.FR            0              21
                                  TCSSLVL.            0              21
                                  BBOLR.F            11              17
                                  LSCOM.FR            0              17
                                  BBPAGE.F            0              15
                                  BCPAGE.F           14              14
                                  BCMAINT.            0              13
                                  BCBSFN.F           10               9
                                  BCBMI.F             6               6
                                  SCASEU01            0               5
```

**Figure 11-3.** Continued.

| FRAME NAME | SPC .COPYs | TOTAL .COPYs |
|---|---|---|
| TCSEXCN. | 0 | 5 |
| BCEXCN.F | 4 | 4 |
| TCSCTCS. | 0 | 4 |
| TCSGCT.F | 0 | 4 |
| TCSSACC. | 0 | 4 |
| TCSSP.FR | 4 | 4 |
| BCSPROGS | 0 | 3 |
| BBMENU.F | 2 | 2 |
| BBMODCHK | 0 | 2 |
| BCPBMI.F | 2 | 2 |
| SCASER02 | 0 | 2 |
| SCNC01.F | 0 | 2 |
| SCNI01.F | 0 | 2 |
| SCNU05.F | 0 | 2 |
| SQRTYR01 | 0 | 2 |
| SSACCR01 | 0 | 2 |
| SSACCR02 | 0 | 2 |
| TCSCAFI. | 0 | 2 |
| TCSCAFL. | 0 | 2 |
| TCSCNM.F | 0 | 2 |
| TCSCNT.F | 0 | 2 |
| TCSCNTX. | 0 | 2 |
| TCSFITM. | 0 | 2 |
| TCSLNKC. | 0 | 2 |
| TCSSACM. | 0 | 2 |
| TCSTCLS. | 0 | 2 |
| BBMOD10. | 0 | 1 |
| BBPAGEM. | 0 | 1 |
| BCPAGEM. | 0 | 1 |
| BCSMC.FR | 2 | 1 |
| BNCICS.F | 1 | 1 |
| DS303.FQ | 1 | 1 |
| DS314.FQ | 1 | 1 |
| SCASER01 | 0 | 1 |
| SCASEU02 | 0 | 1 |
| SCCAR01. | 0 | 1 |
| SCNMR01. | 0 | 1 |
| SCNR01.F | 0 | 1 |
| SCNTR01. | 0 | 1 |
| SCNTXS01 | 0 | 1 |
| SCNU01.F | 0 | 1 |
| SCNU02.F | 0 | 1 |
| SCNU03.F | 0 | 1 |
| SCNU04.F | 0 | 1 |
| SCSACR01 | 0 | 1 |
| SCTCSR01 | 0 | 1 |
| SLNKCS01 | 0 | 1 |
| SSPR01.F | 0 | 1 |
| SSPSPR01 | 0 | 1 |
| STCLSR01 | 0 | 1 |
| TCSADE.F | 0 | 1 |
| TCSBUCH. | 0 | 1 |
| TCSCNPR. | 0 | 1 |
| TCSFET.F | 0 | 1 |
| TCSGLA.F | 0 | 1 |
| TCSGLFT. | 0 | 1 |
| TCSGLSA. | 0 | 1 |
| TCSMACT. | 0 | 1 |
| TCSMADJ. | 0 | 1 |
| TCSMCH.F | 0 | 1 |
| TCSMCNP. | 0 | 1 |
| TCSNFE.F | 0 | 1 |
| TCSTCXR. | 0 | 1 |

REUSE TOTAL          FRAMES:          113     SPC:    100              1474

.COPYs FROM K:\NETRON\PVCS\CS\REF\                              1474
------------------------------------------------------------ = ------- = 13.044
DIFFERENT FRAMES FROM K:\NETRON\PVCS\CS\REF\                     113


GRAND TOTAL          FRAMES:          136     SPC:    212              6068

TOTAL # OF .COPYs FROM SPC                                       212
------------------------------------------------------------ = ------- = 8.480
TOTAL # OF DIFFERENT FRAMES COPIED FROM SPC                      25

**Figure 11-3.** Continued.

130

Treating programs as timeless theorems caused structured programming to be incomplete. Software will continue to appear brittle, and the vast potential of structured programming will go unfulfilled until we recognize that code must be engineered for change, not immutability.

## Software's Tower of Babel

Finally, we turn to programming languages themselves. We focus on three issues that strongly impact software adaptability.

### 1. Languages Fixed

With most programming languages, adding new syntax or semantics is simply not an option. Programmers become frustrated when they find that, although their intentions are clear to themselves, their equivalent code is obscure, awkward, or tedious. These situations are missed opportunities to improve the language's expressive power for a given domain.

Natural languages, such as Latin, die out because they fail to keep up with their evolving environments. It is natural for human languages to become enriched with sublanguages that use a mixture of old and new vocabulary. These sublanguages continually spring up around new disciplines (e.g, computer science, astronautics). Imagine NASA trying to use Chaucer's English to control space shuttles. Yet programmers have suffered the same way when trying to control computers. The resulting programs are overly detailed and hence difficult to understand and modify.

From this perspective, frame technology is a simple metalanguage for extending any existing language. A frame is a way of packaging new vocabulary. Nouns (data structures) and verbs (methods) are defined generically, their semantics hidden within frames. Frame parameters provide the context-sensitive modifiers, analogous to singular/plural, tenses, adjectives and adverbs, and so forth.

### 2. Scalability

Many languages—code generators, fourth-generation languages, I-CASE, and graphical user interface tools (GUIs)—exhibit a lack of scalability. By this I mean, within the scope of the domain for which they were designed, you can use these tools to whip up solutions in no time. But they become increasingly frustrating as the size and complexity of the application grows, or as solutions must incorporate enhancements outside the tool's scope. Such tools are rich in "sledgehammer" verbs: one blow does a lot. With two or three mouse clicks, an end-user can extract statistics from a database and display them as a color graphics pie chart, all nicely labeled and presented.

The sophistication in a system derives from the attention that subtle side effects and fussy details require. The side effects of a sledgehammer verb can outweigh its main effect. In particular, the side effects frustrate the fine-tuning of complex applications. In other words, when it comes to building high-volume, industrial strength systems, high-level languages also need tackhammers.

This observation is not to find fault with high-level languages. Quite the contrary. We need to operate at high abstraction levels. The more abstract, the easier it is to see patterns. It's rather like looking at the world from 30,000 feet; distracting details shrink into invisibility. The mistake is in thinking that the world really is as it appears from 30,000 feet. As we perceive lower-level details, we cannot expect them to be consistent with the simpler view from above. Nor will these details be independent of each other. Thus, effective high-level languages allow "same as, except" details to override and fine-tune the overly simple high-level expressions.

This framelike strategy allows specifications to cascade from level to level, as shown in Figure 11-4. Each level has the capability to override, as well as to extend, the inherited specifications. By packaging them in framelike structures at each level, we can automate the integration of the overrides into the flow from high to low level. The key is to be able to change the higher-level specifications without losing the lower-level overrides.

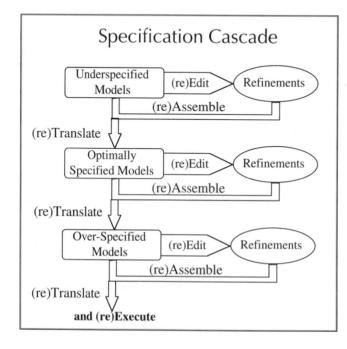

**Figure 11-4.** Underspecified models deliberately leave out details so you can see the forest. In optimally specified models, what you see is what you get. 3GLs and binary models are overspecified— easy to get lost in the trees. The key is to be able to refine and recascade the higher-level specifications without losing the lower-level refinements. Frames do this.

## 3. Function to Algorithm to Program

The last, deepest issue is that, just as we confuse numerals with numbers, so we confuse softwares with algorithms, and algorithms with functions.

Numbers are abstractions. They can be represented (denoted) in many ways, of which numerals are the most common. In a similar fashion, software represents abstract algorithms, and algorithms represent still more abstract functions. Fortunately, the number-numeral confusion is benign because the properties of numbers are so familiar. But, as we know, the properties of most algorithms and functions are far from obvious.

Just as a number can be represented in endless ways, any function, if computable at all, can be computed in an infinite number of algorithmically distinct, yet functionally equivalent ways. Each algorithm not only models a function (which inputs produce which outputs); it also has algorithmic properties (how much time, how much memory). These properties help us distinguish the good algorithms from the bad.

What about the ugly? Well, there is another one-to-infinity relationship, this time between algorithms and software. Each component not only has functionality and algorithmic properties; it also has construction properties (how generic, how adaptable). Distinguishing good algorithm components from ugly ones depends on reuse criteria.

Programming languages make it all too easy to confuse these three abstraction levels. Too bad, because functions, algorithms, and software constructs collectively define software engineering's scope. The good news is that, for virtually any language, frame mechanisms can help us optimize construction properties, independently from the purely algorithmic and functional.

When you first contemplate the solution to a problem, your mind roams freely over a range of variations on an algorithmic theme. You converge on the one you feel best fits the current constraints. Over time, the constraints change and so the solution evolves through successive variations on the original theme. In other words, it is algorithmic themes that have relative permanence, more than any particular program instance that happens to execute at a point in time. This, of course, is why frames have a role to play.

# Plain Talk, Not Smalltalk: An Object-Oriented Primer

## CHAPTER 12

> *The policy of letting a hundred flowers blossom*
> *and a hundred schools of thought contend is*
> *designed to promote the flourishing*
> *of the arts and the progress of science.*
>
> Mao Tse-tung, 1957

Object-oriented programming and its companion subjects, analysis and design (OOP, OOA, OOD), have done much to raise the awareness of reusability and its key role in software engineering. There is a huge and growing literature.

OO concepts germinated with the language Modula-2, taking a generation to come into bloom. The Smalltalk-80 language developed at Xerox PARC is considered one of the "pure" OOLs. There are over 60 others: C++, Eiffel, Objective-C, Neon, Mesa, Object-Pascal, Cedar, . . . . Another tower of Babel has sprung up around the OO paradigm as a new generation faces many old software engineering issues.

Dogmatic fervor fueled Mao's infamous Cultural Revolution. OO is undergoing a similar spell of political correctness: Cobol is dead; long live C++! Fads, oversold before they have a chance to mature, inevitably backfire; remember 4GLs, 5th-normal form databases, and, most recently, CASE. Let's hope OO avoids this fate, for there is much of value in the approach.

The good news is that you can practice an advanced form of OO using frame technology, and do it with any 3GL. To see how to do this, we start by demystifying OO jargon. Armed with a clear vocabulary, we then examine OO issues that are vital to reuse. It turns out that a slight change in the way OO handles object *components* and *generalization* simplifies the entire modeling process, from analysis and design through construction and execution.

Many expositions, having defined the words object and class, proceed to use them interchangeably, treating OO primarily as a run-time phenomenon. Such an emphasis blurs the distinction between run time and construction time, causing important issues to be confused. This primer provides a balance.

## OO at Run Time

At run time, these terms are the important ones (others are explained in passing):

- object
- object-instance
- method
- message
- encapsulation
- polymorphism
- dynamic binding

### Object

In essence, an object is a named, executable group of data structures and the  operators that manage them, as diagrammed in Figure 12-1. In OO parlance, an object plays both noun and verb roles: it is a model of something and it may act upon other models, including itself.

For example, a bank-account object may open an account, close it, accept a deposit, make a withdrawal, calculate interest, charge service fees, and so on. It manipulates its own data when it does these things. It may also report a current balance to a teller object or request overdraft authorization from a credit-manager object. The credit-manager object may, in turn, request data from the bank-account object while fulfilling the original credit request.

An object may model anything, from physical things like jet aircraft, to abstractions such as bank accounts, and, of course, the object concept itself. This remark is not profound. Software, in its various guises, has always had this potential.

Notice that the methods in one object can be called independently by other objects. That is what the arrows on the left-hand side of Figure 12-1 mean. In an ordinary program, the subroutines linked with it cannot be called from outside that program. Such programs are described as single-entry. Programs behave as objects to the extent that they can have sub-

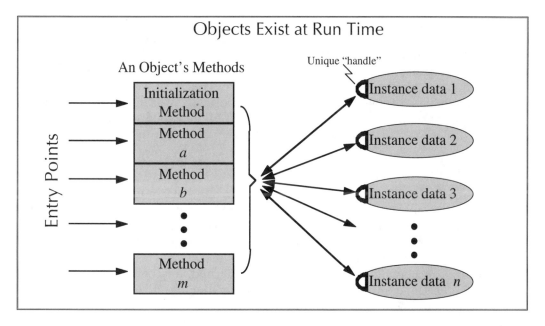

**Figure 12-1.** Any of the methods in the executable object can operate on the data contained in any of the object instances, each identified by a "handle."

routines callable from other programs (i.e., multiple entry points or the equivalent, as in CICS pseudo-conversational mode). Dynamically linked (subroutine) libraries (DLLs) also can be made to mimic objects.

## Object Instance

Like cars and appliances, objects come in different models, each with one or more exact copies. Thus, a checking account object would have many checking accounts, and a savings account object would have many savings accounts, each account being a different object instance. Each instance of the checking account object shares the same set of operators, but uses a separate data storage area, as shown in Figure 12-1. As you might expect, object instances (data storage areas) can be created and destroyed at run time.

A conventional program that manages a file (table) may be thought of as an object whose instances are records (rows). Thus, new customers result in new customer object instances, each containing the relevant particulars for one customer. Opening a new bank account allocates fresh storage for that account's number, owner, current balance, and so forth. Once created, each instance has its own unique state—the values of all its data, instance data, and temporary working storage, at a moment in time—as when various bank accounts show different owners, deposits, withdrawals, balances, statuses, and so forth.

Instance names are termed *handles*, akin to record keys and serial numbers. Data fields are called *attributes*. Because we don't want to lose data between object activations, automatically writing instance data to some permanent store (e.g., a disk file) is called *persistence*. Object instances can be stored in OO databases, but do not have to be.

## Method

A method is an operator, a function. In non-OO languages it would be termed a subroutine, as it has a name and argument list, and a body—data structures and procedural statements. Methods can call each other (recursively), whether they exist in the same object or in other objects. An object's *properties* are true statements about its methods. Through the process of *inheritance*, explained later, the same method may belong to many different objects. At run time, OO systems consist of objects that consist of interacting methods.

## Message

A message is like a subroutine call. It consists of a method name, an object name and handle, and a list of actual arguments needed by the method (possibly including references to other methods). Methods request data and services from each other by sending messages.[1]

## Encapsulation

This term means an object's methods are solely responsible for reading and writing its instance data.[2] Think of an object as a medieval castle whose guards, the methods, protect their castle's treasure, the object-instance data. Other castles cannot get their hands on the treasure; the best they can do is send emissaries, the messages, who return bearing (partial) copies of the treasure (Figure 12-2). Localizing responsibility for data integrity is a very important technique for avoiding errors and hiding complexity. This idea is not new, but OO enshrines it as a central tenet.

---

[1] Henceforth, the reader should assume that a reference to an object usually implies a reference to a particular method and a particular object instance, although for brevity, this may not be explicitly stated.
[2] Encapsulation illustrates the data-function duality. Object data's semantics are its methods' behaviors, and, conversely, object methods' semantics are their input/output data pairs.

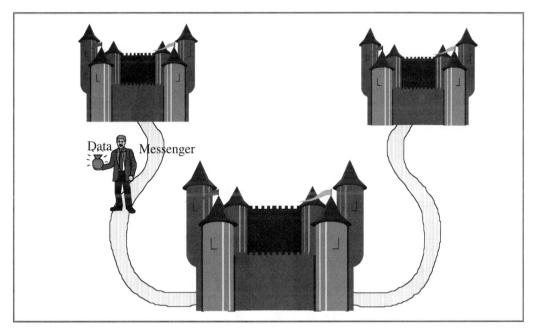

**Figure 12-2.** Encapsulated objects guard their data.

## Polymorphism

Polymorphism occurs when different methods have the same name (and usually the same argument list). Such methods are called *polymorphs*. This is not to be confused with "aliases," where the same method has different names. When a message is sent to a polymorph, which one responds? Most OOLs use the fact that each polymorph resides in a different object; if each message specifies a method and an object, there is no ambiguity. Another way to choose a polymorph involves inheritance, explained below.

Banks have many types of bank accounts: checking, savings, loans, GICs, and so forth. Each type is different, yet each involves similar services: opening an account, closing it, updating the balance, and so on. Thus, while the method for opening a savings account may be different from that for opening a current account, it's often possible to hide the differences inside the polymorphs, and so allow them to have the same name.

Polymorphism is powerful. It increases both object interoperability and isolation. The former facilitates usability (as distinct from reusability); the latter helps protect objects from each other when their properties change. The Noma case study in Chapter 17 illustrates how polymorphism simplifies EDI (electronic data interchange), isolating order processing from variations among customer purchase orders.

But that power is also dangerous; the bodies of two polymorphs can be arbitrarily different. Like wolves in sheep's clothing, innocuous-looking data can still get through polymorphic interfaces and wreak havoc on the system.

## Dynamic Binding

Finally, dynamic binding means that the linkages between methods are resolved during execution, as opposed to static binding, where they are resolved prior to execution. Most OOLs support dynamic binding; C++ and others support both. Non-OOL execution environments also support analogous mechanisms such as DLLs.

Dynamic binding greatly facilitates interoperability. Client-server architectures depend on dynamic binding, as do cooperative processing systems in general, systems with small memory regions, and the like. So-called object request brokers enable objects running on different platforms to use each other's services. Software whose architecture supports high interoperability is likely to be more flexible, extensible, and robust than monolithic systems.

Dynamic binding also supports the myth that the later the binding, the better. This issue is discussed in the next chapter.

## OO at Construction Time

Reactive elements, such as sodium or chlorine, when combined with other elements, form substances with very different properties. The situation should be similar when forming objects, but alas, it usually is not. Once we describe OO's basic construction vocabulary, we shall be able to explain this somewhat enigmatic remark. The important terms are:

- class
- single inheritance
- multiple inheritance

## Class

A class is the source-code definition of a complete object, an encapsulation of data structures and executable methods.[3] This one-to-one correspon-

---

[3] From a computer science perspective, a class denotes an abstract data type.

dence between classes and objects explains why those words are often used interchangeably. Shortly, we shall see its serious implications.

Defining a class begs the larger question: how should domains be partitioned into classes? Businesses, for instance, can be partitioned many ways: physical objects, work units, data flows, and more. An employee class might define properties, such as the ability to exchange messages with other employees, update calendars and files, and so on. But is this the best partitioning, or should employee behaviors and conditions be split and grouped in other ways? Such analysis and design questions are very important, the subject of Chapters 14 through 16.

## Single Inheritance

Classes often share common properties, e.g., "female" and "woman," so why reinvent the wheel? A class can declare itself to be a subclass of another. By so doing, the subclass inherits—implicitly defines—all of the parent class' methods and data structures. Thus, "female"'s properties become part of the definition of "woman" simply by declaring it to be a subclass of "female." "Woman" explicitly defines only its own unique and/or specialized properties, such as being an adult.

*Single* inheritance means a subclass has exactly one parent class. This permits classes to be organized into trees; the closer to the root, the more general the class. "Woman" is a specialized kind of "female person," which ISA "person" (shorthand for "is a specialization of," and "is a subclass of"), which ISA "mammal," and so on, as in Figure 12-3. Because each class inherits from its parent, "woman" inherits all properties of all its ancestors: "female," "person," "mammal,". . . , to and including the most general class.

In most OOLs, methods must be inherited as-is. So, what happens when an inherited method is not exactly what the subclass needs, e.g., a savings-account calculates interest for whole months, whereas its bank-account superclass works from date of deposit? There are two options:

1. Make changes globally to the superclass' method and retrofit all impacted classes;
2. Create a local version of the method in the subclass, using the same name and argument list; this option avoids retrofits and creates polymorphs.

These options are discussed in the next Chapter.

**Inheritance is OO's reusability mechanism.**

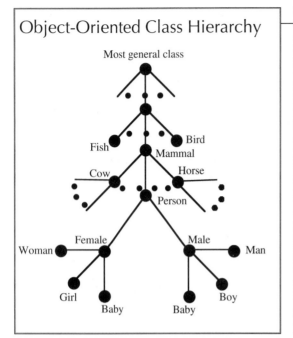

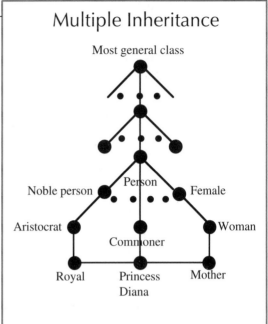

**Figure 12-3.** In object-oriented programming, a class, such as "girl," inherits properties from classes above it in the class hierarchy, in this case, "female," "person," and so on.

**Figure 12-4.** In multiple inheritance, a class, such as Princess Diana, inherits properties from the superclasses of which it is a subclass.

## Multiple Inheritance

Many OOLs support multiple inheritance: a class may declare itself a subclass of more than one parent, as in Figure 12-4. "Princess Diana" ISA "royal," ISA "commoner," ISA "mother,". . . . As you might expect, the Diana class inherits everything from all its parents and all their ancestors. There are problems with multiple inheritance. Yet, as we shall see, multiple inheritance is important for reasons that lie at the heart of software engineering.

Whereas single inheritance organizes classes into a tree, multiple inheritance produces a more complex network of classes.[4] The term *hierarchy* describes both single and multiple inheritance organizations.

With this basic OO vocabulary, we are in a position to discuss in the next chapter issues of high relevance to software engineering.

[4] Called a *lattice* or *acyclic graph* in mathematics. As explained earlier, a lattice can always be represented as a tree, provided each *n*-parent node is cloned into *n* one-parent nodes.

# Extending the OO Paradigm for Reuse

## Inheritance: Single or Multiple?

Some OOLs, notably Smalltalk, discourage multiple inheritance. One rationale for this policy is that we can organize the universe into a single, consistent classification scheme or taxonomy. Take biology, for example. We have organized all living things into six levels, or taxa; from most to least inclusive they are: phylum, class, order, family, genus, and species. Taxonomists may argue over what is descended from what, but single inheritance is a central dogma (although hybrids are common among species of bacteria and plants).

Likewise, single-inheritance OO taxonomies always start with one most general class (which may be empty). All subclasses are descended by a process of incremental specialization—each class descends from a parent that differs by only one or two properties.

Suppose you want to define a new class, say *current account*, but no existing class closely resembles it. No problem. Choose the largest extant class whose properties are a subset of *current account*, e.g., *account*, then design a series of incrementally specialized subclasses—perhaps *bank account* ISA *account*, *checking account* ISA *bank account*, and finally *current account* ISA *checking account*. Since there are many ways to do this

143

(OO taxonomists have arguments, too), this "pure" classification dogma denies the need for multiple inheritance.

The problem with the dogma is that in practice it works only in limited, simple domains. The information content of any physical system, even the tiniest we know—a quark or electron—is infinite! [19] Unfortunately, our memories, and hence our capacities to form models, are quite finite. It follows then, that software models of real domains must ignore all but a vanishingly small fraction of the potential information.

## Rogues and Pigeon Holes Don't Mix

Therein lies the rub. Any real-world domain will contain "rogue" objects that clash with the existing categories of any finite taxonomy. Suppose "customer" is a specialization of "external-agent," and "employee" is a specialization of "internal-agent." Now an object that is both a "customer" and an "employee" cannot be defined in a single inheritance taxonomy without duplicating "customer" and "employee" properties, or fragmenting them into clusters of smaller classes. Either way reduces the taxonomy's overall cohesion and manageability.

These issues become show-stoppers for domains, typical in business, whose properties are conflicting and/or temporally unstable. In such domains, single inheritance over-constrains the modeling process.

## Conformance to Set Theory

A second rationale for single inheritance is a desire to conform to the rules of elementary set theory: $X$ ISA $Y$—a jet "is a" plane—implies all members of $X$ are also members of $Y$, that $Y$ must strictly include $X$. $X$ may restrict membership by defining more properties, but may not ignore (delete) any of $Y$'s properties on pain of disqualifying $X$ from being a subset of $Y$.

Multiple inheritance corresponds to set intersection. For $X$ to be a subclass of both $Y$ and $Z$, all of $Y$'s properties and all of $Z$'s must hold in $X$. But if $Y$ and $Z$ clash (e.g., $Y$ = "external agent" and $Z$ = "internal agent"), then $X$ is null or not well defined. The rules of elementary set theory may be simple, but ironically, their very simplicity leads to problems, as Bertrand Russell's famous paradox proved.[1]

For example, ostriches and griffins are types of birds; a griffin is also a kind of lion. Princess Diana is at once a royal and a commoner (as shown in Figure 12-4). In order to accommodate such rogue classes, a conventional multiple inheritance architecture must be designed extremely carefully. In particular, as I noted above, related properties are duplicated or

---

[1] The set of all sets that are not members of themselves is a member of itself if and only if it is not!

fragmented into cousin classes. This is tolerable for isolated cases like griffins.

But, as analysis and design proceed, more and more rogues inevitably surface. Designers quite properly eschew redundancy. This is why OO design rules actually promote the disintegration of the natural graininess of the domain into tiny classes—one or two properties each. Either you duplicate existing properties or sprout ever bushier hierarchies of atomic parts. This Hobson's choice occurs often.

## Need for Exceptions

Because of the desire to conform to set theory, we can easily add properties to derived classes (same as, plus), but not so easily delete. Worse, even the slightest modification to a method requires its complete redefinition into a separate class. Here comes redundancy again. Consequently, differences among very similar methods remain implicit. For large domains, comprehension drowns in a sea of detail.

Suppose classes *Horse* and *Donkey* are distant cousins. See Figure 13-1. The greater the distance, the greater the chance that Horse and Donkey inherit from specialized ancestors properties that are mutually incompatible. There is nothing wrong with such conflicts; they are a natural consequence of being finite, of defining approximate models, of ignoring context-sensitive information that could have prevented clashes.

Indeed, the more reusable a class, the more context-free it is.[2] Context-free classes ignore their contexts and each other. Trouble is, ignorance is not bliss. Dysfunctional objects arise from inherited incompatibilities, just like sterile mules. If context-sensitive objects are to be built from context-free classes, an inventory of highly reusable and independent (orthogonal) parts, how should the inevitable clashes be resolved?

Short of changing the way inheritance works, the way people avoid this problem is to limit each class to one or two properties. So what's wrong with swarms of tiny objects? Interclass complexity increases, as related properties are scattered across many classes. Performance suffers. Reuse per class decreases.

The "same as, plus" style of inheritance is just not strong enough to resolve conflicts stemming from parents that are distant cousins. Subclass Mule in Figure 13-1 must be able to delete clashing or irrelevant properties inherited from Horse and Donkey, and amend others in order to force them to fit Mule's context. This brand of multiple inheritance we have called "same as, except."

---

[2] Proof: if *A* reuses *B*, *A* provides a context for *B*, and *B* can be reused in other contexts.

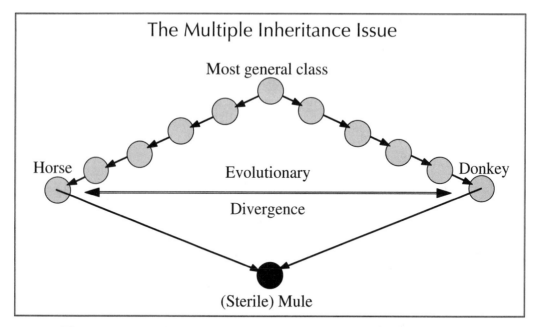

**Figure 13-1.** In the course of evolving a long series of subclasses, Horse and Donkey are likely to acquire incompatible properties that then conflict in their Mule offspring.

## Part-Whole Relationships

There is an even more compelling reason to strengthen the multiple-inheritance mechanism. As illustrated in Figure 13-2, a jet HASA fuselage, two wings, and a tail. (HASA is shorthand for "has a component class called. . .") Being able to detach a jet's wings in flight, as dynamic binding theoretically permits, endows the plane with novel properties, to say the least! Joking aside, while some objects merit this kind of fluidity,[3] the structural relationships among the parts of most objects *simply don't change during execution. If something is truly part of a seamless whole, it does not merit encapsulation as a separate class.*

Clearly, something is wrong with this picture. It begs two questions. What determines run-time modularity? How does it relate to construction-time modularity?

---

[3] HASA is often confused with "contains." A jet may contain passengers, a garden may contain plants, a playpen may contain toys, a database may contain data. Confusion arises because containers contain their parts as well as other things. But these other things are distinguishable. Container parts are static, necessary elements of the containment process; containees come and go at run time.

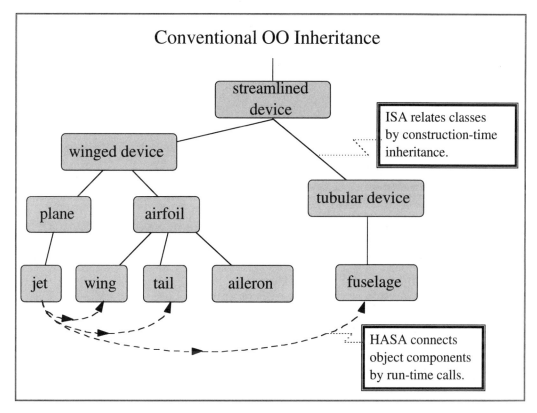

**Figure 13-2.** Abstractions are related by inheritance (ISA), whereas separately encapsulated objects are aggregated by exchanging messages (HASA).

We subdivide executable systems into subsystems, programs, internal and external subroutines, and objects in order to optimize usability. This involves complex trade-offs including the need to:

- provide common services to different executables;
- minimize rebuilding software that has not changed;
- distribute subsystems over parallel processors, e.g., clients and servers;
- improve flexibility through dynamic binding;
- improve clarity through explicit, formal interfaces;
- avoid single points of failure through encapsulation;
- run large systems in small memories;
- trace executions during testing (an intermittent need);
- others that I'm sure the reader can list.

Part relationships are designed to vary during assembly much more than during execution. Obviously, a plumber can move all of a faucet's parts, but not when you turn it on. At run time, too much variability is detrimental. "Too much" means variability that is not required by functionality and ease-of-use, plus the architectural and pragmatic considerations such as are listed above.

We want our objects to be seamless wholes, tuned for performance. So-called late binding obviously has its place, but can be done to a fault. Applied excessively, we saw earlier why it causes scalability and performance headaches. Given that HASA defines all the structural relationships necessary for assembly, most of which are invariant at run time, common sense would suggest that OO implement HASA at construction time.

So, why not? HASA at construction time demands multiple inheritance, an idea rejected by some schools of thought. Moreover, since inheritance is already dedicated to encoding ISA relationships, there is no choice but to use message passing instead.

## Frames Are Classes on Steroids

Frames are like generic classes, but equipped with the active inheritance mechanism called "adapt," described in Chapter 8. On the one hand, inheritance provides an adequate way to model relatively stable domains—physical objects such as (graphics) I/O devices, operating systems, process control, standard mathematical functions. On the other hand, business applications, systems whose requirements are in perpetual flux, need the adapt mechanism.

### Adapt Away Unwanted Properties

It is too easy for classes to inherit unwanted properties. If, for example, "penguin" is a subclass of "bird," and bird is a subclass of "flying vertebrate" then penguins will be able to fly! Software is rife with such exceptions. And, as we have seen, multiple inheritance can bring similar but incompatible properties together from divergent class lineages, resulting in nonfunctional offspring. That virtuoso class designers may stretch themselves to avoid these difficulties is beside the point. By making inheritance more adaptive, frame virtuosos can scale significantly higher peaks, and the rest of us can get on with routine software engineering!

Unwanted properties, such as penguins' ability to fly, are simply adapted away. Adapt also makes both multiple and repeated inheritance natural. Because a frame stores SELECTable properties, dramatically fewer frames span a given application, reducing overall complexity and increasing reuse per frame. A typical industrial-strength application domain contains about 200 functional frames. When combined with a like number of system architecture frames, the amount of custom programming needed is below 10%.

Adaptive mechanisms make multiple inheritance systemic, which is why frame hierarchies show the most specialized classes (context-sensitive frames) at the top. Related properties go from being fragmented to being grouped together. The class hierarchy can directly reflect the context-sensitive structure and granularity of its information domain.

Frame architectures make it easy to accommodate rogues. Selecting griffin properties from *bird* and *lion* classes is straightforward. This is because domains are organized by archetypical components rather than by set-subset abstractions.

## Adapt Permits Functional Normalization

A method is the smallest heritable property, and it must be inherited as-is. If you don't want an inherited method, you write a complete polymorphic variant. In order to avoid redundancy, method grain sizes are kept small. Yet it still happens, as with subroutines, that many similar but subtly different versions evolve. Ultimately, it takes more time to research the differences than to write yet another version. This defeats the very purpose of reuse.

Adapt takes the reverse approach. Adaptor frames, e.g., specification frames, highlight what is different about inherited methods, avoiding unnecessary duplication without fragmentation. This allows the graininess of methods to match the natural coupling and cohesion of the domain.

The word "normalization," when applied to data, refers to the elimination of redundancy and the highlighting of data relationships. A similar effect can now be achieved with software. Generic frames containerize function types and data types to remove redundancies. The adapt mechanism highlights component relationships.

In order to achieve such normalizations, we need to partition software along boundaries that do not necessarily correspond to calling interfaces (e.g., object aggregation). Whereas a class defines *one encapsulated object*,[4] a generic frame defines *an unencapsulated component of many objects* (e.g. data structures without methods and vice versa). A complete object arises from the assembly of its component frames. (This is why the most specific

---

[4] Strictly speaking, so-called abstract classes do not define any objects themselves, leading some to think them framelike. But they are used to define calling interfaces for all their subclass objects, the very encapsulation boundaries that often inhibit normalization.

frame in any parts-explosion diagram, the specification frame, is always at the root. In contrast, a class hierarchy, organized by generalization rather than component relationships, places the most general class at the root.)

## Build More with Less

A worthy normalization goal is to implement a maximum diversity of functionality with a minimum of common components. Software is already complicated enough without adding the burden of finding and managing huge parts bins. Tom DeMarco says that "a library of 30,000 components is virtually useless." We have the luxury of a much lower threshold. I worry long before a frame library reaches 1,000 members.

## Fusing ISA with HASA

In other words, *adapt* fuses HASA and ISA into one mechanism. Figure 13-3 illustrates how this fusion permits frames to represent real-world objects

**Figure 13-3.** Both abstractions and component relationships are captured in one domain partitioning.

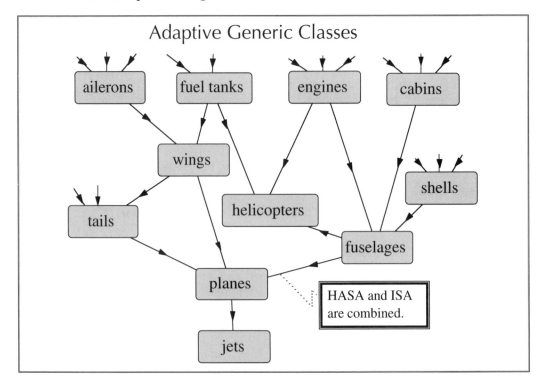

in a natural manner. A plane naturally HASA fuselage, two wings, and a tail. Wing HASA fuel tank, flaps, and zero or more engines, depending on the model. Each of these components is generic—adaptable, say, to jets and helicopters. Without this ability to combine part relationships with abstractions, we would need a much more elaborate partitioning of the domain, with all the complexity issues that that entails.

The frame approach thus simplifies the flow from OO analysis through design to construction. In a nutshell: real-world objects are analyzed for similarities that, during design, are consolidated into generic frames from which the original objects, and, more importantly, their ever-changing versions can be automatically (re)constructed. The next four chapters take this nut out of its shell.

## Class Evolution

What happens when existing classes need to evolve? A good answer to this question is essential if we are to handle the kind of volatility that business systems routinely experience. The simple answer—spawn additional classes—expands the sea of look-alikes. A better one is to have each component retain past differences from its current version. This allows it to evolve as necessary without spawning look-alikes, and without forcing existing objects to retrofit. Whenever an object is reconstructed, it sees only the version that was current when the object was defined. This is a special case of a frame carrying SELECTable variations, something that OO currently does not permit.

## Optimize Usability

My constant emphasis on construction time may give the impression that frames do not support highly modularized run times. Quite the contrary is true. The whole point of frame technology is to enable decisions about run-time architectures to be based on purely functional, ease-of-use, and performance requirements—usability. To the extent that dynamic binding, for example, satisfies such requirements, frames routinely build DLLs. Frames have even been used to build object-oriented execution environments for supporting the behavior of OO-Cobol-like objects. Tell me what you want to build and I will show you how frames can build it.

But to the extent that execution environments are co-opted to support behaviors that relate to generality and adaptability that is not needed during execution, I draw the line. Reuse issues do not belong there. Remember the duality. By separating run time from construction time, we can eat our cake and still have it. That is, we can optimize usability without compromising reusability and vice versa.

## Complexity Management

A clean separation of run time from construction time permits a new perspective on two important OO concepts, polymorphism and encapsulation, and on the general issue of complexity management.

### Polymorphism

Powerful but dangerous, a set of polymorphic methods, despite having identical interfaces, can still play havoc with a system because of differences in their behaviors. Some protection can be provided through runtime state checking, but there are difficulties: determining all the legal state transitions is difficult because they change with context, and with time; checking at run time degrades performance; preventing errors is preferred to merely detecting them.

At construction time, frame parameters can help prevent polymorphic aberrations. GUI- and report-painter front-ends, for example, enforce parameter settings such that all and only legal combinations are allowed. The resulting polymorphic methods for windows and reports are virtually guaranteed to work. Further, frame parameters consume no run time, and they can be tailored to suit a particular instance without disturbing the generic rules.

### Encapsulation

This capability is vital at run time, but, as I have hinted, counterproductive at construction time. Why? If some frames encode generic data structures while others encode generic processes, then each can be mated to frames of the opposite type, further enhancing reuse and avoiding redundancy.

In practice, this partitioning of a domain is quite effective. In EDI (electronic data interchange), for example, a supplier's customers have different product ordering formats, yet the supplier's generic order processes should be adaptable to each format. Say 100 customer data frames combine with 10 process frames to produce 1,000 useful polymorphs; then only 110 frames need to be managed, not 1,000 classes. Noma Industries uses this technique to great advantage (see Chapter 17).

### Frameworks Address Life-Cycle Issues

Complexity has a time dimension. At a moment in time, the more complexity you can hide behind object interfaces, the better. As a system evolves, however, it changes in random ways that occasionally do violence to its run-time architecture. There is no recourse but to revert to a construction-time view. When we do, we see that change happens on multiple time scales.

We can stratify unencapsulated components (frames) on the basis of how quickly they change. Even though an object is encapsulated at run time, different parts of it are subject to different evolutionary pressures and rates of change. Interface types tend to be more stable than interface instances. It is similar for data types and function types.

In exploiting this stratification, construction architectures, also called *frameworks*, organize components differently than execution architectures organize objects. In having frameworks to complement the run time, we limit complexity and reduce errors. Put another way, we extend the size and complexity of what we can effectively build.

## Lasagna Code

OO programmers complain about the "lasagna code" problem. That is, there are so many layers of small methods involved in satisfying a given service, each method calling another in some remote object, that it is very hard to understand what is going on. With frames as the unit of assembly, objects tend to package more related pieces of functionality. This practice can do much to alleviate the lasagna code problem during testing, although it can show up again in the framework.

## Behavior Predictability

A one-to-one correspondence between classes and objects aids predicting a system's behavior from its class definitions. Unfortunately, the power of an encoding is inversely correlated to its perspicacity [20].

Take biology, for example. DNA is clearly a powerful way to encode extremely sophisticated organisms. But the biologically important properties of proteins are very hard to predict from their nucleotide definitions. Frame-built objects can suffer this same fate. How does Nature cope? By automating a construction process that reuses robust, well-tested components—the development of an organism from a single egg through to its adult morphology is not left up to the organism!

The same applies to frames. That is why the destiny of reusable components is bound up with the development of rich frameworks. Odeseus (a pseudonym), a very large (over 5,000 programs), sophisticated client-server system to manage customers, was designed with such frameworks. Reusing the frameworks were over a hundred geographically dispersed developers. Odeseus was memorable because it cranked out *100 to 200 lines of unit-tested code per developer per hour*. Alas, Odeseus died because its parents (a consortium of purchasers and a major computer manufacturer) could not limit its growth (also known as requirements turbulence).

## Pushing the Envelope

In summary, frames are adaptive generic classes. Frame technology is an object-oriented construction system in which you are free to design whatever run-time architectures you like. You are never forced to use particular dynamic-binding, API, or DLL protocols; frameworks will support what is best for any situation.

Client-server is a good example of a family of architectures that lend themselves to this approach. The diversity of distributed, heterogeneous communications and computing platforms requires adapting to the needed architectural variations, as well as isolating the different sources of variation. The more complex and changeable the computing environment, the more such an approach is needed. Ample evidence exists that the frame approach does indeed scale up.

# Domain Analysis

## CHAPTER 14

> *A specification is a subset of points selected from a continuous portion of an infinite multidimensional space. The object itself and its total future history is the only complete specification.*
>
> Robert A. Frosch, 1969

W e want to build systems from reusable components. Fine, but where do we start? What are the system's executable components—its objects? What are their components? How do we generalize components? Make them adaptable? Underlying all these questions is the fundamental reuse question: what are those fewest components from which I can build the solutions I need?

Open-ended questions, by their nature, lack definitive answers. In this chapter and the next three, I present an empirical approach, driven by reuse, based on "archetypes and deltas." Evidence from over 10 years of successful practice confirms that the approach simplifies important analysis and design issues, described below. There is a huge and growing literature on various approaches to analysis and design. I suggest Coad and Yourdon [21], [22], and Booch [23] for further reading.

## Back to Basics

For every good analysis, many are awful—too detailed, too late, too wrong. Despite the many rules you find in books like this, there can be no substitute for a good grasp of the problem domain. Many insights come from talking to real domain experts or being one yourself. Even more derive from building things and trying them out, as per the iterative design refinement process explained in Part III.

We start with a fresh look at key analysis and design issues. This perspective shall give us a strategy, a *way* of doing domain analyis. To discuss the issues and form the strategy we need a bit of vocabulary.

## Information Domains

An *information domain* is a fancy name for a group of problems to be analyzed. Most interesting domains are untidy, oddball mixtures of stable physical and mathematical laws, somewhat unstable technological and computing environments, and even less stable application environments—business objectives, power and control issues, competitive pressures, government regulations, and the like. Although most interesting domains are chaotic and inconsistent, they usually posses relatively stable subdomains of similar elements, which we shall call categories.

Virtually anything induces an information domain! That should be obvious from the definition. To take a silly example, "the green pencil in my top desk drawer" induces a domain to the extent that you want to explore the relationships among that pencil's properties.

Examples of commercially important domains are also legion: customer management, product distribution, manufacturing planning and control, launching a space shuttle, insurance policy administration, power plant process control, and on and on. To take customer management, some example categories are customers, orders, deliveries, post-sales services, and relationship management. Each of these could be broken down into subcategories, if the problem warrants.

If anything can induce a domain, isn't the concept trivial? A domain gains utility through the process of identifying objects and properties you want to include and exclude from the domain. And, since each inclusion can induce a subdomain, the process may recurse indefinitely. As we shall see, the beauty of archetypes is that they are the "more concrete" examples that give meaning to a domain.

## Bridging the Chasm Between Domain Analysis and Object Design

To quote from Frosch again, "The real world is, however, highly non-linear, and unless real attention is paid to this fact, the linear decomposition treatment will fail catastrophically, because the interaction terms may be as large as the subproblems and not reducible to simple interfaces." [24]

Frosch identifies a key issue, which, over twenty years later, Coad and Yourdon eloquently bemoan[1] as the "major chasm between analysis and

---

[1] Pages 24–26 in [21].

design." This chasm is really between vagueness and precision. On one hand, executable systems are paragons of precision. Every character must be exactly so, or things might not even compile. On the other hand, domains contain inherently vague and inconsistent properties. Things true in one context are often false in another.

We need a bridge that makes crossing from vagueness to precision as smooth and painless as possible. As things at either end of the bridge change, and change they will, we shall have to recross it many times. Which is to say, we require models that can do two things: (1) characterize the properties of a vague domain at all relevant scales of granularity; and (2) easily combine and recombine into executable systems that accommodate our ever-changing perceptions of the domain.

## Archetypes and Deltas

In Chapter 8, we glimpsed this bridge. At the vague end are archetypes; at the precise end are frames. For convenience the definitions are repeated here.

**Archetype.** "The original pattern, or model, from which all other things of the same kind are made; prototype."

*[Webster's New World Dictionary]*

Think of an archetype as a "best example" of some sub-domain or category of similar constituents. Complementing archetypes are deltas.

**Delta.** A small difference between two things.

*[from mathematics]*

For us, a delta is a set of additions and subtractions, which, when applied to an archetype, convert it into a different example in the same category. So, deltas specify the differences between an archetype and "other things of the same kind"—its category of similarity.

When you think of reports, what comes to mind is one or a few generic examples that, for you, typify all reports. You can easily classify specific reports because they are small deltas from your archetypical reports. The same is true for systems in general, provided the system's components combine to serve some overall function or related set of functions. That overall characterization, together with the half-dozen or so major components or subsystems, form an archetype, from which specific systems in the same category are deltas.

Cognitive psychologist Eleanor Rosch's work [25] provides strong evidence that in our minds we represent categories as archetypes (she called them "prototypes"). Linguist-philosopher George Lakoff convincingly shows Rosch's ideas simplify our representations for languages [26]. These results support my hypothesis that software engineering should make use of archetypes and deltas because they are part of our natural "epistemology"—theory of knowledge. Let's examine my hypothesis.

## Vague Domains Beget Vague Categories

Think hard about any realistic category and you discover how fuzzy are its boundaries. Take the "bird" category. Penguins are birds but we don't think of them as archetypical examples. Even further out are (mythical) griffins. Are they birds, lions or something else? Even such an obvious category as "living" trails off into shades of gray. Are viruses alive? Prions?[2] Ecosystems? Spores? Embryos? People whose hearts have stopped? Frozen organisms? Artificially intelligent systems? My point is that there are no absolutely right or wrong answers to such questions. Right and wrong vary with context and over time.

Archetypes and deltas allow us to hedge our bets. We can model each category with a good example, one from which we can easily add and subtract as necessary. The larger the delta, the farther from the "center" of the category, the more the result could also belong in other categories—i.e., result from other archetype-delta combinations. In other words, archetypes model the way categories overlap in real domains. In practice, stretching an archetype too far is self-limiting. The more work involved, the more you will look for an archetype with a smaller delta.

The ability of archetypes to have arbitrary deltas may sound sloppy, ad hoc, but it gives us our best chance to adapt to variations in requirements and design that have yet to occur to system stakeholders. Moreover, a vain search for categories with just the "right" properties leads to analysis paralysis. Rather, as we shall see below, it's much easier and faster to pick reasonable examples, and use deltas to create instances that satisfy the stakeholders. Also, if and when requirements stabilize enough to justify the extra analysis effort, you can always go back and refine your archetypes.

If we get lucky and find our domain is well behaved, great! The archetype approach works whether or not the category boundaries fit together neatly. In particular, mutually exclusive categories are just overlapping categories that happen to have no overlaps.

---

[2] Prions are smaller than viruses. They are infectious agents that have no DNA or RNA, but reproduce in brain cells, causing fatal diseases: scrapie in sheep, "mad cow" disease, and Creutzfeldt-Jacob disease in humans.

## Archetype Decomposition

Archetypes, being specific examples, can be broken into pieces. Not broken as with a hammer. We want the pieces or parts to be as similar as possible to (pre)existing archetypes. By decomposing an archetype into such parts, we can replace their voluminous details with much smaller deltas to the existing archetypes.

Something interesting is happening. Archetypes are being composed from (component) archetypes, forming framelike hierarchies. By the same token, categories are composed from categories. A delta expresses an explicit relationship between main and sub categories. Because in practice, a delta is small, ranging up to 15% of its archetype, we can not only eliminate redundancies, but also clarify the relationships among categories at different levels.

Ideally, an archetype would be at the "center" of its category. In principle, if we knew all the members of a category, we could find its center—the member such that the sum of the deltas from that member to all others is minimized. Of course, this calculation is rarely, if ever, possible in practice. And unnecessary! All we really need are examples whose deltas to most instances are small compared to the example. In practice, these are reasonably easy to find/invent because they are already "close" to solutions that work in specific contexts.[3]

## From Archetypes to Frames

In general, while an archetype is explicit, it may have no group of properties that defines its category "categorically." Any property may be modified or deleted in the process of making "other things of the same kind." Must a living organism be able to reproduce? Repair itself? Feed itself? The answers are mostly yes, but not always.

Likewise, a report program archetype probably contains page header lines and trailers, data group headers and trailers, detail lines, total and subtotal lines, as-is and derived data details, and so on. A particular report may modify or omit one or more of these properties. Similarly, for a category of systems, particular subsystems are highly likely to be tailored,

---

[3] Recent work in the theory of evolution indicates that mutations (deltas) occurring in fit individuals (archetypes) are far more likely to be helpful than harmful. Conversely, mutations in unfit individuals tend to be more harmful than beneficial, but because the unfit die faster, the overall result is positive. Why do complex, nonlinear domains seem so well behaved? Perhaps the "anthropic" (from the word anthropomorphic) principle is at work: chaotic domains may appear well behaved to us because we and our systems can operate (survive) only in sufficiently benign regions.

some to the point of omission. In order to keep the deltas small, it is useful to span some categories with multiple (overlapping) archetypes.

What is the relationship between archetypes, deltas, frames, and objects? An archetype exemplifies a category. Deltas give rise to other category members. A frame is a formal generalization of an archetype, and hence represents a category implicitly. A frame $F$, also embodies deltas. $F$ uses: INSERTs and REPLACEs to add and subtract properties from its descendent frames, SELECTs to choose among multiple archetypes jointly spanning a component category, BREAKs and frame variables to allow deltas in $F$'s ancestor frames to vary the archetypes and deltas of $F$.

Frame subassemblies specify how categories combine to form new categories. Complete frame hierarchies specify how to build executable objects. We have our bridge.

Frames exemplify a domain's basic vocabulary of noun forms and verb forms. With frames in hand, we can automatically build objects so we can test and refine our analysis and design, and get on with delivering a robust system. Part III is devoted to this process.

## The Functional Analysis of a Domain

Our first goal is to understand the macroscopic properties of the domain well enough to be able to design the architecture of the run-time environment—the inter- and intrasystem interfaces, behind which complex behaviors can be encapsulated in objects.

On a visit to Long Island Lighting Co., Peter Fidleman observed to me that one of the software industry's mistaken notions is that of a "system." His point was that their boundaries are often artificial, creating interface problems that would not otherwise exist. Peter envisions independent polymorphic objects communicating with each other via a common infrastructure with no preconceived physical or logical boundaries as in "systems." He has a point; vague domains do not have well-defined boundaries. A single business process often involves multiple systems. For convenience, however, to the extent that a (not necessarily fixed) collection of objects interact with each other in order to model an information domain, we shall refer to them as a system.

For our purposes, an object is an executable analogue of a (semi)antonomous agent[4] in the domain. It consists of a coherent set of methods that manage a shared data structure. An object can have multi-

---

[4] An active entity, capable of interracting with other agents and behaving in various ways.

ple instances, the same methods accessing a distinct set of values for the data structure. All external access to an object's data is via messages to and from the object's methods.

Functional analysis in a nutshell: Scope the domain. Resolve its important agents. Partition the set of agents into internal (executable objects) and external (users, customers, other systems, etc.). This partitioning results in a de facto system boundary, within which we try to decide the interfaces among its objects and to the outside agents. The aggregate of such decisions constrains the run-time architecture.

We focus on defining the novel states of archetypical objects, and the rules that govern their transitions. We next exemplify the archetypes' constituents—data attributes and methods. Then we are ready for the next chapter, to resolve archetype components, leading to frame design.

## Write a Scoping Document

The first step in requirement setting is to scope the domain of relevant concerns. What are the high-level goals and global constraints, including deadlines? What problems do we want to solve, and what do we want to avoid? Which solution aspects are critical success factors (must haves), which are secondary (should haves), tertiary (might haves), and explicitly outside the scope? What are the likely risks, benefits, and opportunity costs?

There can be no mechanical rules for scoping a domain. Requirements are changeable, partly explicit and partly implicit. The effectiveness of a scoping document lies in how well it guides stakeholders. As requirements and clarifications emerge, a well-characterized scope makes it easy to agree where each suggestion fits (must, should, might, not applicable).[5]

Listen to, and immerse yourself with, people who work effectively in the subject domain, be it some aspect of banking, retailing, manufacturing, or whatever. Learn the jargon of the trade. Identify the agents and focus on their most important activities, information flows, and the temporal relationships among them. For banking, agents might include tellers, customers, bank officers, current accounts, and asset management. The temporal relationships cover time scales ranging from seconds to years. Finding all the meaningful relationships and grouping them appropriately is an empirical process.

---

[5] Stakeholders need to agree up front on the consequences of requirements "turbulence": new and changed "musts" can directly impact the implementation schedule and/or costs, or even abort the project; new "shoulds" ought not to affect the schedule (a buffer usually exists to accommodate surprise "shoulds"); "mights" come after satisfying the other two categories.

Test your discrimination between major, minor, and irrelevant details by asking domain experts to critique how you would deal with specific situations. What conditions should trigger updating currency exchange rates? Underline key nouns and verbs from the known requirements and connect them with the jargon of the trade.

Often there will be examples (ideally archetypes) of systems within the domain, and without ("near misses"). Scoping the domain as deltas from these actual working examples often forces out many otherwise hidden assumptions.

Good scoping documents should be brief. They contain only the highest level requirements, and they list as many assumptions as stakeholders can think of (it's usually the implicit assumptions that cause the most problems). Altering any of these requirements or assumptions can be grounds for aborting the associated project.

## Identify Agent Archetypes

In banking domains, agents would include customers, accounts, loans, securities, tellers, managers, officers, investors, and regulators. Not all agents in a domain map into system objects. Which ones belong inside a system depend on what services the system is required to provide, a question whose answer is not fixed in stone. But some common sense guidelines apply:

1. We want to find the domain's persistent agents. System requirements are volatile, especially during early analysis. This volatility can be exploited. Functionality that remains relatively stable despite requirements turbulence should form (parts of) the system's main agents. Given that everything changes over time, one of our jobs is to discover the relatively stable elements, then engineer them for maximum (re)use.

2. Another way to recognize persistent agents is that they have histories—they manage data accumulated from prior invocations. Objects, managing encapsulated history data, will become executable models of those agents.

3. Behaviors involving repetitive search, retrieval, calculation, update, and display are good candidates for modeling as system executables (objects). Conversely, making judgments, integrating ad hoc information, and recognizing patterns are relatively harder for computers to do, and so are usually assigned to external (human) agents.

4. Categorize agents by matching them with pre-existing archetypes. In mature reuse environments, many archetypes—customers, for example—will already be embodied by frameworks such that novel customer species are deltas from a generic customer category. And such categories, in turn, nest within even more generic categories, say, containing support for databases, screens, reports, network protocols, and the like. The expertise encoded into such prestratified, pretested frameworks will greatly reduce your analysis and design work, and allow you to focus on the true novelties of your current domain.

5. Speaking of novelties, determine whether pairs of archetypes can be fused, modeled as one object. Can a bank teller be a loan officer? It is important not to take "no" at face value. Our habits and beliefs are based on implicit assumptions that may be invalid or outdated. But no one has noticed. By challenging such assumptions, a good analyst can often discover simplifications that not only save money, but create new wealth-generating opportunities. From a system's point of view, if two agents are so similar that their differences can easily be characterized by a few properties governed by executable rules, then make a case for fusing them.  A loan officer can be thought of as a bank teller plus a few more rules for creating credit!  Can customers be their own tellers? Certainly, as in ATMs.

6. Each agent interacts with a set of other agents. If two agents interact with the same set of agents (or one set is a subset of the other) then consider fusing them.

   Two agents may also be fused into one object if they are tightly coupled. The ideas of *coupling* and *cohesion* [27] can help us decide what belongs in one object and not another.

   Objects should be *loosely coupled* to each other. This means objects that talk to each other need only send short messages in order to effect desired results. I think of these interfaces as "hourglass" points. See Figure 14-1. On either side of its narrow neck, an hourglass swells to encompass methods that are interdependent. The boundaries of objects, then, are pinned down by loosely coupled interfaces.

   On the other hand, within an object, its methods should have *high cohesion*. That is, each method performs one succinctly described function; each complements the others; taken together, they are necessary and sufficient to manage a common data structure (which suggests they may be tightly coupled). Deciding the cohesive properties of objects is a subject in its own right.

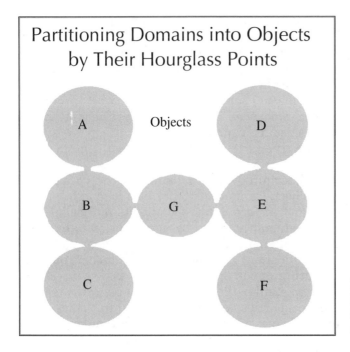

**Figure 14-1.** Objects should be loosely coupled to each other and have high internal cohesion.

### When in Doubt Leave It Out

Any interesting domain contains an unlimited number of properties and relationships among them, most of which are irrelevant. Domain knowledge and experience are vital when choosing appropriate properties. Does a bank need to know the color of a customer's shoes? The names of relatives? The answers are yes and/or no, depending on what types of business the bank is in, which changes with time. Many property choices will be obvious; others will be visible only with the hindsight of experiencing the consequences of your current choices.

Given all the uncertainties, go for the "must have" properties. Get a rough idea built and tested so you can learn from the dynamic interactions of the system with itself and its environment. When in doubt leave it out. Adding a property is always easier than removing one upon which some objects now depend. Ruthlessly simplify. Life is already complex enough.

### Describe Agents by Their State Transitions

To prepare for designing and building dynamic models, you can document your proposed objects using *state transition diagrams*. The technique is summarized here. For more details see Booch [23, ch. 5].

An object's state is the value of all its variables (also called *attributes*) at an instant in time. The state of a jet in flight includes its position, air speed, ground speed, direction, altitude, pitch, yaw, roll, fuel in each tank, engine thrust, . . ., to name a few. We can group variables into "private" and "public." Public variables are external, used by other objects; private ones are internal, local to the methods within an object.

*State transition rules*, a fancy phrase for program logic, define how to change the state of an object. Our jet object will have rules involving air speed, altitude, orientation, and engine thrust. During execution, these variables change, and so our jet object simulates the way a real jet operates. (Whether or not the simulation occurs in real-time depends on whether variables change state in synchrony with a real jet.)

Objects change each other's states by sending messages to the methods that update each others' public variables. Our jet's pilot sends messages to the jet via her control stick, switches, and knobs, and receives messages from the jet via its dials and displays. We represent each state transition in the diagram as a labeled arc connecting two object nodes, as in Figure 14-2; arcs also represent messages.

**Figure 14-2.** Three objects exchange messages, thereby updating each other's states according to specific rules.

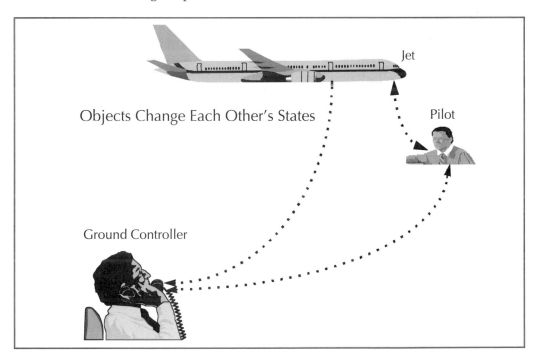

Objects Change Each Other's States

Jet

Pilot

Ground Controller

State transition diagrams are static models of dynamic properties, useful for sketching (novel) relationships among agents. Given a reuse environment, such diagrams need only specify the novel relationships among archetype objects. The state transition lines highlight new and changed behaviors. The rest are subsumed within existing frameworks. Of course, where there is much novelty, the diagrams are more detailed.

The next step is to convert the state transition information into examples of how the archetypical objects work. This design step moves us from static to dynamic models.

The architectural design of a run-time environment should attempt to maximize the *usability* of objects—functionality, performance, ease-of-use. There are many ways to gauge usability. Usability is also subject to many practical operational constraints: fixed physical interfaces, a desire to minimize recompiles, network characteristics, existing systems and their interfaces.

## Sanity Check

Where are we in this discussion? We started with an approach to identifying the archetypical agents in a domain, then trying to decide what their properties—interfaces, attributes and methods—should be. If some archetypes seem like functions while others look like data, some of your boundaries are in the wrong places. Executable objects are encapsulations of both data and process—loosely coupled, internally cohesive models of persistent domain agents.

We noted that we should avoid reanalyzing similar wheels, that we should fuse agents and simplify their properties at every turn. Our goal, constrained by existing reusable architectures, is to get from a static model to working versions of the most critical parts of a system as fast as we can. Each version provides dynamic feedback needed to analyze what the next version should be.

# Parts-Oriented Analysis and Design

## CHAPTER 15

*The poet must become more and more comprehensive,
more allusive, more indirect,
in order to force, to dislocate if necessary,
language into its meaning.*

T.S. Elliot, 1921

I have often pointed out the dual nature of run time and construction time. Domain analysis resolves behavioral archetypes—categories of run-time objects. They are assembled from data and logic structures—categories of construction-time parts. How do we resolve behavioral archetypes into frame parts? That is the subject of this and the next two chapters.

We start by decomposing behavioral archetypes into their major pieces, frame subassemblies. We design framework architectures—subassemblies layered for change isolation. Finally, we generalize the frames for adaptive reuse within the scope of their categories.

We shall often refer to a (sub)assembly as if it were a single frame. We can blur the distinction between frame and frame assembly because the details in component frames can be adapted as if they were all in the (sub)assembly's root frame. This blurring allows us to resolve components in a top-down fashion, starting by treating each behavioral archetype as a single frame. It also gives us a great deal of latitude to change our minds about frame sub-hierarchies, as we learn how the categories are nested.

## Resolving Reusable Parts

We need defensible answers to software engineering questions like: Should wholesale and retail customers have separate definitions or should a more generic definition be adaptable to both? Should a customer record definition exist as a separate frame or be encapsulated with the methods that maintain it? Should customer identification—key, name, address, etc.—be a fragment of the customer definition or packaged as a separate frame?

Before we can begin to answer such questions, we need to distinguish functional from structural similarity analyses. First, let's review functional similarity analyses such as we saw in the last chapter.

### Functional Similarity

Accounts receivable resembles accounts payable. They are functional inverses of each other. Managing loans is the same as managing deposits, except. . . . Airlines, hotels, and other reservation applications are kinds of inventory control. Order processing is order processing, whether it's a sales order, a work order, or a purchase order. Government revenue departments manage taxpayer cases like insurance companies, gas utilities, and lawyers manage their client cases. From a functional point of view, the universe fairly glows with similarities.

We modeled our archetypical agents with state transition diagrams that constrain their functionalities. One issue is that there are many different algorithms that are functionally equivalent. Choosing good ones depends on modularity and usability criteria, which here we shall take for granted.

### Structural Similarities

To understand what structural similarities offer, let's digress briefly, as we did in Chapter 11, to the notions of genotypes and phenotypes. In biology, a *genotype* is "the fundamental constitution of an organism in terms of its heredity factors" [*Webster's New World Dictionary*]. In other words, genotype means genes, DNA, construction-time properties. Again from Webster's, a *phenotype* is "the manifest characteristics of an organism. . . that result from both its heredity and its environment." So, phenotype means run-time properties.

Fact: *similar genotypes may give rise to dissimilar phenotypes*. Indeed, a point-mutation (a change to one DNA codon) in certain genes can cause profound differences in your health. In software, as in biology, large run-time differences can result from tiny differences in structural definitions. This nonlinearity adds a new dimension of power to similarity analysis.

## ACME Sales

Let's consider a small example. ACME Sales has regional offices. Each region maintains its own databases. Head office periodically uploads regional data in order to do corporate-wide analyses of their customers, some of whom deal with multiple offices. After uploading, regional information is consolidated in various ways, such as:

1. Global:  a master file of all customers.
2. Multi:  a file of all multi office customers.
3. Local:  a file of all single office customers.

From a *functional* point of view, we notice that Global and Multi can be used to define Local = Global – Multi. Without a structural similarity analysis, we would probably go ahead and code Global and Multi, then define Local in terms of the other two.

Now think for a moment about how Global might work. Assuming the input files are sorted by customer and open together, Global would check customer keys for duplicates and output exactly one record per customer. But if we simply omit the step that outputs a record whose key is duplicated, Eureka! We have a version of Local that is at once simpler, needs no temporary output, and executes twice as fast. Genotypically, Local is a very small delta from Global, even though phenotypically, they have quite different effects.

While somewhat contrived, the example illustrates the power of *structural* similarity analysis to simplify both the genotypes and the phenotypes of a domain. A deeper structural analysis of this category shows that methods corresponding to the so-called primitive operators of set theory (union, intersection, and difference) are all small genotypic deltas from Local.

How small must exceptions be for two parts to be considered similar? As mentioned in the last chapter, experience shows that "similar" implies genotypic differences up to 15%. Why? Below 15%, the work of understanding genotype $X$ and figuring out the delta to $Y$ seems less than creating $Y$ from scratch. Above 15%, it seems more effective to roll your own than to spend so much time figuring out $X$'s irrelevencies and wrong structures. On the other hand, changing 15% of a genotype can take you a very long way from the default phenotype. (Remember, according to Professor Stebbins, the DNA delta between us and chimps is less than 3%. For those who find this hard to believe, see the footnote on page 41.)

What follows is a process for analyzing the structures and designing the components of the behavioral archetypes resulting from the domain analysis. To focus the discussion, let's pick one of these archetypes and call it Archie. In principle, we can break Archie into pieces—groups of data structures and/or methods—in many different ways. Both functional and structural similarity analysis will help us choose good pieces.

## 1. Match to Existing Use-as-Is Parts

First, look for parts of Archie that are, or can be made, functionally equivalent, possibly identical, to existing data definitions (relational data models, object-oriented databases) and existing executables (objects, operating system services, programs, statically or dynamically linked subroutines, etc.) Cleave away as much of Archie's structure as possible by referring to existing data structures and calling existing executables.[1]

## 2. Match to Existing Same-as-Except Parts

Look for the largest remaining pieces of Archie that are small deltas from existing frames. Further cleave away as much as possible from Archie by same-as-except, referring to those frames.

## 3. Match to Other Behavioral Archetypes' Parts

In the remaining pieces of Archie, look for the largest same-as-except analogues to pieces in other archetypical agents. For example, if a domain has customer, supplier, and employee archetypes, we will find all three contain similar identification information—key, name, address, phone number, etc.—along with methods for managing that information. We can cleave all such similarities from their archetypes because we will be framing them. After replacing all such structurally similar pieces with same-as-except references, any remaining pieces of Archie become part of Archie's specification frame.

## 4. Frame the Most Reusable Pieces First

They are easiest to spot because they crop up the most. There is an 80:20 rule here: 80% of the reuse comes from 20% of the frames; framing them first provides the largest benefits. Conversely, avoid designing frames whose reuse is largely hypothetical (less than three known reuses), unless there are compelling reasons, such as the need to isolate different sources of change. You can always frame a piece later when its need is proven, whether or not you go back and cleave its analogues from their specification frames.

---

[1] At first glance, this process might appear to be nothing more than "subclassing" Archie to multiple parent classes. However, here the classes are not abstractions of Archie. They are Archie's parts.

Just as we want to maximize the usability of executables, we want to maximize the reusability of their parts. One reuse measure is the ratio:

**(# frame reuses)/(# reusable frames)**

Another common ratio is:

**(total ESLOC – specification frame ESLOC)/(total ESLOC)**

The larger these ratios, the higher the reuse.

The most reusable frames are the most context-free, the ones toward the bottoms of hierarchies. This is because higher frames supply context for lower ones but not vice versa. Is there a way to spot context-free frames before we know their hierarchical positions? Yes. They are needed in most, if not all, contexts of reuse; however, most contexts do not have to be aware of their presence in order to adapt them. This is because context-sensitive frames (SPCs) set values to frame variables, such as "target environment," whose effects cascade throughout a hierarchy, including the deepest frames. However, these effects are *implicit*—specification frame writers are normally unaware of their effects on context-free frames.

## 5. Normalize

To avoid needless exceptions and overlaps, normalize similar data definitions [28, 5]. Or, if applicable to your run-time environment, consider object-oriented database design techniques [29]. As with data, you may be able to normalize similar methods. That is, if you can make them functionally equivalent, you can design frames to encapsulate the functionality in a separate object or (DLL) routine. In this way, you enhance usability, and when its functionality evolves, there is only one module to be reconstructed (compiled and tested).

## 6.  Frame Context-Related Deltas

Notwithstanding step #5, domains resolve into many same-as-except categories of data structures and methods, where the "except"ions cannot be eliminated. With frames, the instances of such categories do not have to be, and normally should not be, designed to be separately executable polymorphs (as current OOLs require). Rather, we design frames to be components of larger executables (objects). There are several reasons for this.

**First: context.** Suppose $f_1, f_2, ..., f_n$ are deltas (customizing arguments) to independent frames, $F_1(x)$, . . .,$F_n(x)$, respectively. And suppose corresponding instances, $F_1(f_1)$, . . .,$F_n(f_n)$, are (sub)components of Archie. Because all the $F_i(f_i)$ must work together in the context of Archie, it is likely that the $f_i$ are interdependent, even though the $F_i(x)$ are not. By bringing all the $f_i$ together within Archie, it's easy to see exactly what changes were necessary in order to make the $F_i(x)$ collaborate in Archie's context. Later, should Archie or any of the $F_i(x)$ change, we have one place to look—Archie—in order to determine if there are any side effects on the other collaborators in that context.

On the other hand, if Archie invoked the $F_i(f_i)$ as separate executables, it would be hard to understand their interrelationships because the $f_i$ would be both implicit and scattered. Localization of related deltas allows us to understand why various (polymorphic) instances from different categories are necessary.

**Second: uncallability.**  Frames that contain data definitions without methods or, conversely, methods without data definitions are reusable, but not callable. I cannot emphasize enough that reusable components do not necessarily cleave along callable interfaces.

**Third: surplus properties.**  Frames often deliberately contain more properties than any one object needs. They are SELECTable alternatives within a component category, and they evolve as a unit.

**Fourth: graininess.**  Last, but not least, we want our objects to mirror the natural graininess of their domain. Pragmatic limitations aside, if a component object is used in conjunction with only one composite object, then the separate component adds unnecessary execution time and complexity (one more entity to manage).

## Frame Organization

Having found pieces that need framing, we need to organize the frame hierarchy—decide what is a component of what. A frame, being a piece of a module, may only be a data structure, or a method, or just commands for adapting other frames. Of course, a frame may be combinations of all three.

Suppose $p_1$ and $p_2$ are pieces of Archie being framed. The question is, should $p_1$ and $p_2$ be in the same frame, or, if in separate frames, should they be siblings, or should one be a component of the other? The choices are diagrammed in Figure 15-1. The logic of reuse helps us decide among them:

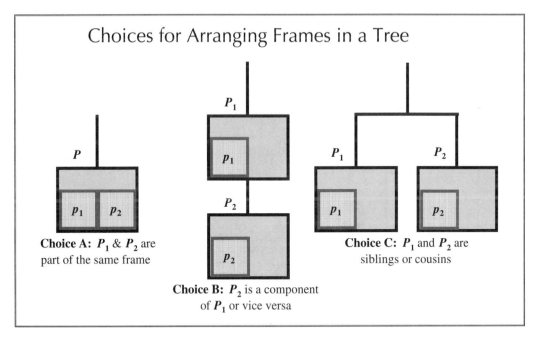

Choices for Arranging Frames in a Tree

**Choice A:** $P_1$ & $P_2$ are part of the same frame

**Choice B:** $P_2$ is a component of $P_1$ or vice versa

**Choice C:** $P_1$ and $P_2$ are siblings or cousins

**Figure 15-1.** The three choices for $p_1$ and $p_2$ depend on their relative reuse. The frames they are housed in are larger as they may contain other information.

If every reuse of $p_1$ is likely also a reuse of $p_2$ and conversely, then they belong in the same frame. Otherwise, they belong to separate categories and we should design separate frames, $P_1$ and $P_2$, to house them. For example, $p_1$ might be a data definition and $p_2$ might be logic to process $p_1$'s data. The domain may contain contexts in which $p_2$, perhaps with small deltas, would also operate on data defined by other frames.

If every reuse of $P_1$ implies a reuse of $P_2$ but $P_2$ can be reused without $P_1$, then $P_2$ is a (sub)component frame of (COPYed directly or indirectly by) $P_1$. This rule reflects the fact that the more reusable the frame, the lower in the hierarchy it goes.

If $P_1$ and $P_2$ can each be reused without the other, then they go into sibling frames. To continue the above example, it could also turn out that data structure $p_1$ (with small deltas) could be operated on by methods in separate frames. Siblings, depending on the further decomposition of the frames, may actually turn out to be cousins. That is, they will have a common ancestor frame, but may be COPYed by different parent frames.

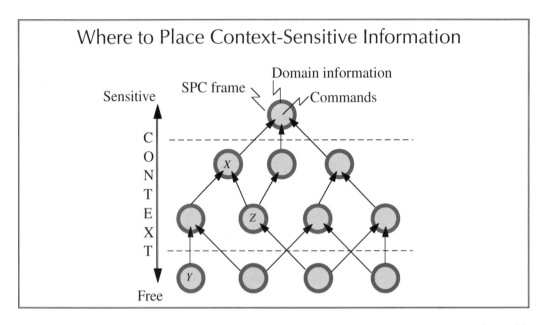

**Figure 15-2.** If $Y$ and $Z$ clash, $X$ is the nearest common ancestor and would normally be the place to resolve the context-sensitivity. This spares the SPC from unnecessary detail.

## Where to Resolve Context Clashes

Two or more context-free parts often clash[2] because they satisfy conflicting constraints. Minor issues, like a missing message argument, or incompatible data formats may be irrelevant in many reuse contexts, and therefore not the "fault" of any one part. Inter-frame issues that arise only in certain contexts are ideally resolved there. "There" is usually, but not always, the nearest ancestor frame that can adapt the relevant components.

Suppose in Figure 15-2, there are two clashing frames, $Y$ and $Z$, at different levels. Then they could be resolved by the nearest common ancestor frame, $X$. The steps taken to resolve the clash can be highlighted within any frame that spans the context of the clash. Potential reusers of the $X$ subassembly, the SPC in the case of Figure 15-2, have to be concerned only to the extent, if any, that the $X$ subassembly clashes with the rest of the hierarchy.

There are exceptions. The fix does not go into $X$ if the clash depends on the context in which the $X$ subassembly is reused. Then it goes into the closest ancestor frame in which the interference is manifested, (i.e., in this

---

[2] Such clashes can be very subtle and may not be detected until run time.

case, the SPC).

## A Real-World Example: Overdraft Protection

Imagine a banking system involving three archetypical processes OD, SC, and CA (See Figure 15-3). OD scans accounts for overdrafts. In some bank products, OD attempts to eliminate overdrafts by transferring funds from other accounts belonging to the same owners. To do this, OD invokes CA, which retrieves accounts belonging to a given customer. SC also scans accounts, calculating service charges for checks, money orders, overdrafts, automatic withdrawals, and other transactions. Again, depending on the banking product, if an account's balance is more than some threshold value, SC may waive service charges.

Being reusable, OD and SC are involved independently in various banking products. However, when reused together, OD and SC may clash. Specifically, OD sometimes causes an account to fall below its SC threshold balance, even though the overdraft could have been covered by other accounts. This is a context-sensitive interaction. Such side effects seldom increase customer satisfaction, especially when told "it's the computer."

To resolve the clash, OD needs to minimize threshold crossings. The proper solution is neither to modify the generic processes, thereby compromising their context-free reusability, nor to program around the clash, thereby increasing complexity and run-time inefficiency. In the solution

**Figure 15-3.** Two frame subassemblies can get reused in many banking products (contexts).

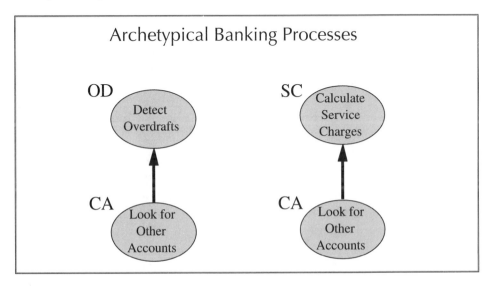

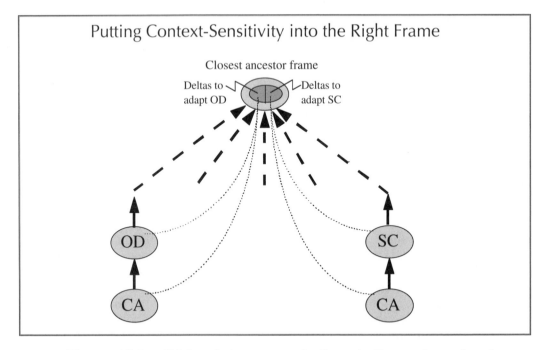

**Figure 15-4.** Clashes between overdraft protection and service charges should not be resolved by modifying those frames. Rather, resolve them in the nearest common ancestor that is reused in banking products where the clash happens.

(Figure 15-4), the nearest common ancestor frame spanning the clashing components provides the context in which to localize the refinement to OD and/or SC. The refinement does not undo any of what OD and CA do; it creates the best algorithm for that context. It reworks rather than works around. The algorithm's complexity is minimized, its execution is optimized, and its construction-time components remain generic, reusable. It seems that we can eat our context-free parts and have them too!

Detecting context clashes is a haphazard business. If the run-time environment is imperfectly understood (always true in practice), the side effects may be noticed only after the components have been designed, built, tested, and standardized. What's nice about frames is that, while the side effect's closest spanning frame is ideal, any frame closer to the SPC, including the SPC, can also deal with it. It's just that the context may be more specific, and hence the delta less reusable than it could be; another context may experience the same side effect and the delta would have to be expressed redundantly.

# The Second Dimension: Reuse Across Time

## CHAPTER 16

> *A system is never finished being developed*
> *until it ceases to be used.*
>
> Gerald M. Weinberg

I n the previous chapter, I dealt with reuse across a domain of behavioral archetypes. We might call this reuse across space, so to speak, the *first dimension*. It is first because execution domains are the primary focus of our design. Decomposing archetypes in this way provides the "vertical" dimension of frame hierarchies.

Reuse across time, which we might call the *second* (or "horizontal") *dimension*, is at least as important. If we can minimize the impact of change, which occurs over time, we don't have to be nearly so worried about flaws in our current understanding of the domain, nor about unpredictable requirement changes. One of the strengths of frame technology is its propensity to accommodate change.

Requirements change unceasingly, driving ever more "same-as-exceptions" into our frames. Different sources of evolutionary pressure cause frames to evolve asynchronously. End-users cause endless changes to their specific applications. Managers change departmental business rules. Executives change corporate system standards. Computer and software suppliers change technologies—database interfaces, network protocols, GUI APIs, and the like.

These different sources of change form a set of broad categories that are orthogonal to the domain categories we have been discussing until now. Each category of changes will correspond to a layer of frames. These layers constitute the second dimension of reuse, cutting "horizontally" across the "vertical" archetype decomposition. By ensuring that parts affected by different sources of change are isolated in different frames, we can minimize the impact of change.

End-user changes, for example, are confined to specification frames. Changes to corporate system standards are usually independent of business rules and vendor-specific technologies. While never perfect, it is straightforward to isolate separate sources of change into separate frame layers. By freeing each layer to evolve independently of the others, you reduce complexity and increase the speed with which you can respond to change.

Moreover, we shall see below how to protect existing executables from changes to their components. New executables will incorporate these changes without compelling us to retrofit.

Taken together, these two orthogonal reuse dimensions result in what is called a layered component architecture. It is designed to handle change, both systemic and temporal.

## Wrapper Frames

Wrapper frames, as the name suggests, are intended to hide the complexity of other frames "inside the wrapper." See Figure 16-1. Suppose after reusing $P$ several times, you determine that $p_1$ and $p_2$ in $P$ can be independently reused. In this event, you change $P$ into what is called a "wrapper" frame. $P$ simply COPYs two new sibling frames, $P_1$ and $P_2$. This ability to exploit 20-20 hindsight implies that you should be conservative, not breaking frames into smaller and smaller pieces unless there is a good case for independent reuse of the pieces. Wrapper frames have two other important purposes.

The first is to hedge developers' learning curves against changes to widely reused frames. When changes are proposed to such a frame, rather than embedding the changes directly, thereby forcing people to change their understanding of the frame, put them in a wrapper frame. Users of the wrapper are those who perceive the need for a change. For their purposes, it's as if the underlying frame has been modified. For everyone else, life goes on as usual; they continue to use the underlying frame directly. Periodically, say every year or two, you can look at the reuse statistics and decide whether or not to consolidate the wrapper as a permanent change to the underlying frame (under version control, see SELECT below). Chapters 19 and 20 explain the frame maturation process in more detail.

The second and most common purpose of wrappers is to hide the complexity of another frame. A file-handling frame (hierarchy), for example, may be able to handle a variety of database schemas, as well as flat files,

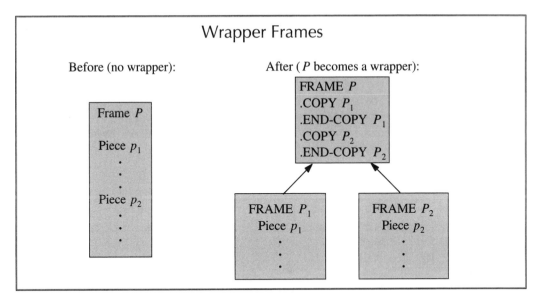

**Figure 16-1.** If $p_1$ and $p_2$ turn out to be reusable, they can be framed, with $P$ containing nothing but references to $P_1$ and $P_2$. Such changes are invisible to other frames.

ISAM, VSAM, and so on. A given computing environment may need only one schema. A separate wrapper frame for each schema would set parameters for the file frame in order to adapt it to that schema. Thus application programmers in a given environment only see a simplified set of choices. To them, the wrapper frame is the file frame tailored for their needs.

## Templates

A template is a special kind of wrapper frame, intended to simplify the process of defining SPCs. In most domains, it turns out that there are relatively few behavioral archetypes, with plenty of instances of each.

Let's assume the application layer of a component architecture is implemented by SPCs (i.e., all business rules are unique). Then archetypes typical of business domains would include data entry, batch update, reporting, enquiries, . . . ; after a few more you run out. For each behavioral archetype there will be a characteristic frame hierarchy.

By providing developers with a template for each framework, they no longer need to remember what frames they need or what parameters they need. Rather, each template remembers these items for them. It invokes the appropriate frames, lists the frame parameters developers typically need to fill in, and documents how and when to set the parameters.

The difference between a template and a wrapper is that programmers copy and modify templates, whereas a wrapper is a read-only frame, and is adapted by higher level frames (e.g., specification frames).

The template concept generalizes to suites of executables. In other words, a system template can be defined that, when parameterized, automates filling in specification frame templates for every executable in a given archetype system, e.g., client-server.

## Frame Generalization

This section presumes you are familiar with the frame commands explained in Chapter 9.

When framing archetypes, each method and data structure is surrounded by a (BREAK. . .END-BREAK) pair. Thus, each frame becomes a list of parameters whose default values are methods and data-structures. This enables adaptor frames to INSERT deltas that can delete, modify, or extend whatever properties they require. This includes INSERTing generic properties—data structures and methods—that contain frame variables and commands. (You may recall that INSERTs are evaluated in the context of their BREAKs, so the text of an insert has exactly the same effect as if it had been coded directly in the frame containing the BREAK.)

A "nice to have" design goal would permit frames that customize subframes to localize each delta to a single INSERT. Unfortunately, this is often not possible. For example, suppose you frame an archetype as a subassembly of existing frames that have not been reused together before. Component frames are likely to clash because they are mutually context-free, as illustrated by the banking example at the end of Chapter 15.

The deltas that make a subassembly mesh smoothly will probably require multiple INSERTs. You should localize them as a contiguous block, but where do you put it? As I mentioned, in principle, you could put it in any frame that is ancestral to the subassembly in question. The natural frame within which to put it is the root of that subassembly. Putting the block into a more distant ancestor, such as the specification frame, reduces its reusability and exposes application builders to needless complexity.

## Generalizing with SELECTs

Whereas BREAK allows for unpredicted deltas, SELECT allows for predefined deltas, known in advance to be needed. A BREAK is an "open" parameter, a SELECT is "closed." Open means an unlimited number of deltas could be INSERTed. Closed means a fixed number of predefined deltas can be chosen by setting a frame variable to one of the values the SELECT uses to identify each alternative. In the next chapter, the EDI example goes into details.

Unpredictable deltas belong in the frames that define the contexts giving rise to the exceptions—hence they are INSERTed from relatively context-sensitive frames. Predefined deltas belong in the frames where the predefinitions take effect, i.e., where the BREAKs would have gone. A frame should contain SELECTable alternatives when one or more of the following occurs.

## 1. More than One Archetype

Suppose domain analysis reveals that a component category is typified by more than one archetype. For example, we represent sparse matrices as linked lists, and nonsparse ones as arrays. Some details of each matrix operator will vary with the matrix representation. Thus, in the category of matrix operations, each operator will be a pair of archetypes, one for linked lists, the other for arrays. Some operator properties will be common to the pair and others different. You should carry each pair of differences in the frame (hierarchy) within a SELECT, parameterized by a frame variable "SPARSE," say, whose values are either "yes" or "no." WHEN "yes," the variations associated with linked lists are SELECTed; WHEN "no," those associated with regular arrays are SELECTed. In this manner, all variations of the alternative archetypes are controlled with a single parameter.

## 2. Similar INSERTs

Suppose you discover that many frames are inserting a small set of similar INSERTs into the same BREAK. This redundancy indicates a pattern of reuse that deserves to be made generic and localized in the component frame (containing the BREAK). You embed the set of INSERTs in a SELECT at the BREAK, with the BREAK embedded in the OTHERWISE clause. Instead of INSERTing a delta, ancestor frames just set the option they want. They can still ignore the options and INSERT an arbitrary delta.

## 3. Distributed Deltas

Often a delta must change multiple properties, scattered across a frame hierarchy. For example, you are designing a system to run on mainframes with 3270s and on PCs with GUIs. This will affect many points within each of many frames. You localize control over such distributed deltas by putting a SELECT in every affected position. Each SELECT will contain mainframe and PC alternatives relevant to that position. Thus, a single point in the root of a hierarchy (perhaps a specification frame) can set the target-environment frame variable to, say, the PC, causing hundreds of polymorphic variants to be seamlessly stitched together, producing the PC version of the module.

## 4. Version Control

Version control is a special case of (3). Having reused a component frame, C, in many modules, can we make arbitrary modifications to C without having to retrofit those modules? As Figure 16-2 illustrates, we can accomplish this by embedding each changed property of C in a SELECT, parameterized by a version parameter, CV. (CV typically encodes a date.) Because no existing module will have REPLACEd CV with the current version, they SELECT the original (OTHERWISE) version of each modified property, thus guaranteeing no retrofits. On the other hand, because (the templates for) new modules REPLACE CV by the current version, such modules SELECT the current version of C.

If C should undergo further version changes, nested SELECTs controlled by CV in effect provide an evolutionary audit trail, a precise history of how C evolved to its current form. Modules can always upgrade to later versions of C, but the default is to let sleeping dogs lie.

**Figure 16-2.** Using SELECTs to make C's changes invisible to modules that were defined before 1996.

---

Frame C

frame text that was not modified

.SELECT CV
.WHEN > V1995_12_31
        frame text encoding the post-1995 version of a property
.OTHERWISE
        frame text encoding the original version of a property
.END-SELECT

more unmodified frame text, interspersed with ".SELECT CV"s for each property that was modified.

---

Wrapper frames complement the version control technique. They allow frame engineers to hedge their bets, letting the test of time determine which proposed frame enhancements are widely reused and which are local to their proposers. The widely reused enhancements are periodically consolidated under version control; the local ones are left in their wrappers.

### 5. Dual Run-Time/Construction-Time Variability

Depending on the context, some properties may be static at run time, others may be dynamic. For example, in some contexts, interest will always be compounded monthly. In other contexts, you may need to compound monthly, quarterly, semiannually, and annually while the interest calculation is executing. You can use SELECTs so frames can construct modules for either case.

## The Role of WHILE

Recall that frames can be reused repeatedly within a given hierarchy. Sometimes the number of repetitions is variable, depending on the context. In most windows applications, for example, data-entry fields are displayed, entered, validity-checked, and error-handled in a similar fashion. What varies from field to field are the display and storage attributes, and, of course, each window contains a different number of fields. What we want is a single encoding of this pattern that can appropriately instance every field in every window.

To set up such a pattern as a generic frame, you first define the archetypical process for a particular data-entry field. Next, you replace each reference to a specific field attribute with a corresponding indexed frame variable. Finally, you make this generic process the body of a WHILE that indexes through the frame variables.

To exercise the WHILE, some adaptor frame, such as a window definition frame, sets the indexed frame variables to the attributes of actual data-entry fields. Then, the frame containing the WHILE will construct an instance of the process for each field.

The WHILE construct is particularly valuable when tools translate data-dictionary (DD) entity-attributes into frame-variable settings (REPLACEs) automatically. A data-dictionary's high-level model then becomes your primary control point. The nice thing about frames is that models-to-code construction is a "gray box" generator—your SPCs can (re)customize the (re)generated frames. SPCs are your fine-tuning control points. The Noma case study in the next chapter illustrates these ideas.

## Generalizing with Frame Variables

We have already seen important uses of frame variables in conjunction with SELECTs and WHILEs. More generally, any element of a frame can be a variable. Often these elements are names: data (structure) names, names of program blocks and sections, frame-names, break names, and even the names of frame variables and commands.

The range of uses for frame variables is enormous. Below are three not covered in SELECTs and WHILEs.

### 1. Avoiding Name Clashes

Frame-names must be unique. To ensure other names are unique across a frame hierarchy, you should prefix (or suffix) all names (including frame variable names) with a frame variable, *FN*, whose default value is the frame-name. This simple convention not only enables uniqueness, but also allows a frame to be reused repeatedly within the hierarchy. For example, several different instances of a generic file definition (or data structure) frame *F* may be declared within a program. At each invocation (COPY *F*), set *FN* to another unique value, and all names within each instance of *F* will be unique.

### 2. Parameter Passing

A frame should declare and initialize all its variables to default values each time the frame is invoked (COPYed). To wit, a "parameters" BREAK occurs right after the above initialization. This permits adaptor frames to INSERT local overrides to the initialized frame variables. Right after the parameters BREAK, the frame checks bounded frame variables for legal values. It can report/override illegal settings, and set error severities that permit frame processing to continue with or without module assembly.

### 3. Adaptability

I advocate an "only as necessary" approach to parameterizing frames for adaptability. Beyond framing archetypes in the manner described so far, you substitute frame variables for specific archetype elements that you know will vary across its category. This means that lots of elements remain static at first that later may need variability.

Not to worry. New frame variables can be introduced later almost for free. All you have to do is initialize them to what used to be the static element. Ancestor frames ignore descendents' frame variables unless their values need overriding. This "studied ignorance" means making an element variable that used to be static will not affect ancestor frames that existed prior to the introduction of that variable because they now get the right element by default rather than by having it "hard wired." So, you can relax. Don't worry about not generalizing frame elements "right" the first time.

## When in Doubt Leave It Out

There is a natural tendency to overgeneralize. In keeping with the conservative advice regarding frame variables, refrain from "throwing in" features and capabilities unless you know they are needed. Otherwise, you stand to burden frames with unnecessary complexity. Worse, having put in a questionable "feature," a few application developers will come to depend on it. Later, when you feel the need to simplify the frame, it becomes much harder to get rid of such "features." Remember, adding a real feature later is always easy.

Having persevered through three relatively abstract chapters, we make the principles of analysis and design more concrete through the experiences of Noma Industries.

# Noma Industries

*The time to begin your reuse program is now.*
Martin Griss and Marty Wosser

oma Industries is perhaps best known as "the Christmas Tree Lights people." While they are one of the world's largest manufacturer of Christmas trees, lights, and ornaments, they have also manufactured a diversity of products, ranging from wire and cable to automotive parts and garden equipment. In 1981, Noma gave birth to Netron, and completely outsourced the management of its IT (Information Technology) facilities to it. As a result, they are the longest consumer of systems built with frame technology. (Netron's other cofounders bought Noma's interest in Netron in 1992 and Netron is now independent.)

While Noma's revenues are (or were until a recent divestiture) in the half-billion dollar range, the total number of people involved in software development ranges around a dozen and a half. They use no user intermediaries. They have small groups of people working directly with key users at the divisions needing software development. A typical project team consists of one person. However decentralized these small groups may sound, IS is actually a hybrid organization—most frames are reused across all sites. As with other cultural reuse (Level Four) organizations, almost all developers are frame engineers and vice versa; there is no need for a separate frame engineering department.

Because so much of the complexity of Noma's diversified divisions has been captured in standard frames, developers are freed to "concentrate on rapid building of systems." They conservatively estimate having 200 frame-built systems in production, comprising about 20 million lines of code, and are churning out new or replacement code at the rate of about 4 million lines of code per year.

The teams use no tools for planning, analysis, and design. The need is not there because they never design from the ground up. Everything is a delta from existing frame models, and iterative design refinement is de rigueur. Noma uses packages where the package "can be reasonably isolated," meaning not much work is needed to use the package as is. They also avoid the "islands of technology" disease so common in large organizations.

David Kerner, one of the systems managers, says that in gaining proficiency with frames, the biggest challenge was the "different thought process or outlook" required to create effective frames. His change in perspective had to be absorbed by osmosis, because the frame analysis and design process was undocumented until I wrote these chapters. Yet, that so much could be accomplished with such a "seat of the pants" approach is testimony to its intuitive nature.

The key to Noma's IT success lies also in hiring the best people and empowering them to get on with things. As Ed Yourdon and others report, the difference between best and worst performance in programmers exceeds 100 to 1. Compound that difference with effective reuse technology and you can see why so much can be done with so few.

The biggest problem they have is "being asked to do the wrong thing." This problem is exacerbated when you can respond so quickly, and echoes what "The Great Canadian Trust Co." said, and what the "world's best user" said was the final, incompressible problem. The silver lining is that people also find out something's wrong in days rather than months or years.

## A Sample Application: Electronic Data Interchange (EDI)

Noma's EDI system was first developed in 1992 by one person, Steve Juniper. Over a calendar period of five months, he spent about 60 mandays getting from design to production. It is a distributed processing, client-server application, using an object-oriented architecture at run time. Steve reused the design of the "School MIS" architecture (described in Chapter 23) and Netron's standard frame library.

EDI refers to an intranet protocol for linking the computers of buyers and sellers so they can do business electronically. Noma receives electronic purchase orders (POs) from many of its customers, such as Beaver

Lumber. This company places large orders for a variety of products using an ANSII x12 850 format, which is one EDI standard for purchase orders. These incoming data were stored in a PC file called EDIPC.

The problem with EDI is not the protocol, which is industry standard and works well. The problem is that each customer has a custom way of using the protocol, and no supplier is about to force its customers to conform to the supplier's way. Nor do suppliers want to patch their software every time a new customer signs up, and every time an old one changes their ordering practices. This problem did not arise with paper POs because human data-entry clerks automatically do the conversions using the computers between their ears. But EDI systems are supposed to automate that step. In practice, many suppliers trivialize EDI by dumping out the electronic POs as they come down the line, then manually keying them back in!

The trick is to systematize customers' idiosyncrasies in order to minimize the work of adding and updating order translators. Steve analyzed what an archetypical order should look like. It comes as no surprise to business analysts that its components are an order header and a set of order detail lines. (At this level of abstraction, sales orders, purchase orders, work orders, etc. are all *same as, except.*) Purchase orders have several detail-line types. One type specifies a product, order quantity, and unit of measure; another describes the product; still others specify drop points, freight charges, volume discounts, general comments, and so forth. Because each customer is an independent source of change, Steve modeled each customer order translator as a separate polymorphic object. (These objects are subroutines, which, if they were dynamically linked, as in a DLL, could be created and modified without taking Noma's PO system down.)

Having defined the archetypical data structure and creation process, how did Steve systematize the idiosyncrasies (deltas)? After looking at various actual orders, he discovered most deltas involved nonstandard meanings for the EDIPC data elements, for example, strange units of measure. Steve chose to highlight such deltas in customer objects' specification frames.

With this strategy in mind, Steve began to analyze, design, and construct the generic components to be reused in each customer polymorph. Figure 17-1 shows his overall system architecture, including the main flow of data from customer PCs to Noma's computer, where the orders are converted and processed. We shall focus on how Steve designed the customer objects. He formalized a pattern common to all customer objects, an archetypical object consisting of four main components (subassemblies). Each object consists of a set of methods, including a pair for each data field in Noma's standard PO. In outline, they are described in the following sections.

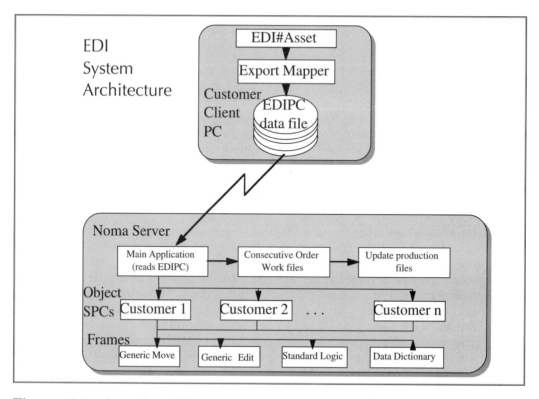

**Figure 17-1.** A portion of Noma's Electronic Data Interchange system translates incoming purchase orders into a format Noma's systems can handle.

## Generic MOVE Frame (STEMV.FE)

STEMV.FE is the set of default methods (Cobol sections) for moving customer data into the standard-order data fields, be they header or detail fields. Each default method contains one or more statements to (combine and) MOVE customer data field(s) into a standard data field, possibly converting data types and formats in the process. There will be one method for each data field defined in the data-dictionary frames (described below).

Each default method is surrounded by a BREAK so customer specification frames can extend or, if required, override the default. For example, a customer might use a nonstandard unit of measure, or a conversion algorithm might depend on the value of another data field. This mechanism provides every customer with a uniform way to isolate and highlight any kind of delta.

## Generic EDIT Frame (STEDT.FE)

Analogous to the generic MOVE frame, EDIT contains a generic method for editing (error checking, validating) each standard data field. Again, there is one per data field defined in the data dictionary, and they can be further adapted by customer specification frames.

## Data-Dictionary Frames

There are three frames: F021.FI defines order header data fields; F022.FI defines order detail fields; EDIPC.FI defines any other EDI data fields that are relevant to Noma's order processing. (F021 is the name of the order header record; F022 is the order detail record name.) Each frame contains nothing but a series of frame variable assignments. The following illustrates F022.FI, which orders the data fields within their proper record types (a percent sign indicates a comment about the construction process):

| | | |
|---|---|---|
| .REPLACE I | BY 0 | % I indexes F, a field-names table, |
| | | % & T, a record-types table |
| | | % Each defined TI starts a new |
| | | % record type (group of data fields) |
| .REPLACE I | BY ( ;I + 1 ) | |
| .REPLACE F;I | BY LOCKOUT-22 | % F1 = the name of the record's |
| | | % lockout flag; T1 is undefined |
| .REPLACE I | BY ( ;I + 1 ) | |
| .REPLACE T;I | BY ' "SALES-22" ' | % T2 = "SALES-22" (quotes included), |
| | | % sales detail record type |
| .REPLACE F;I | BY PRODUCT-22 | % F2 = the name of the product code |
| | | % data field |
| .REPLACE I | BY ( ;I + 1 ) | |
| .REPLACE F;I | BY QUANTITY-22 | % F3 = the name of the product |
| | | % quantity data field |
| .REPLACE I | BY ( ;I + 1 ) | |
| .REPLACE F;I | BY . . . | % T3 is undefined |

.
.
.

etc. For all required F022 data fields, segmented into record types, defined in the order they need to be processed.

Notice that the frame could have been written without using the *I* index. This index reduces errors when modifying the frame. For example, should Noma ever need to introduce a new field into an existing record type, it is a simple matter of inserting two lines into the frame. Had *F* and *T* been V indexed with *I* automatically, every line of the frame below the introduced field would have had to be re-indexed manually.

## Generic Logic Frame (EDIFM.FE)

This subassembly contains methods, such as file I/O, that are common to all customer objects. It also contains optional methods, embedded in SELECTs, that are included or excluded as required by each customer specification frame. Finally, it stets up the "performs" for all the methods created by adapting the generic MOVE and EDIT frames. The WHILE below expresses the "Performs" sufficient to move the order detail fields. (The emitted text is Cobol. An asterisk indicates a comment that describes things at run time.)

```
.COPY F022.FI SAMELEVEL.      % Define the F and T tables for use by the
                              % WHILE. (The last "." means "END-COPY".)
.R STEMV BY STEMV             % Initialize prefix
.R STEDT BY STEDT             % Initialize prefix
 If TRUE                      * This dummy If handles the first group
                              * of data fields

.REPLACE I BY 1
.WHILE ;F;I                   % Exit when ;F;I is undefined, having processed
                              % every F entry

.SELECT ;T;I
.  WHEN <>                    % When ;T;I is defined (not = null)
 End-if                       * Complete the If for the prior group of
                              * data fields

 If RECORD-TYPE-22 = ;T;I     * If the input is record type ;T;I
.  END-SELECT % ;T;I
   Move "Y" to ;STEMV-OK      * Initialize error flags
            ;STEDT-OK         % Note: hyphens terminate frame variables.
   Perform ;STEMV-;F;I        * Move customer field to ;F;I.
   If ;STEMV-OK = "Y"
      Perform ;STEDT-;F;I     * If the input was successfully moved,
                              * validate ;F;I.

   End-if
.REPLACE I BY ( ;I + 1 )
.END-WHILE % ;F;I
 End-if                       * Complete the If for the last group of
                              * data fields
```

Each WHILE iteration indexes the list of frame variables (set by COPYing the data-dictionary frames SAMELEVEL). In this manner, each iteration emits a new pair of custom perform statements (which, when executed, will convert a specific PO data field). When the index passes the end of the list, the WHILE exits, and the list of perform-pairs for converting purchase-order details will have been constructed.

Similar setups will construct the perform-pair lists for header data and other EDIPC fields.

The frame fragment on the facing page emits the following:

```
If TRUE                          * This dummy If handles the first group
                                 * of data fields
    Move "Y" to STEMV-OK         * Initialize error flags
              STEDT-OK
    Perform STEMV-LOCKOUT-22      * Move customer field to LOCKOUT-22.
    If STEMV-OK = "Y"
        Perform STEDT-LOCKOUT-22  * If the input was successfully moved,
                                 * validate LOCKOUT-22.
    End-if
End-if                           * Complete the If for the prior group of
                                 * data fields
If RECORD-TYPE-22 = "SALES-22"   * If the input is record type "SALES-22"
    Move "Y" to STEMV-OK         * Initialize error flags
              STEDT-OK
    Perform STEMV-PRODUCT-22      * Move customer field to PRODUCT-22.
    If STEMV-OK = "Y"
        Perform STEDT-PRODUCT-22  * If the input was successfully moved,
                                 * validate PRODUCT-22.
    End-if
    Move "Y" to STEMV-OK         * Initialize error flags
              STEDT-OK
    Perform STEMV-QUANTITY-22     * Move customer field to QUANTITY-22.
    If STEMV-OK = "Y"
        Perform STEDT-QUANTITY-22 * If the input was successfully moved,
                                 * validate QUANTITY-22.
    End-if
    .
    .
    .
End-if                           * Complete the If for the last group of
                                 * data fields
```

The careful reader will have noticed that "If RECORD-TYPE. . ." statements are emitted only when a new record type begins. This works because the F022.FI frame has defined the ;T;I frame variables only in association with the first data field of each record type.

## Customer Specification Frames

At run time, each customer object converts customer purchase orders into standard orders, data field by field. A customer object converts each purchase-order field by performing a customized pair of (MOVE and EDIT) methods. The following is the essence of a template for all customer SPCs. (The line following each COPY is a set of REPLACEs, treated as an INSERT into the PARAMETERs BREAK. This is a convention for narrowcasting overriding frame variables locally, as explained on pages 117-118.)

```
.COPY EDIFM.FE          % Bring in standard logic and list of performs
.   REPLACE . . .       % Select any optional methods this customer needs
.   INSERT . . .        % Any custom method extensions/overrides
.   INSERT . . .
.
.
.
.END-COPY % EDIFM

.COPY STEMV.FE.         % Bring in all move methods
.   REPLACE . . .       % Select any optional methods this customer needs
.   INSERT . . .        % Any custom method extensions/overrides
.   INSERT . . .
.
.
.
.END-COPY % STEMV

.COPY STEDT.FE.         % Bring in all edit methods
.   REPLACE . . .       % Select any optional methods this customer needs
.   INSERT . . .        % Any custom method extensions/overrides
.   INSERT . . .
.
.
.
.END-COPY % STEDT
```

The following (Table 17-1) lists the executables for the EDI PO conversions. BEAVR is the subroutine object for Beaver Lumber, to show what is typical for all such Noma customers. The table illustrates the amount of reuse Steve obtained in this project. The average, 95%, typifies mature reuse cultures. Steve spent the two man-months in analysis and design, and in writing the key frames that implemented his ideas for isolation and automation. The architecture has since been reused on other supplier/customer situations, including the invoicing function, which are the "same as, except" purchase orders.

**Table 17-1   Noma's EDI Project Statistics: Sample Executables**

| Module | Total ESLOC | SPC ESLOC | % Reuse |
|--------|-------------|-----------|---------|
| BEAVR  | 3835 | 171 | 95.5 |
| CERR   | 106  | 6   | 94.5 |
| EDERP  | 1289 | 73  | 94.4 |
| ESERR  | 1755 | 34  | 98.1 |
| EDI00  | 885  | 4   | 99.6 |
| EDI21  | 1082 | 24  | 97.8 |
| EDIDC  | 57   | 7   | 88.2 |
| EDIIO  | 1400 | 228 | 83.7 |
| EDILG  | 2317 | 20  | 99.2 |
| ERCVT  | 173  | 15  | 91.4 |
| F21ED  | 1100 | 68  | 93.8 |
| FINVP  | 881  | 87  | 90.1 |
| MERCD  | 2401 | 12  | 99.5 |
| PGEDI1 | 429  | 103 | 76.1 |
| PGEDI2 | 752  | 44  | 94.1 |
| **Totals** | **18462** | **895** | **95.2** |

# PART 3

# REUSE CHANGES THE SOFTWARE ENGINEERING PROCESS

Frame technology, the focus of Part II, provides the technical means for reuse, but it is only the first step. Technologies are neutral with respect to the good they can do and the harm they can cause. Well applied, frame technology can deliver hundred-fold improve-ments. Misapplied, it can wreak havoc. Believe me, I have seen both.

It is people who make technolo-gies work, and people function through processes supported by an infrastructure and a culture—in our case, an infrastructure and culture predicated on reuse. What processes and infrastructures make reuse work? Which don't? Part III focuses on these issues.

The existence of adaptable building blocks changes the way we think about software and how we develop it. In fact, there are two interlocking processes. One involves refining applications from reusable components. The other process involves refining the components themselves. These two interlocking processes are collectively known as iterative design refinement (IDR).

Traditional software development calls for analysis, design, construction, and testing to be done in a sequential manner, the "waterfall" model. This "tried and untrue" process is beset with difficulties, largely stemming from the implicit, yet false, assumption that we can get things right the first time.

IDR starts from the premise that software risk stems from our unavoidable misunderstanding of requirements, which themselves are forever changing. IDR's principal aim is to minimize this risk by continually reducing the gap (delta) between what we currently have to reuse and what we currently think is the need.

Some people think developing reusable parts requires a large investment up front. This belief is not only a deterrent but also wrong in approach. True, the quality of a frame is proportional to the effort invested. But that effort should be invested in stages.

The iterative design refinement process ensures that reuse more than pays for itself as it goes. Even better, the process seasons frames with a diversity of actual problems, rather than trying to "get it right the first time." You may be thinking, "but if I don't freeze my components early, keeping up with all the retrofits will kill me." In truth, retrofits can be deferred indefinitely, and their costs can be hidden in upgrades the users are willing to pay for. This property of frames is what enables IDR to work.

From IDR's perspective, the very idea of software "maintenance" is harmful and unnecessary. By being able to engineer software to evolve indefinitely, IDR unifies development with evolution. Both are manifested in a cycle of analysis, design, and test that never stops.

Part III concludes with a case study of a controversial application built by people who apply the techniques in this book.

# People Make Technology Work

## CHAPTER 18

> *Even the best planning is not so omniscient*
> *as to get it right the first time.*
>
> Fred Brooks, 1975

I n the era of global competition, adaptability to quickly changing needs and opportunities is key. For information systems, the reality has unfortunately been otherwise. It's ironic that such systems, having propelled organizations of every description into the automation age, are now themselves millstones around many organizations' necks.

Part of the solution is to enable computers to capture insights in adaptable models such as frames. These models can then be quickly and easily applied in a routine, yet effective, fashion, the essence of good engineering.

What's needed is a return to basics. A reexamination of the very purpose of software development will uncover assumptions that no longer apply. Changing those assumptions to capitalize on reuse technology is a much harder task than simply procuring reuse technology. The stakes are high: survival. Those who master reuse will have a decided competitive edge.

Whether technologies result in benefit or harm depends on people. People function through processes based on an infrastructure supported by organization. Consequently, if frame technology is to benefit the software community, appropriate processes, infrastructure, and organization must all be in place. Instrumental to a strategic use of frame technology are a series of relationships:

1. A working partnership between developers and users as a means of refining requirements to meet the users' real needs;

2. An organizational structure that supports this partnership;

3. One fundamental technology and supporting infrastructure, for people work together effectively only through well-understood patterns;

4. A development pattern based on iterative refinement (sometimes called *protocycling*, or *rapid application development*), for requirements are never perfectly clear at the outset;

5. Minimizing risk by designing with adaptable software components.

## A Partnership with Users

The results users care about start with requirements. And obviously, the users are one of the principal sources of requirements. In the course of development, as we have noted, requirements always change. Thus, any process for building systems must involve users on an ongoing basis, as well as other stakeholders. Hence the need for a partnership.

### Refining Requirements

The existence of systems that are easily refinable by use of frame technology puts the realm of ill-defined and/or transient phenomena within reach of our modeling capabilities. Business systems, because they deal with a fluid mix of needs and opportunities, are part of this realm. This fluidity, well known to users, is why they have a strong interest in participating in the refinement process.

Professional software developers, of course, are just as vital to the refinement process, but for different reasons. They must ensure the integrity and security of a system and of the other systems with which it interacts; they must achieve acceptable performance, robust designs, graceful error recovery; they must be able to implement subtle features and control side effects within and among systems; and they must engineer the components, which evolve in the course of development, for generality and adaptability.

Timely interactions between users and developers are of the essence. Neither should feel dominated by the other. Each needs to trust that the other is working for the greater good of the organization. Each needs to better understand the other's issues.

## Barriers to Partnership

Nevertheless, there are many barriers to developing a partnership between users and developers. Three are important at this point:

1. User skepticism: a history of strained relations makes users skeptical, even cynical.

2. Too busy: users have full-time jobs operating the business and begrudge spending time working with developers.

3. Intermediaries: large organizations commonly have a group of people between the developers and the actual end-users. These surrogate users work with developers to map out the detailed needs of each system. Unfortunately, intermediaries often add "noise" to the communications channel. Overcoming the noise may cost real users more time than if they had dealt with the developers directly.

Quality, deadlines, and costs are at risk in direct proportion to the lack of cooperation between users and developers. The volatile nature of software requirements demands cooperation throughout the refinement process, not just at the beginning. Refinement of requirements and design iterates quickly and, between iterations, the timely resolution of questions requires further cooperation.

Once users see that progress can be rapid and that they can steer the design as the system takes shape, the greatest skeptics become the greatest fans of the process. They realize, every bit as much as the developers, that the cost/benefit of the result is their responsibility and under their control.

## Joint Application Design

Garbage-In-Garbage-Out was coined to describe the execution process of systems. GIGO is even more apt when applied to the system construction process. Quality systems demand quality specifications.

Quality specifications are hard work! Modern businesses are irrational in many ways. Different parts of the business are constrained by different regulations, competition, isolation, and so forth, to operate in conflicting ways. For example, the tax laws in different countries often compel multinationals to apply mutually conflicting accounting rules.

Like people, businesses are rationalizing, not rational. Different groups of users see the same system from very different perspectives. They legitimately argue over which features should or should not be in a system. It's hard to see the global picture. Sorting out issues in such an environment requires a facilitator (referee) who has the respect of all parties. He or she must combine the understanding of what is technically, operationally, and financially feasible with the communications skills to reconcile conflicting views of business needs.

On any given issue, one user's view may be right and another's wrong, or they may both be wrong, or both may be right. In the latter case, we need two system variations to accommodate two "right" views. Mixed with the technical disputes are the political implications of features that alter who controls what information. Few people in any organization have a strong enough mix of business, technical, and communications skills to resolve such conflicts. Failure to cope with these conflicts properly often results in systems that do damage.

Joint application design (JAD) is an effective way to expose and resolve conflicting requirements. [30] JAD is a structured seminar process led by a trained facilitator, often brought in from the outside to ensure neutrality.

JAD's purpose is to gather the right group of people in one spot at one time and extract a consensus understanding of what is needed. In a matter of one to three days, a JAD forum can produce results that might otherwise take weeks or months! The output of a JAD forum can be turned into working software by use of frame technology, often in a matter of days.

## The Hybrid IS Organization

There is a perennial debate in the software industry over whether to centralize or decentralize Information Systems development. Centralizers argue that corporate standards can be enforced and there is more control and economy of scale. Decentralizers counter that organizations should not isolate developers from users, that large bureaucratic shops are inefficient, and that development units need more autonomy to cope with the diversity of user needs.

The pendulum keeps swinging, because neither extreme is optimal. Until recently, a means of stabilizing the pendulum near the middle has not existed. Frame technology enables you to retain the strengths of both, while using each to offset the other's weaknesses.

### Centralization

Many IS functions should remain centralized. A central group provides overall direction and strategy. It provides quality assurance in hiring, training, and promoting IS professionals. It ensures that a common set of tools and techniques is employed throughout the organization.

Most importantly, the central group is proactive in software engineering, providing and supporting common libraries of reusable components—systems and applications "architectures." Frame administrators are responsible for the development, testing, documentation, distribution, and support of corporate frames. They also establish policies for promoting frames from application-wide to corporate-wide reusability.

## Co-location

Development projects should be decentralized. One-to-four-person "SWAT teams" (Skilled with Advanced Tools) are immersed in end-user environments. This immersion is necessary to achieve the timely clarification of missing or ambiguous requirements. It also promotes trust and cooperation; implementers learn about business issues, and end-users learn about systems issues.

Burton Napier, when he was senior vice president at Toronto Dominion Bank, used the term "co-location" rather than decentralization. The term "co-location" puts the emphasis on the fact that SWAT team members physically work at end-user sites, but continue to have solid-line accountability to the central IS group. They have a dotted-line relationship to end-user management. Central accountability preserves continuity and ensures peer review and ongoing professional development.

A major benefit of this arrangement is that portable programmers can be easily shifted from area to area to balance demand. Individuals seconded to engineer frames are placed in various SWAT teams to play three roles:

**1.** Ensure that standard frames are being effectively applied;

**2.** Write new frames that are needed by the project;

**3.** Coach novices on the job.

Conversely, applications developers who are budding frame engineers can spend time in frame administration, learning the processes for maturing standard frames and architectures, and looking after the frame repository.

Each co-located group iteratively refines the applications "owned" by a given business unit. (Systems spanning multiple business units, such as "back-office" systems, will still be owned by some business unit, not the central IS group.) By forming a hybrid organization, we can balance the dual goals of communality and diversity.

## One Reuse Infrastructure

A common infrastructure for software development is like a common road system or standard time zones. Without a common road structure, the growing number of incompatible left-hand/right-hand drive vehicles would result in a growing number of confused drivers. Without a common reuse infrastructure, the growing mass of incompatible software systems will require a growing mass of incompatible people to look after them.

An effective reuse technology should support an infrastructure within which all other technologies—graphic user interface, client-server, database, pen computing, multimedia—can co-exist. Its purpose is to facilitate sharing while hiding complexity, especially of other technologies. To have incompatible infrastructures co-exist within a single economic unit defeats the very point of reuse.

With the invention of automobiles, for example, a progression of increasingly strategic questions had to be addressed:

- Technical: What do I do with my buggy whips and footmen?
- Infrastructural: How do carriages and roads need to change?
- Paradigmatic: What new patterns of commerce do trucks and cars enable?

Replacing manual programming with engineering technology begs similar questions:

- What do I do with my existing systems and programmers?
- How does the development process need to change?
- What new competitive edges does adaptability and quick time-to-market enable?

Noma Industries, the subject of the previous chapter, is an example of the application of such an engineering technology. During the eighties, this diversified manufacturer experienced sixfold growth, from less than $100 million to over $650 million in annual sales. Yet, its information systems staff, using frame technology, hovered around 20 people. With well over 20 million lines of code in production, Noma's entire budget for systems, including hardware, software, and operations, is still well under one percent of sales.

The reasons behind these remarkable statistics have little to do with the nature of manufacturing. They have everything to do with skills, organization, and technology—in that order. We need the skills to (re)engineer a business effectively; the organization to mediate the interactions among (users and systems) professionals; and the technology to mediate the interactions among hardware, software, and people.

Reuse changes fundamental relationships among people, tasks, and time. Harmonizing these relationships is necessary; otherwise, displaced bottlenecks will rob reuse of its effectiveness. Here are some examples.

## Hurry Up and Wait

During development, resolving the inevitable gaps and ambiguities in the specifications takes time. Resolving these in a manual programming environment is off the critical path, as there is always plenty of things to keep programmers busy. But in reuse environments, the critical path changes dramatically. During the two weeks, say, that it used to take to get clarifications and changes approved, the automated program assembly line may come to a crashing halt!

## I Did It My Way

Many actually prefer to start from scratch because they perceive an opportunity to "get it right this time," to avoid "the mistakes of the past," and because by remaining independent, people reinforce their autonomy. This attitude is fatal to a reuse environment. Requirements determined in ignorance of existing reusable components are likely to be incompatible with those components. Thus, the time and cost to build new systems are far higher than they should be, and the environment becomes clogged with components that overlap existing ones, increasing complexity and support costs.

## Reuse Power Politics

Agreeing to abide by a set of common standards requires serious cooperative behavior that may be foreign to the culture. Some may not like the standards and insist on going their separate ways. Those unaccustomed to compromise will perceive a threat to their comfort and power. "Why should other groups be able to tell me what to do?" Reuse requires striking a new balance between communality and diversity.

# The Waterfall Is Our Downfall

Software has had a long tradition of being designed from scratch and constructed one character at a time. As systems became ever larger and more sophisticated, manual methods had to be scaled up. Accordingly, we borrowed a familiar methodology for building solid structures, such as cars and TV sets.

It's known as the "waterfall" methodology (Figure 18-1). While its variants partition development into different phases, they are all sequen-

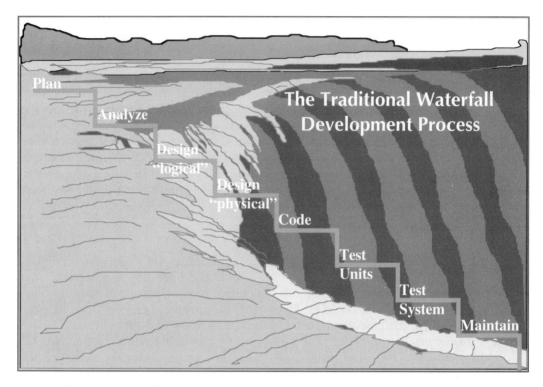

**Figure 18-1.** The development of hardware is more suited to the traditional waterfall because backing a physical product up the waterfall into redesign is difficult and costly.

tial—first analysis, then design, then construction, then testing, then maintenance. Each phase must finish before starting the next. Conventional engineering requires a cascading sequence of phases because of the following factors.

## Abstract

Analysis and design are abstract—diagrams, blueprints, technical narratives. Converting abstractions into physical substance is a complex and expensive process. Construction should not commence without a high probability of success.

## High cost

The cost to climb back up the waterfall is high, increasing the need to "get things right the first time." In the case of physical systems, often you can get close to this ideal. Physics and chemistry can precisely predict many aspects of complex system behavior.

## Stable Form

Physical constructs achieve a stable final form. Thereafter, periodic "grease and oil" maintenance and repairs restore them to their "like new" states.

The risk in building physical systems lies in the expensive and irreversible materialization of abstract specifications. Offsetting this risk are the mutually consistent and unbreakable laws of physics with which to analyze, stabilize, and constrain the design issues, and to predict the outcome of the materialization process reliably. The waterfall model is predicated on consistency, and completeness.

So much for conventional engineering. In contrast, software requirements are inherently hard to define and unstable to boot. Business systems, which account for the bulk of commercial software, are quintessential examples. A business exists in a man-made environment, subject to man-made laws, using man-made technology, competing with other man-made businesses. Man's desires, perceptions, conventions, and rules are always in a state of flux. This constant flux is why software engineering differs from other kinds of engineering.

Stakeholders have different and often conflicting visions of what a system should do. Compounding all this are the hidden agendas driving the politically powerful visions. Unrelenting pressures for responsiveness in the volatile world of business, along with the growing diversity of computing environments—mainframes, graphic workstations, database schemas, networks, and communications protocols—combine to overwhelm the waterfall approach.

Analysis and design are prone to exhaustive specifications, "paper products" that are out of date before a single line of code is written. Late projects, 60-month development backlogs, and 80% maintenance burdens confirm this approach works poorly. Why?

With its emphasis on completeness and consistency, the waterfall encourages the over-analysis and over-design of software. So-called "upper-CASE" (computer-aided software engineering) tools worsened the situation by automating it. As James Martin said, "such tools are not user-friendly, they are user-seductive." Some analysts literally diagram themselves into oblivion, losing themselves in intricate "wallpaper" whose validity goes untested and whose relevance is questionable. The result is either "analysis paralysis" or a false sense of security from a six-inch stack of official specs—the project bible.

Requirements are never perfect. Even if they are right today, they will be wrong tomorrow. The trick is not to try for the perfect system; rather it is to engineer it for change. It is to use a development process that discovers major flaws early, rather than after most of the time and money has been spent. Nasty surprises late in a project are very costly to fix. Most are swept under the rug and the project declared a success. Of course, the users will harbor their own opinions.

## Minimizing Risk

The risk in software design lies in the instability and vagueness of the constraints on a system that, nonetheless, must run in a timely and effective way on that paragon of rational, well-defined behavior, the computer. Given this risk, it is foolish to expect that you will "get it right the first time," or even that you have understood the problems correctly.

### Our Fundamental Risk

The ever-present risk is that of solving the wrong problems. You can offset this risk by using a method that makes it quick and cheap to get from an abstract specification to a working version of the system. You find out if this version provides the expected results. You refine the software as the stakeholders, trying out the working version, discover its deficiencies.

The key to minimizing risk is being able to automate the translation of partial designs into executables. Given reusability-based construction tools, people need only express the novel part of specifications, not all the mundane details. Frame technology suits this approach. The novel specifications are isolated from the generic models. When the current version of the system needs refining, its novel aspects are front and center, minimizing the cost of change.

We have embodied this risk-containment idea in a process we call "iterative design refinement," elaborated further in the following chapters of this part. This process is "iterative," because it is a cyclic process of improvement, based on reusing the current "design" models (frames), thereby producing a new "refinement," as Figure 18-2 shows.

### Feedback Is Key

The issue is building cost-effective systems cost-effectively. It is often said that the earlier we detect design flaws, the cheaper they are to fix. It is also said that coding is only 20 to 25% of the effort in major projects, hence automating code construction is not strategic.

These observations, while true, miss the point. Given the vagaries of the design problem, we need the feedback from a working prototype to guide requirements and the subsequent design. Code automation greatly

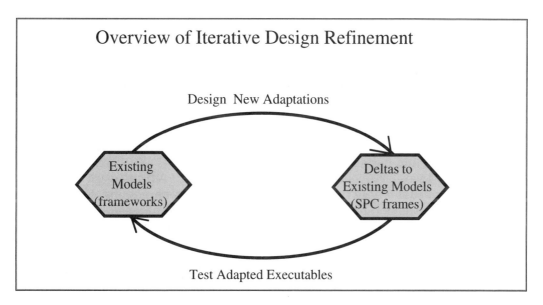

**Figure 18-2.** Starting with existing models (frameworks), the iterative design refinement methodology applies deltas (SPCs) to the frameworks. The loop closes when new executables cause further refinement of the frameworks.

enhances our chances of early detection, not of defects in code particularly, but of flaws in requirements and design. It is this point that is strategic.

There is an irony here. The waterfall is considered a systematic, conservative, safe approach. Yet, because it delivers executables so late in the process, it produces systems built to stale specifications; it increases risk! IDR, by iteratively refining already proven models called frames, reduces risk, as illustrated in Figure 18-2.

## Designing from Adaptable Models

People in mature fields of engineering do not design structures down to every last nut, bolt, and washer. As I have said, designing from scratch is not called engineering—it's called research!

In current software practice, it is normal to begin the design process with a virtually clean slate. Experienced designers certainly have an understanding of previous systems, and have seen many examples of good and poor design. But there is not yet an engineering handbook of standard designs such as we find in mature engineering disciplines.

## Established Models

Engineering design normally starts with a proven model—e.g., a civil engineer would start with a cantilever model or suspension-bridge model. Such standard design models already embody hundreds if not thousands of lower level details. The presence of a model enables the designer to focus on the unique design elements, rather than being distracted by details that can and should be taken for granted. Combining unique requirements with standard models is a conservative, common-sense strategy that combines top-down and bottom-up design techniques.

Software engineers can design the same way. A framework is a proven design model whose parameters provide the design options. Frames hide the mundane details that can be taken for granted. Instead of drowning in detail, the design task reduces to adapting existing, proven models to new requirements. Because the adaptations themselves can be packaged in frames, they can also become proven models in the designers' "handbook." Feedback enables each iterative cycle to build on the results of the previous one. Now we can say that the first cycle builds upon the handbook.

## System "Delta"

Critics of rapid-application-development methods object to building software too soon. They have a point. Analysts need to understand the forest before the trees. One forest issue is how different the proposed system is from its predecessors—its delta. The amount of preliminary analysis and design, prior to a first iterative cycle, correlates with this delta. On the one hand, the delta of a system designed from scratch is the system itself! On the other hand, the deltas of even large systems, when the systems are derived from generic data and process models, can be relatively small. In other words, the "forest" is already structured as generic frame-trees (please excuse the pun).

What if you are just starting off, and have no frame models? Chapters 14 and 15 in Part II partly addressed this question. The next two chapters in this part address it again in the larger context of co-evolving frameworks and systems that incorporate them.

In these ways, frame technology provides a formal mechanism for transferring common models and common skills to diverse application domains. Key intellectual assets of the organization can be distilled into frames to provide fast responses to competitive situations.

# The Iterative Refinement of Frameworks

## CHAPTER 19

> *Total grandeur of a total edifice,*
> *Chosen by an inquisitor of structures*
> *For himself. He stops upon this threshold*
> *As if the design of all his words takes form*
> *And frame from thinking and is realized.*
>
> Wallace Stevens, 1950

H aving examined frame analysis and design in Part II, this chapter and the next describe a practical frame development process. Chapter 21 presents a parallel process for system development.

## Frames Co-evolve with Systems

While frames must exist before we can reuse them, we cannot suspend system development until our frames fully mature. Even if we could, we would be wrong to do so. The most effective reusable components arise through their co-evolution with the systems that reuse them.

Co-evolution is one of many relevant biology metaphors. Software systems correspond to organisms; executables—programs, objects—play the role of organs. Organisms function at "run time" until they die. Their capacities to respond to various stresses are limited by their fixed morphologies—skeletal architectures, neurological connections, organ functions, circulatory systems, and so forth.

Genes at "construction time" are essential to survival, both moment-to-moment and generation-to-generation. During morphogenesis and throughout life, genes specify how to assemble proteins, copy and alter the

211

various types of stem cells in the (re)generation of entire organisms (virtually every cell in your body is replaced every seven years or so). Two useful illustrations are the immune and the reproductive systems.

The immune system responds to unforeseeable (microscopic) invaders. Four "mini-gene" types assemble a combinatory explosive variety of antibodies [31]. A similar effect occurs in reproductive cells—gametes. Genetic mutations in gametes respond to unforeseeable environmental stresses by providing a combinatory explosion of variations to what is normally invariant at run time. This strategy is the only chance a species has of transcending the structural and functional limitations of individual organisms.

Software frames are analogous to genes. They specify how to (re)assemble all of the executables in a system. Just as organisms share common genes, systems share common frames. When environmental stresses cause systems to evolve, frame engineers (currently) supply the frame "mutations"! Thus, with our help, frames co-evolve with the systems they define. (If systems evolved their own frames, they would probably need the combinatory explosion strategy.)

## Time Domains

A key measure of well-engineered software is its adaptability to stresses at all graininess levels. We have seen how to adapt to graininess in structure size, from symbols to systems. Now we look at how to engineer for variability. Figure 19-1 portrays the duality of run time and construction time at three nested time scales:

1. *Executable* run time is the construction time of the data.
   Time scale: subseconds or longer.

2. *Framework* run time is the construction time of the executables.
   Time scale: seconds or longer.

3. *Frame-engineer* run time is the construction time of the frameworks.
   Time scale: hours or longer.

What role do variables play in implementing these three levels? Program variables are necessary to handle changes during program execution. Likewise, from duality, frame variables are required to handle changes to programs, changes that remain invariant at program run time. Finally, frame engineers are required to change the frameworks, changes that remain static at framework run time. Because the three time scales are nested, there are many opportunities for engineering trade-offs and for dual ways to handle change.

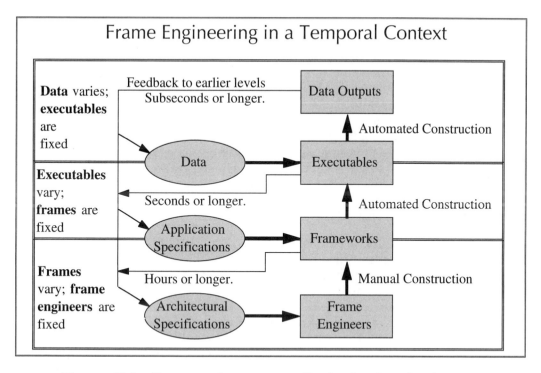

**Figure 19-1.** Frame engineers manually develop frameworks, using input from architectural specifications. Frameworks automatically assemble executables in accordance with application specifications. Executables then operate on data.

The feedback loops of Figure 19-1 are said to be open, requiring human input and judgment. If we could close the loops, we would have solved the fundamental problem of artificial intelligence—self-adaptive systems. This problem is left as an exercise for the reader! (Hint: look to biology for further insights.)

## Data or Function

The above duality clarifies a deeper question about the difference between function and data. If data are what vary, and functions transform data, then a stable system requires its functions to be invariant.

Indeed, it's very common to define systems in terms of their mutable data and immutable functions. But immutability is mutable! "Functions" become "data" when other "functions" transform them, for example, software tools or ourselves.

Confusion can be avoided by keeping track of which role a module plays in a given context: if it's being created or modified, it is data (an operand); if it manipulates data, it acts as a function (an operator). It cannot do both at the same time and remain well defined.

To clarify further, I shall try to restrict my terminology: we *vary* data, *adapt* programs, and *evolve* frames.

Frame engineers, then, evolve new frameworks for adapting software automatically. People are conditioned to associate such automation with magic. There is no magic. The following set of principles constrains the evolution and explains what to expect at each stage.

## Setting Realistic Expectations

Left to themselves, project managers are unlikely to invest serious efforts into making things reusable. Quite rightly, they are paid to deliver working systems within tight resource budgets and deadlines; previous projects have conditioned them to expect overruns. They believe specific systems are much easier to implement than generalized components. Such parts must incorporate hard-to-anticipate future requirements that might or might not benefit the organization, but certainly not this project. Who needs this reusability aggravation? The project and the organization as a whole, that's who. The good news is that reuse should pay as it goes. Then project managers and the organization can profit from it quickly.

### Making Reuse Pay as It Goes

One commonly held fear is that reusing imperfect components proliferates problems. This belief "front-end loads" the investment, creating its own barrier to success. The evolutionary process explained below should greatly alleviate this fear.

Perfection is a utopian impossibility. For certain domains, such as mathematics, the perfect-components approach may work for a while. But even here, perfect software is a fiction. Proof: mathematical functions are abstractions that occupy no space, consume no time, and have infinite precision. In contrast, software consumes both memory and time, and computes finite results. Clearly, a perfect model is an oxymoron. Believers in perfection are simply choosing to ignore those properties that a model either does not or cannot implement.

In reality, all software, including frames, needs to evolve. Some frames will be used in hundreds or thousands of different programs before evolving, others in only one, and everything in between. The more diverse the scope of reuse, the more a component costs to approach perfection.

On the other hand, *new frames* typically generate "*profits*" on a *single project*! They have obvious deficiencies, but can be evolved without affecting the current beneficiaries. Frames in stark contrast to use-as-is functions, can be far from perfect and still be reusable.

When an organization needs more reusability, it can make a further investment, provided it is less than its expected payback. If you can't make the numbers work, then the anticipated reusability benefit was never really there. This principle has an important corollary: it reduces the risk of overengineering a frame.

The more potential for reuse, the more engineering effort will ultimately be required, and is justified. Specification frames, being non-reusable, should be very easy to create and evolve. If you know that a potential frame is going to be reused more than three times, then you can invest up to three times the effort that a single use requires. You can still be confident of "making a profit." If you know it's going to be used more than 10 times, your investment can be correspondingly higher. Frames lend themselves to economic justification.

Let's assume that some source code, written for a single instance of use, requires one person one time-unit to design, write, and test. What guidelines are reasonable for investing in a reusable frame?

- If an application frame will be reused at least four times within one system, you should time-box its creation and evolution to something less, say two or three units.

- A department-level frame (more than 20 reuses) merits investing up to 10 units.

- A corporate standard frame (more than 100 reuses) merits up to 30 units.

As diagrammed in Figure 19-2, the investment goes up by a factor of three while the return on investment (ROI), evaluated conservatively, goes up by a factor of five.

## Time-Boxes

The management technique for making reuse pay as it goes is called time-boxing. Its purpose is to combine essential progress with contained risk. It involves setting short deadlines and expecting less than "perfect" results. The technique encourages the most critical results to be produced first, and leaves the rest to subsequent time-boxes. I like time-boxing software development projects because requirements are moving targets. As in photography, the longer the exposure, the blurrier the subject.

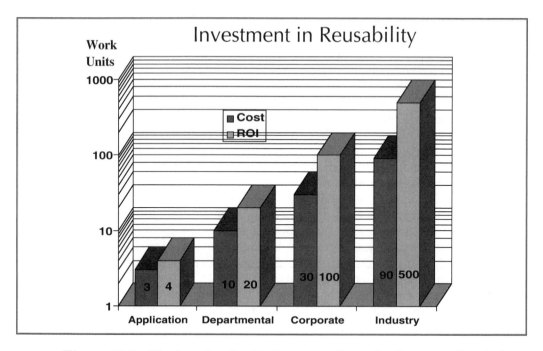

**Figure 19-2.** The broader the likely applications of a frame, as listed along the horizontal axis, the higher the return on investment relative to the cost. Note that the logarithm scale on the vertical axis means that the ROI line grows much more rapidly than the Cost line.

Time-boxing improves the result and avoids waste because:

1. Requirements have less time to change, to get out of focus;

2. Early feedback from the most critical executables helps us better understand the requirements before we build too many wrong things;

3. The "20%" of the system that delivers "80%" of the benefits are in the hands of users sooner, producing benefits sooner.

As we shall see, frames go through a time-boxed maturation process that ensures that each stage realizes a positive ROI. Thus, it becomes easy to justify investments in reusable frames.

## Exposure = Risk/Volatility

New components undergo numerous changes. Developers discover bugs; users discover side effects, missing features, inappropriate solutions, performance problems, and so on. Volatility, the frequency of construction-time changes, is highest when software is youngest and declines to a nonzero steady-state, characteristic of its environment (see Figure 19-3).

We intend to expose reusable frames to many contexts and easily adapt them every time. But when such frames are new, such exposure can be dangerous. The last thing you need is to have to rewrite a component that is already part of several deadline-critical projects. The resulting frustration and wasted work kills confidence. As shown in the bottom graph of Figure 19-3, exposure should be very limited when the frame is very young, and increase as the volatility decreases. This relationship can be summed up in the following "equation":

$$\text{Risk} = \text{Volatility} \times \text{Exposure}$$

You reduce overall risk by ensuring volatility goes down faster than exposure goes up.

**Figure 19-3.** Volatility, or frequency of construction-time changes, is high when software is first coded, declines during unit testing, and reaches a low level during production. When a frame is first coded, limiting its reuse is wise because it contains many defects. As wider use enhances its reliability, it can be safely used in a larger number of applications.

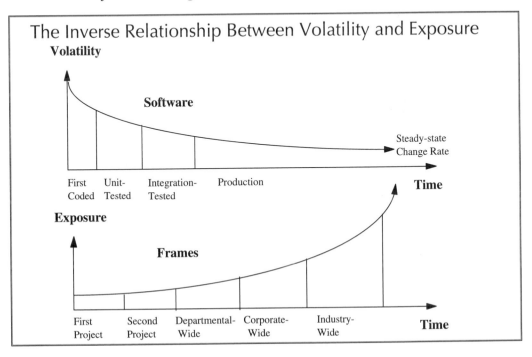

## Undersell New Frames

Pride of authorship is one of the worst frame-engineering sins. When a frame is new, an invisible crevasse opens between the "framer" and developer "framees." The framer, on her side, can make the frame jump through some amazing hoops, and she thinks everyone can make it do similar tricks. She doesn't realize how much her feats depend on knowing frame internals that others don't, and perhaps shouldn't ever need to know.

On the other side of the crevasse, myriads of requirements and constraints, familiar to framees, are terra incognita to the framer and her newly minted frame. Thus, the frame, whose capabilities have been oversold, crashes into the crevasse; everybody loses and reusability gets a black eye.

No one likes calling someone's baby ugly, so "pride of authorship" needs sensitive management attention. Framers must be humbly aware of how incredibly diverse are the demands to be made on their frames. Rather than overselling, the framer should demand suggestions for improvement as the price of trying a new frame. Rather than expecting brilliance and clarity, framees should regard a new frame as a diamond in the rough, in need of further cutting and polishing.

Forewarned is forearmed. Much unnecessary rancor can be replaced by goodwill and cooperation.

## Frames Must Work at Two Levels

Ordinary source code is designed only for proper execution. How well it works depends on the usual criteria: functionality, performance, ease-of-use, and modularity constraints.

Frames must work in both the execution and construction domains. Frames incorporate two sets of formal parameters, one for variability and the other for adaptability. Thus, in addition to usability, frames must satisfy reusability criteria: generality, ease-of-reuse, and conformance to standards, at both run time and construction time. Designing and testing this extra set of criteria is the extra price of reusability.

Applications are (unit, system, integration, and user-acceptance) tested against a *variety of data*. In addition to these kinds of tests, frames must be tested for reusability (generality and adaptability). The only way to test for reusability is by testing against a *variety of application domains*. That involves real projects.

## Real Projects

Generic frames emerge from the analysis and design techniques described in Part II, but stop.

**Always design frames for real projects.**

It is all too easy to invent "castles in the sky," elegant and general frames that just aren't practical. Knowing what parts of a frame need parameters and what parts should be unadaptable, knowing how to organize a frame so that 80% of the adaptations are handled with 20% of the frame variables—these and similar engineering issues require grounding in specific system requirements.

## Ownership and Resource Issues

The cliché, "knowledge is power," applies to frame technology in spades. It empowers the organization not only to automate the automators, but also to extract information from your best people and package it as adaptable corporate assets. This simple fact raises many power-related issues. Who owns what frames? Who administers them and how? How is frame sharing maximized, both during initial development and after general release? Who is responsible to make changes to frames? Who pays for frames?

## What to Frame

Frames with the highest reuse potential clearly have the highest priority. And they are the easiest to identify because they are ubiquitous. Given a run-time (object) architecture, framework architectures typically resolve into at least three strata:

1. The *system architecture* contains generic components for interfacing to devices—workstations, printers, data storage, operating system platforms, and communication networks. System architecture components are normally corporate frames.

2. The *application architecture* contains generic process components (data entry, update, inquiry, report, . . .) and data components (transaction-types, master-record types, parameter-tables, . . .). These can be corporate frames as well, but application types may be peculiar to a department or line-of-business. In this case, application architecture frames may exist only at the departmental or project level.

3. The *business architecture* specifies the rules and data structures that model various business applications (manufacturing, engineering, banking . . .). Many, if not most, will be reusable only within a project or application.

As framing proceeds from (1) to (3), their potential reuse increasingly depends on noticing local patterns, after the fact. For example, you may notice that the next specification frame is similar to a couple of others.

There is nothing wrong with parameterizing one of them to make it reusable.

### Sources of Frames

Many frames from all three strata can be vendor-supplied. Databases, GUI, network protocols, and the like are common to particular computing environments and are available from software vendors whose business includes multiplatform support. Package vendors sell frames common to particular industries, such as banking. Figure 19-4 illustrates the spectrum of levels and sources of frames.

Just as vendors enjoy real profits from reusability, an enterprise applies the profit motive to each of its internal levels of reuse. The profit rules exemplified by Figure 19-2 combined with the limited risk equation,

$$\text{Exposure} = \text{Risk/Volatility}$$

yields the frame promotion principle. That is, application frames with the potential to become corporate standards should be groomed through a disciplined process.

**Figure 19-4.** Software architectures divide into layers based on the likelihood of reuse and the source—self or purchased.

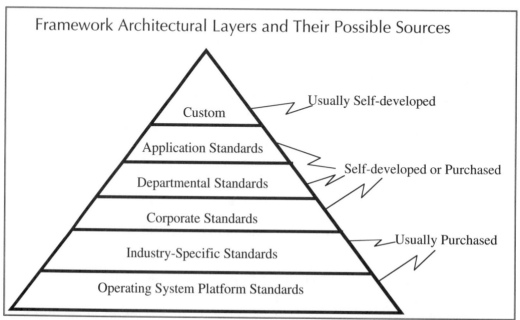

## Frame Ownership

Who owns and pays for frames? Ownership and support for project frames resides with the project (application) manager whose budget pays for creating the frames. This implies that a frame engineer seconded (full or part time) to the project team is paid for out of the project budget.

Ownership gains teeth when the owner's budget retains some of the "profits" from the frame's reuse. For example, by calculating QSM's productivity index for a frame-based project and subtracting the baseline PI (an average over projects that did not reuse frames), it is straightforward to convert the difference into the effort (cost) saved due to reuse (as we saw in Chapter 1). Should another project reuse the originating project's frames, the owner, in return for supporting the frames, can charge "royalties."

When a project frame is to be groomed into a corporate (or departmental) frame, ownership transfers to the central frame administration group. One measure of effective corporate frames is that "royalties" from development projects more than fund the many activities of the central group. It is a natural profit center, as it provides a product and services it too.

Reuse should not be coerced. Frames are a commodity, to be traded in proportion to their value. Their value should be perceived as fair to both supplier and consumer. Automated accounting together with reuse metrics should enable the internal market to make rational decisions easily. This approach motivates people to regard frames objectively, as true capital assets. Handling frame development in this way promotes a culture of sharing. It makes people portable among application projects. It avoids creating an "ivory tower" elitist group, resented by project developers.

# The Frame Refinement Process

## CHAPTER 20

> *The greatest invention of the nineteenth century*
> *was the invention of the method of invention.*
>                                   Alfred North Whitehead, 1925

C hapter 19 discussed the infrastructure and management aspects of developing frames.[1] Now we turn our attention to the process of frame maturation. As with application development, frame maturation is iterative. When frameworks merit promotion to departmental or corporate-wide reuse (or to the world beyond), the central frame management group undertakes frame consolidation and support. Infrequent postrelease versions are refined, based on the actual reuse experience of individual frames.

Whether or not a frame is destined to be a corporate standard, it starts life in some system development project. Thus, framing must occur early so project executables can take advantage. The time-box principle scopes the framing effort to ensure expeditious delivery and to avoid overengineering.

## The Initial Application Project

Let's assume a time-box of three time-units. That is, the frame-to-be will be reused four or more times and each instance would otherwise need one

---

[1] As usual, the word "frame" can also mean "frame subassembly." A "framework" is a library of frame subassemblies, designed to isolate different sources of change.

unit to design, build, and test.[2] The three units need not be consumed in one fell swoop. One frame engineer may be working on several frames in several projects. Time is allocated to different time-boxes as her attention switches from frame to frame.

How should three units be allocated over a frame's two aspects—usability (functionality, ease-of-use, performance) and reusability (generality, adaptibility)? Most of the three units is invested in meeting the initial project's usability needs. The rest is invested only as necessary in generality and adaptability.

A reusable frame's first version might arise simply from splitting a specification frame (which, in the extreme, can be a whole program) into a smaller SPC and a generic subframe. Another developer, working closely with the frame's author, then tries it in his own program (executable).

After two or three more successful reuse instances, the frame's usability should be stable enough to be packaged and reused by the rest of the project. Formally, reaching this stage means it has *application*-frame status. The frame author continues to support others as they reuse it. By support, I mean the frame's author documents, coaches, and makes further refinements as required. If the changes are general improvements, she changes the frame directly (and helps with any retrofits). (Version control is inappropriate until the frame demonstrates reusability across projects.)

Once its time-box limit is reached, the frame is frozen, a discipline essential to prevent wasting time on "frills." Now if general improvements are needed, application developers, not the frame's author, make them in "temporary wrapper" frames. Specification frames are reserved for customizing a single instance. Wrappers formally isolate thought-to-be-reusable enhancements from thought-to-be-custom ones. This tactic highlights potential frame reengineering options for later analysis. In the meantime, wrapper-frame reusers can pretend the enhancements went into the base frame because the two forms are functionally equivalent.

This approach gives developers a stable frame even though it is, and will always remain, "imperfect." It also enables management to track and control the frame development process:

- A frame that has used up its time-box, yet is still too immature to be frozen, warrants an immediate audit and remedial action.

- Time spent on temporary wrappers is part of the investment in the underlying frame. That is, the "profit" from reusing the frame is offset by the cost overruns of the wrappers.

---

[2] In practice, life is more complicated, as we shall see later in the chapter.

## Refine Alternate Versions

Just like fast-track executives, project frames with corporate potential need grooming in a variety of business areas. The number depends on the inherent diversity of the enterprise. Single-product companies, for example, may find the first project produces an acceptable version of a corporate frame. More typically though, version-one of a frame is merely a reuse reference point. The frame needs seasoning in other projects, chosen because their requirements differ from the first project. The frame probably needs significant changes and extensions, even though it produced a profit in its first project.

Business priorities often conflict with your ideal choice of grooming projects. Then you must fall back upon the competence of your frame engineers. Immature frames that cannot get full direct exposure to your organization's diversity are another reason why frame engineers should already have that exposure.

Whether a frame is exposed to different projects in parallel or serially, each project should be free to rewrite it, using the time-box strategy. Short of complete rewrites, emphasis in these versions shifts from usability to reusability. Its different versions are given names that reflect their provisional status. These "guinea pig projects," testing experimental versions of a frame, are part of the organization's deliberate investment in reuse. And the project managers should not mind their "guinea pig" status, since each guinea pig gets an ROI from its own version.

Might too many cooks spoil the broth? Not likely. Worse than most disciplines, software engineers must stir a witch's brew of ambiguities, conflicting constraints, and changing expectations. Each chef avoids duplicate effort by starting with the currently best recipe. Moreover, confidence that a recipe has global appeal comes from liking its taste in different meals. At the risk of one-too-many clichés, Fred Brooks was so right: no silver bullets—frames are brass bullets that must be bitten.

## Consolidation and Stable Release

Having stabilized two or more versions of a frame at the application level, the central frame engineering group decides whether or not to consolidate the versions into one standard frame. Consolidation may not be appropriate if the versions turn out to address different problem categories, or if further divergence seems likely.

For example, a conglomerate may ostensibly need a sales-order frame, but current versions exhibit little commonality among product and market structures. One division sells bulk petrochemicals, another offers custom software services, and so on; the conglomerate is too eclectic.  Not to despair, each division's sales-order frame returns a tidy application development profit.  This is where departmental frames are the right level at which to stabilize your components.

Figure 20-1 shows the maturation path for frames. Because department- and corporate-level frames are refined in a similar manner, we refer to both as corporate frames. Differences between them are explained as we proceed.

To decide whether or not to undertake a consolidation, you estimate your alternative ROIs.  For example, suppose:

- 10 applications will be able to reuse a frame an average of 10 times each;

- the cost of writing and stabilizing an application frame is time-boxed to three (units of functionally equivalent, nonreusable effort);

**Figure 20-1.**  Several versions of one frame may get created in guinea pig projects. Wrappers and version control are two ways to stabilize frames. Version control eliminates wrappers.

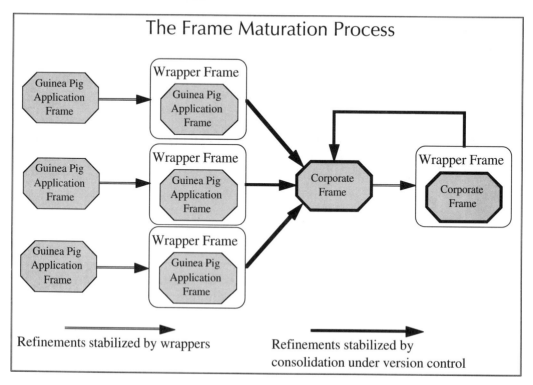

- the marginal cost of consolidating a corporate frame from three application versions is time-boxed to eight units;

- the adaptability cost is 0.15 units per reuse of an application frame;

- the adaptability cost is 0.05 units per reuse of a corporate frame (i.e., it has higher ease-of-reuse and is probably not adapted by most SPCs).

Assuming you consolidate one corporate frame from three guinea pig projects (without retrofitting), and you reuse it in seven more projects, your total investment over 100 reuses is:

$$(3 \times 3) + 8 + (3 \times 10) \times 0.15 + (7 \times 10) \times 0.05 = 25$$

Since the nonreuse alternative cost would be 10 x 10 units, we have a profit of 75 units, an ROI of 300%. Alternatively, should you elect to develop 10 application versions with no consolidation, your total cost would be:

$$10 \times 3 + 100 \times 0.15 = 45$$

for a profit of 10 x 10 - 45 = 55, or an ROI of only 122%.

Of course, we have ignored important factors, such as the costs of managing 10 versions rather than four, the central frame administration overhead, the extra quality of a corporate frame, the reduced application maintenance costs, and using nonframe-reuse techniques as the baseline of comparison.

Specification frame writers prefer adding to component frames rather than modifying their behavior. They feel this way because the additional functionality would be necessary in any case, but modifying a component requires understanding the frame author's thinking. (We take for granted the work that such frames save.)

As reflected in the above cost model, the further a frame is from the SPC, the smaller is its cost per reuse. SPC writers usually are not even aware of the more context-free frames, because intervening frames do the customizing automatically.

The central frame engineering group consolidates the submitted versions by writing one frame whose core is common to all versions, and whose SELECTs contain the variations found in the different versions. Reusers should be able to simply set a software switch to select a desired variation.

Which temporary wrapper frames to consolidate depends on the amount of reuse they experienced. If a version is always reused with a certain wrapper, they are consolidated together. But if a proposed improvement was too seldom reused to justify consolidation, then it becomes a permanent wrapper of its frame version prior to consolidation, and/or is rewritten to wrap the consolidated version. The decisions depend on a frame-by-frame cost-benefit analysis.

During consolidation, most of the activities are related to a frame's reuse properties:

- ensure the frame conforms to corporate coding standards;

- provide corporate-standard documentation on how to use it, both at run time and at construction time;

- update or create standard template(s) for ease of reuse (as explained in Chapter 16, a template is a prototype SPC that may incorporate the new frame into a frame hierarchy and provide a linear list of parameters for the whole hierarchy);

- add version control (as explained in Chapter 16);

- regression-test the consolidated frame as a functional superset of its precursor versions, using their test suites; the consolidated frame may not replace its precursors, but equivalent functionality is a minimum goal;

- officially register the frame, and any wrappers and templates, into the appropriate framework library, and announce its general availability.

The corporate frame now needs to be centrally supported as it enters its stable, steady-state phase.

## Manage Evolutionary Refinements

In spite of inevitable evolutionary pressures, the need for long-term stability is now paramount. The maturity process now pretends the frame is perfect, even though it is not. This pretense flattens its learning curve. Software developers do not have to worry about the frame having changed since the last time they reused it. The more they can build its patterns of reuse into their habits of thought, the more productive they will be, the less effort they will need each time they adapt it, and the fewer errors they will make.

### Freeze the Frame

For a year or two, handle all evolutionary pressure using the "temporary" wrapper tactic. One wrapper can incorporate all the suggestions for improvements for an entire community of developers. Each suggestion is SELECTable, keeping the number of wrappers to a minimum. Developers reuse the wrapped frame as if the changes in its wrapper had been made to the wrapped frame. Because the details in the wrapper are not mixed up with single-use details in SPCs, they are easily analyzed when the underlying frame is finally thawed for possible consolidation.

The frozen period is proportional to how widely the frame is reused. Departmental frames should be stable for at least a year, longer for corporate frames. When the thaw comes, frame engineers analyze the accumulated wrapper suggestions to decide which ones have stood the test of time. Those that gain wide reuse may deserve consolidation with the frame, depending on whether or not the wrapped frame continues to be reused independently of its wrapper(s). Unconsolidated suggestions remain in (their now) permanent wrapper(s).

Figure 20-1 illustrates steady-state iterative refinement cycles. Consolidation of wrappers is performed under version control. This control ensures that all existing systems are protected; by default, only new development can reuse the evolved version. Sometimes the changes are radical enough, such as a complete redesign, that the new version is conceptually a new frame. In this situation, it is wise to create a new frame and continue to protect people's expertise with the old one. As in all engineering disciplines, these kinds of judgements are based on pragmatic trade-offs relying more on experience than fixed rules.

# The Iterative Refinement of Software Applications

## CHAPTER 21

*Ready. Fire. Aim.*

Cadbury's Executive

T he trend these days is to require software developers to conform to process quality control standards, such as the European ISO-9003, the British TickIt program, and the Software Engineering Institute's Capability Maturity Model. These efforts to ensure quality in the process, are to be strongly encouraged. However, such efforts emphasize building systems right rather than building the right systems. This chapter complements the former by emphasizing the latter.

Why bother, when so many methodologies are commercially available? Their highly detailed manuals create the impression that system development can be mechanized by human "computers" carrying out methodology "programs." Unfortunately, most methodologies are oblivious to the fact that the interesting software domains are ill defined. In reality, system requirements are unstable. Consequently, elaborate methodologies leave too little room for error and feedback. We seek an engineering approach that deals head on with ambiguity and instability. We need a way to produce the best systems that limited time and money can buy.

Iterative design refinement is more a guideline than a detailed methodology. In the spirit of adaptability, IDR is meant to be tailored to the size and scope of each project, to the skills of project team members, and to the maturity of the frame library. (The previous chapters explain the frame maturation process. An empty library is a degenerate special case of IDR.)

There is one essential prerequisite. IDR requires software to be automatically assembled from generic components. The existence of those components allows them to serve as adaptable design models. As a result, IDR analysis is guided by existing models, and confined to the truly novel requirements.

## An Overview of IDR

Let's imagine we are engaged in a major software development project using the IDR development process. While IDR (Figure 21-1) iterates indefinitely, the cycles are grouped into three phases: conceptual, prerelease, and postrelease. (This chapter deals with the first two phases, and Chapter 22 discusses the postrelease phase, often called "maintenance.")

In brief, the *conceptual* model provides just enough information to justify, estimate, and segment the project into pre-production releases or *pre-*

**Figure 21-1.** Start with requirements. Guided by existing framework models, engage in joint application development. JAD leads to the design of the most important system elements. These elements customize the frameworks that developers assemble into executables and test. The users also test the results and suggest refinements. After one or two refinement cycles, the next most important pre- (or post-) release is started.

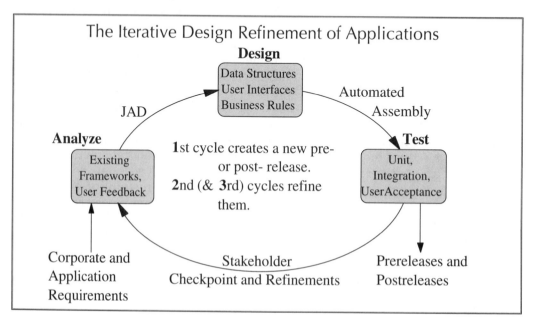

*releases*. Each prerelease is a set of executable modules, constructed and refined to be acceptable to the stakeholders.

What goes into a prerelease depends on its criticality. The functions most essential to the stakeholders and to subsequent prereleases must be built next. Each prerelease normally requires two or three IDR cycles; the first cycle constructs a working set of executables, the next cycle or two refines the executables into an acceptable prerelease. IDR then repeats the process for the next prerelease.

## Phase One: Produce a Conceptual Model

### Analysis

The analysis step is our entry point into the first IDR cycle. This entry being the conceptual phase, we seek a macroscopic model of our putative system, one that puts it into the context of its surrounding environment, including any other systems that may interact with it. Our first analysis step, therefore, asks basic questions about overall goals and constraints, and the general requirements of the system. What is its business case? What deadlines exist? Can we buy off-the-shelf frameworks for some or all of the requirements? What is the anticipated ROI?

Attempting to answer such questions requires the participation of all the stakeholders—the executive sponsor, the system architect, the operations manager, key end-users, perhaps even key external customers. When stakeholder communities are diverse, requirements gathering is best facilitated through joint application development (discussed in Chapter 18).

Requirements should always be determined in the context of existing run-time architectures and frameworks. Otherwise, many requirements will inadvertently turn out to be incompatible with them, resulting in unnecessary extra time and effort, and a proliferation of overlapping components. The best way to test compatibility with existing components is to build an experimental prototype of the system, reusing those components. JAD outputs can be used to construct one quickly, in a few days at most. The prototype highlights necessary points of departure from existing models (frames). Assuming a reasonable fit, subsequent JADs can be conducted on a "same as, except" basis.

### Design

Having gathered the major external requirements in the first analysis step, the first design step identifies the subsystems of the conceptual model, its table of contents. Figure 21-2 illustrates the design flow from a conceptual model on down to an executable system that approximates the

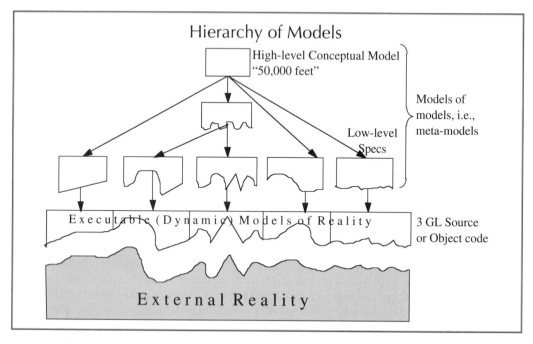

**Figure 21-2.** In the hierarchy of models, the external reality at the bottom is real. At the next level up, that reality is modeled by executable modules. Going still farther up, the executable modules are themselves modeled by several layers, originating in the conceptual model.

real world. In essence, a conceptual model is a macroscopic description of a system that the design group hopes will satisfy the requirements. The model (see Table 21-1) should also identify the benefits and costs of having such a system. The model should demonstrate the fit with what exists, in terms of both external run-time objects and internal construction-time components.

A conceptual model is usually represented by a combination of narratives, Entity-Relationship diagrams, dataflow diagrams, and the like. While more a convenience than a necessity, numerous graphics-oriented tools are available for capturing and manipulating this information on-line.

The conceptual model's structure should group related requirements, and separate independent groups from each other. For example, details relating to specific computing platforms, network protocols, database schemas, and the like should be separated from business process and data rules. Nor should the model redundantly describe similar things.

**Table 21-1  A Conceptual Model Provides the System Context**

Conceptual models determine:

- the system's purpose, scope, interfaces, deadlines, and any other global constraints;
- the business case for and against the system, its ROI, and relative priority;
- whether to build the system or to buy (and customize) a package.

Assuming a system is to be built, the model determines:

- the relative priorities of business benefits correlated to system components;
- similarities and differences among proposed system features and functionalities;
- compatibilities and conflicts with existing frameworks;
- what new frames are needed;
- an estimate of total implementation time and effort;
- a Ganntt chart of subsystems whose development can be overlapped;
- agreed responsibilities of users, developers, and managers, and their expectations about the system and each other.

In a mature reuse environment, a system's conceptual model can be quite terse, needing only to specify deltas to previously identified generic structures, along with the system's rationale.

Having identified and briefly described all the subsystems and their interfaces, each is similarly refined into its executable components. This layering approach is called *breadth-first* analysis and design, because it covers the whole system at a consistent level of detail before moving to the next level, as shown in Figure 21-3. The layering stops at the *function-point boundary*. This boundary is marked by the ability to identify the following list of elements by name and a one-line description:

- windows (i.e., separate screen displays),
- reports,
- interfaces to other systems,
- subject databases.

An insurance policy administration system, for instance, may require policy initiation, premium payments, claims processing, and

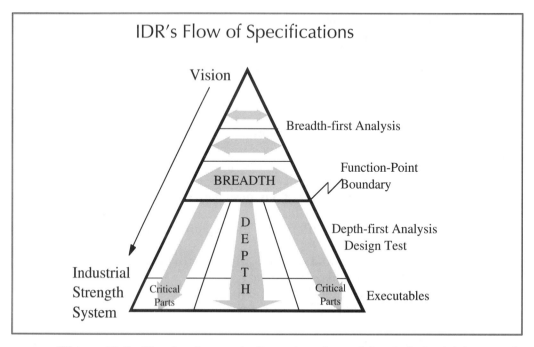

**Figure 21-3.** The development of a system from vision to industrial strength may be conceptualized as a series of layers, analyzed initially breadth-first. Below the function-point boundary, detailed analysis, design and test proceeds depth-first.

interfaces to other systems such as the underwriting and estate-planning systems. Each of these subsystems is resolved down to a description sufficient only to distinguish its function points and their interrelationships, not the details of each function point.

Because the conceptual model is not carried beyond the function-point boundary into great details, patterns of similarity among model structures are relatively easy to spot. Such patterns abound, whether or not they exist as frames. Using a conceptual model to spot frames is one of the most important ways to avoid needless work. As mentioned above, the model should be condensed at each point of similarity, and a demonstration of an existing framework can indicate its relevance (same as, except).

Assuming mature frameworks exist, a conceptual model (including its demonstration) can be completed in a few days, even for a large system. In general, the time and effort spent in the conceptual phase will be proportional to the completeness and maturity of those frameworks (a subject treated in previous chapters).

## Test

The test step obtains feedback and, ultimately, approval for work done and to be done. Stakeholders who can be involved only periodically exert their influence at the test step. And, of course, approval to commence the prerelease phase must be obtained as part of the final review and approval of the conceptual model.

This step raises the question as to the number of iterations required to complete the conceptual model. Small systems, or large systems that are small variants of existing frameworks, will require only one cycle. Systems that incorporate significant novelty may require several breadth-first modeling cycles before reaching the function-point boundary. The number of cycles also depends on the desire of stakeholders, such as the system sponsor, (*a*) to guide the refinement process, and (*b*) to time-box the conceptual model, i.e., to avoid analysis paralysis.

Upon approving the conceptual model, the stakeholders should agree on their mutual expectations and obligations during the prerelease phase. In particular, they should *expect requirements to change during construction and allow for this* in the schedule. The goal is to maximize "bang for buck,"[1] rather than building a system to a set of stale specifications. While the total time and effort can be estimated, only the first prerelease should be firmly quoted.

## From Breadth-First to Depth-First: Gearing for Phase Two

So far, IDR has followed the traditional waterfall with one twist: the conceptual model derives from reusable frameworks. At this point, the two processes fundamentally diverge. Whereas the waterfall continues its breadth-first layering until detailed design is complete, IDR's function-point boundary marks the transition to a depth-first process. In particular, IDR defers the detailed analysis and design of less critical system structures until after the most critical ones execute satisfactorily.

Why? An aeronautical engineer, having determined the global requirements of a new aircraft (e.g., fuel economy, range, passenger capacity), first designs the air foil with simulations, including a wind tunnel model. Only after he is confident of the aerodynamics does he worry about the secondary design issues, such as passenger access and seating. The same is true for software engineering. Fuss over GUI window layouts only

---

[1] "Bang for buck" is Tom DeMarco's charming name for a possibly imaginary, but potentially real, project metric. It is, he says "a quantitative indicator of net usable function from the user's point of view" per unit of development expenditure. [32]

after confirming that the system will keep its enterprise "flying." These considerations are why the first prerelease focuses on critical structures.

Systems usually obey Parieto's rule: *eighty percent of the benefits derive from twenty percent of the system.* Selecting the critical 20% requires some judgment. Which outputs have the highest financial impact on the organization? Which executables must sustain peak-load performance? Which ones involve real-time synchronization with critical external events? Which components need to be framed first because they have the highest work-avoidance potential?

The most critical executables comprise the first preproduction release. While built quickly, a prerelease is not a mock-up of the users' interfaces; nor is it a quick-and-dirty prototype. It is an end-to-end slice through the system, a refined version of which will in time be put into production, because it is assembled from standard frameworks. Once the first prerelease has been refined and stabilized, the next one should likewise comprise the next most critical executables. A final decision about which these are should wait until the current prerelease works well enough to confirm expectations.

When resources permit, a large system should be split into subsystems for parallel development purposes. Using the conceptual model, find its "hourglass necks"—places where data flows are most limited, where processes in the same hourglass lobe couple to each other more than they couple to those in another lobe (diagrammed in Figure 21-4). The outputs of "upstream" subsystems can be mocked up, enabling parallel development of "downstream" subsystems.

Form SWAT teams (Chapter 18) of no more than three or four members. The number of subsystems should be at least the number of teams available. The infrastructure is organized to optimize the productivity of the SWAT teams, as they are on the critical path from "vision" to "industrial strength" software. Anything that wastes their time will delay the entire project. To be sure, the SWAT team can carry on with their own best guesses while waiting for "official answers." But the longer the delay, the more downstream work is likely to be wasted.

## Start New Framing

How do you develop frames that are prerequisites to the first prerelease(s)? The frame engineer(s) should start a step or two (in the three-step IDR cycle) ahead of the SWAT team(s). That is, detailed frame analysis starts before any SWAT team starts detailed analysis of its first prerelease. The staggered start should be just enough to enable each SWAT team to design the executables in which the frames will be tested. In the case of subsystem parallel development, each prerelease's executables, and hence

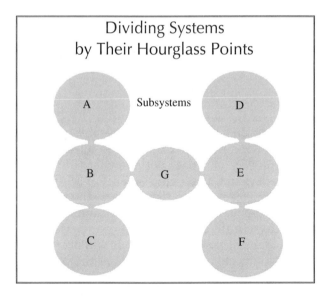

Dividing Systems
by Their Hourglass Points

A     Subsystems     D

B        G        E

C                  F

**Figure 21-4.** Large systems can be divided into subsystems by finding the places where data flows between groups of functions "neck down" the most.

the common frames, are tested in parallel. The frame engineers work with the SWAT teams, refining the frames to satisfy common requirements. This is the co-refinement of frames and systems described in the previous two chapters.

To summarize IDR to this point, accepting the conceptual model marks the end of the first phase. An overview of the system is in hand, resolved down to its function-point boundary. The most critical work to be done has been itemized to become the first prerelease. Now we must drive some stakes into the ground, to get that prerelease working as soon as possible, and find out if it will support the expectations of the stakeholders. Then and only then can they have the confidence to erect the rest of the system.

## Time-Box Each Prerelease Cycle

The size (amount of functionality) of each prerelease depends on several factors, including:

- the minimum functionality required to demonstrate useful or end-to-end results;
- the knowledge and experience of the SWAT team members (a module that takes an expert only a few hours to analyze, design, and test may take a novice a week);
- the desired frequency of checkpoints—the more frequent the check-

points, the smaller the risk of doing wrong things. But each checkpoint consumes stakeholder review and approval time. The more expertise the developers have, the more they can do before requiring a checkpoint. The time-box for a cycle includes the time to do the previous cycle's checkpoint.

Assuming a four-week time-box for the first cycle and a SWAT team with three developers who average one fully tested executable per day, then each prerelease will consist of the next (4 x 5 x 3=) 60 most critical executables. This estimate is simplistic, as it does not allow for things like learning curves, intrinsic complexity, sick time, and so on. An IS department should monitor and revise its project estimation rules as the baseline of frames grows, and as users and developers become more sophisticated.

The first cycle creates the executables, the second, and possibly a third, refines them. The stakeholder checkpoint evaluates the prerelease and negotiates changes. Each refine cycle is typically 50% of the previous cycle time. Thus, if the first cycle is four weeks, the second is two weeks and the third is one week. The prerelease should be scaled and tuned to industrial strength by then or management has a right to question the project's viability.

Unbudgeted extra cycles should be discouraged. When confronted by unexpected delays, the default decision should be to deliver less functionality and get back on schedule. This decision is usually acceptable because the most important parts of the system are being built first anyway. Stakeholders always have the option of deferring the less critical features to the next release. The whole point of each cycle is to time-box the process and avoid the natural temptation to embellish.

## Detailed Analysis

The first cycle's detailed analysis of the function points for the current prerelease involves determining the specific data structures and business rules necessary to this prerelease. To the extent that generic structures and rules already exist, the process becomes one of instancing them, defining the deltas. JADs involving key stakeholders are a popular and effective technique for obtaining consensus and documenting the results.

## Detailed Design

Detailed design involves associating the frameworks (that implement generic windows and screens, reports, database schemas, network protocols, etc.) with the specific requirements stemming from the analysis. The outputs of the design step are specifications that feed into the frame-based software assembly tools.

## Detailed Testing

Notice what has happened. Since construction is automated, we have moved around the IDR loop in Figure 21-1 directly from detailed design to testing. Testing critical system components in the very first IDR cycle enables us to flush out hidden requirement and design errors as early as possible. Limit testing to the SWAT team until the executables work to specifications. Then freeze a separate demo version. Thus, users can be testing while the team is making further refinements.

Unit testing occurs in each create cycle; integration testing with all existing prereleases and external system interfaces occurs in the first refine cycle. User acceptance of the accumulated prereleases occurs in the second refine cycle. Testing should answer questions such as:

- Are you getting the benefits you expected?
- Are there serendipitous benefits that could change our understanding of the system's potential?
- Are there unexpected or hidden development costs?
- Are there performance problems?
- Are there side effects with other systems?
- Are any critical requirements missing or wrong?

At the end of each checkpoint, answers to these questions are input to the next cycle's analysis, where the executables are reworked as described earlier (or the next prerelease is initiated).

As testing occurs in each cycle throughout the project, the testing load is relatively level. We want to minimize piling up testing at the far end of the project. As with the waterfall approach, massive tail-end testing destabilizes the system, because too many executables are changing between test runs. Moreover, since so much of the system results from seasoned, standard frameworks, testing becomes a largely routine checklist. Nonroutine testing correlates with novel system features and interactions among them.

When errors point to problems with the requirements or the design, they are most likely to be local to the current prerelease. That is, the conceptual model is not affected. The reason is twofold:

1. Design models describe frameworks that have proven themselves in previous systems. They are less likely to exhibit serious structural errors than those designed from scratch.

2. By terminating the conceptual model at the function-point boundary, there is less detail to get wrong.

On the other hand, because IDR deliberately goes after the most critical parts of the system, the very first prerelease is where errors with the conceptual model are most likely to be discovered. Should this happen, a (hopefully) short IDR cycle must be inserted to revise the conceptual model and revise plans for the prerelease phase. The silver lining is the time and money saved by catching such errors early.

At the point of satisfactory acceptance of the prerelease, "lock it down." That is, defer further changes until the postrelease phase (unless, of course, subsequent prereleases uncover hidden problems). You can now start developing user documentation and training materials for the locked-down prerelease. This work proceeds in parallel with the next prerelease.

## Software Scaffolding

Because a prerelease may be a thin slice through a system, many executables needed to supply data to the slice will be missing. In order to test the prerelease executables, the missing data are "stubbed" or mocked up. Such temporary scaffolding is much cheaper to supply than the actual parts of the system (that are scheduled for a future prerelease). Developers can quickly use their assembly tools to erect scaffolds upon generic frameworks.

## End-User Roles

Assuming standard templates for menus, data entry, updates, reports, and so forth have been defined, end-users can be trained to use drag-and-drop painting tools. Involving end-users in this way both frees the SWAT team members from fussy cosmetic details, and gives users control over that part of the design that affects them most directly.

To maximize the effectiveness of IDR, end-users must be able to interact with the SWAT team during each step of each iteration. Co-location, as described in Chapter 18, facilitates the needed interactions. In addition to the formal analysis and design JADs, a responsible end-user should be available to the SWAT team, not only to paint interfaces, but also to resolve issues missed during the JADs. Such users should have the power to escalate issues that they cannot resolve, and to force timely responses. This is a very important, but often overlooked, infrastructural bottleneck.

## Releasing the System into Production

Phase Two consolidates a sequence of prereleases into an integrated system. When to release the system depends, in part, on the lead times needed to train users, and on appropriate moments to cut-over existing systems and procedures. In large organizations, this may be another serious bottleneck.

To compound the issue, in many IS environments, the polarity between users and developers is such that users refuse to accept a system until every last feature is present to their satisfaction. With IDR, this polarity should evolve into a partnership that focuses on bottom-line benefits, not features.

## Partnerships Are Based on Trust

Meaningful progress on short time scales can do wonders for morale, trust, and support among users, IS, and senior management. Senior management's "black hole" perception of IS should disappear because projects can be managed more like projects in other departments.

Because IDR refines the most beneficial parts of the system first, users soon notice that the organization is losing those benefits every day they are not released. Thus, there is a strong incentive to adopt a schedule that rolls out the system in stages. Users will trust that the remaining stages will happen in a timely fashion since they have witnessed SWAT teams develop the most significant parts of the system in a timely, flexible, sustainable fashion.

On the other hand, the cut-over to a new system may need to be synchronized with opportune moments in the business, or the release may need to go into pilot testing to see how it works in remote sites. Early versions of a system may need to operate in parallel with its antecedent. By building a system in stages, the options for its deployment increase.

A related potential bottleneck is system operations. The staff may be used to a traditional roll-out process, in which large amounts of functionality are installed infrequently. Now they must accommodate small amounts of functionality installed frequently, to the point where prereleases are temporarily installed for testing, then de-installed for further refinements. These bottlenecks, often ignored, greatly reduce the responsiveness of the organization to external business pressures. Unfortunately, frameworks cannot solve infrastructural problems.

## Maximizing Bang for Buck

IDR puts management in a marvelous position to minimize risk. Rather than committing to the whole budget for a large system, they need only commit to the next prerelease. At the end of each IDR cycle, management, based on tangible results, can judge how on or off track the system is. The evidence provided by each prerelease will either confirm that expectations are still within affordable change tolerances, or reveal show stoppers as early as possible.

As I have already mentioned, at the beginning of each create cycle the project manager should be prepared to fix the cost, and revise her estimate of the overall project cost. Because the most critical parts are delivered first, the estimates-to-actual variances in the schedule and in the cost should shrink as the cycles unfold.

## Gaining Points of Reference

Software projects differ from conventional engineering projects in one very important respect. The problems we are trying to solve are intangible (not to mention volatile and ill defined). Our prereleases give us tangible reference points with which to improve our perception of the problems. In other words, future requirements depend on what currently works. IDR, based on adaptive component assembly, is geared to this phenomenon.

The time-box principle improves management's control over projects by using short deadlines to force trade-offs in favor of the most important results. Given Brook's Law about adding bodies to a late software project, the time-box should be a *resource-box*, limiting effort as well.

## Contracting Out

IDR maximizes bang for buck from an in-house development perspective. When contracting-out for software, the goal should be not to fix the requirements, then award tender to the low-cost bidder; rather the goal should be to set a minimum requirement and a maximum budget and deadline, then award tender, conditional on each prerelease, to the bidder who will maximize your system's ROI (operational benefits over development cost), and minimize your ongoing costs to refine the system as necessary. You have a right to expect the best solution that your limited time and money can buy.

## Requirements Inflation

IDR has a nice problem: end-users, may become excited, seeing rapid progress and responsiveness to their requests. They may get "hot flashes" in the shower, rush in still a little damp, and breathlessly dash off their request, saying "It's easy; you haven't built this part of the system yet."

Of course, uncontrolled requests will upset any schedule. IDR has a natural valve for controlling requirements inflation. Once the JADs for the create cycle produce requirements, freeze them until the end of the cycle. During the JADs for the refine cycles, prioritize requests until the 50% resource allowance is consumed. Users are not unreasonably put off, because their requests are addressed at the analysis step of each cycle, which is never more than a few weeks away. It's fascinating how hot flashes in the shower seem to cool off when seen with decent hindsight.

Developers can further guard against "gilding the lily" because, having built the highest ROI components first, they will be able to estimate the relative costs of additional features, and to credibly negotiate cost-effective trade-offs.

# IDR Benefits

IDR's strategy is to scale up quickly from partial solutions to a system whose quality and completeness is sufficient to release into production, then to continue indefinitely to refine the system with postproduction releases.

Without adaptive component assembly, IDR's strategy could not work. It depends on being able to start, not from scratch, but from an initial design model that is easily refined to the needs of the new system. At each prerelease, what has already been stabilized is reused as part of the framework for further refinements and additions to the system. IDR refines the design and produces the system at the same time. Here are its main advantages:

- *Each prerelease is real*, not a throwaway or shell prototype. It just happens that the first few may not be sufficient to release.
- *Credibility and enthusiasm builds*, due to frequent, visible progress.
- *Cost-effective requests are accommodated* into subsequent cycles while holding firm the cost and schedule of the current one.
- *Users may take less* (in the first release) in order to start getting benefits sooner, confident that the project team will deliver the rest.
- *Risk is limited;* management can dole out money in much smaller amounts; misconceived systems can be aborted early, based on hard evidence.

Look at what IDR avoids:

- *Analysis paralysis* when requirements change faster than the voluminous details can be updated.
- *Wasted work* when wrong requirements and/or designs are detected late.
- *Destabilization* when massive testing trips over co-evolving modules.
- *Gilding the system* with features whose benefits turn out to not be worth their cost. IDR can resolve many disputes over what features are useful by simply trying them.

The bottom line: IDR avoids unnecessary risk on unproven ideas.

# Software Maintenance Considered Harmful

Engineering software to remain soft is perhaps the most neglected design objective of all. Why is maintenance the most expensive end of the life cycle, consuming at least 70% of IS resources and climbing? Part of the reason software fails to remain soft is because we treat it as a kind of hardware. The very word *maintenance* is anachronistic; we never restore software systems to their original forms. Even bug fixing is not maintenance, for a bug is a pre-existing defect, not a result of wear and tear.

According to Lientz and Swanson, changes in user requirements account for 41.8% of maintenance costs, while hardware and operating system changes are another 9.6% [33]. With the advent of client-server, multimedia, GUI, pen computing, and the like, the share of these changes will surely go up. In other words, changes in the system's external environment drive over half of so-called maintenance. The engineering issue, then, is that environments change spontaneously while software models of them do not. Is this not what *evolution* is all about? Environmental stresses force otherwise stable systems to adapt.

If we engineer software for perpetual modifiability, then evolution, not maintenance, best describes the change process, both pre- and postproduction. We shall see below that IDR is also a postproduction change process; indeed, it is premised on software's unending need to evolve. Maintenance as a separate process, done with separate people, tools, and mind-sets, is an obsolete, counterproductive idea.

## Postproduction Releases

Why do people treat software "maintenance" differently from "development?" In addition to plain old habits of thought, are there essential differences between preproduction and postproduction environments?

### Nominal Differences Between Pre- and Postproduction

We examine three differences between the two regimes to see if they are essential or not.

1. Developers with a waterfall mind-set think they can construct systems only after the design phase and before the production phase. Two things are wrong with this positioning. One, much of a system built from reusable components is, in some sense, in existence before its design phase. Two, its major components are already in production in other systems.

   With a reuse mind-set, this distinction between development and production becomes artificial. That is, systems are seen as adaptations of their previous incarnations. Whether or not they are in production, such systems are under perpetual (re)development. They are always in a process of "becoming."

2. Technically, the existence of production data differentiates pre- from postproduction. Changes to a production system must not threaten the integrity of the production data. But the presence of production data is only one of many operational constraints requiring effective testing and effective configuration control.

   Production integrity, not being a construction-time constraint, should be independent of the maintenance process. So maintaining production integrity cannot be at the root of the maintenance mentality.

3. Requirements volatility is considerably higher during preproduction than during postproduction. High volatility derives from the ease with which one idea changes into another. In early prereleases, global requirements have not been validated, hence systemic design changes tend to occur early.

   However, unless the developers misconceived the system, after two prereleases it should then settle down to the inherent volatility of the domain, as we saw in Figure 19-3.

   Volatility is inversely related to the need for fine-tuning. It makes no sense to tune a system that solves the wrong problem. But after a system achieves its needed first-order effects, attention properly shifts to second-order issues. This progression is reflected in all top-down analysis and design techniques. But beware of the devil in the details.

Lientz and Swanson's statistics suggest that small-scale details account for at least half of so-called maintenance changes. Unfortunately, many construction tools generate black-box code—clumsy, if not impossible, to modify. Without the ability to make fussy changes to stereotypic code, a strategy for unifying "maintenance" with IDR cannot work. Lack of control over small, but important, details is one of the biggest complaints programmers have about construction tools. It is the primary reason such tools are ignored during so-called maintenance.

If your tools can handle the large-grain changes, as well as fine-tune down to individual symbols, then this third difference between pre- and postproduction goes the way of the other two.

## Programming by Exception

Specifying exceptions is inherent in frame technology. A reusable frame is a structured collection of defaults. Other, more specialized frames, such as specification frames, specify extensions and exceptions to those defaults.

The exceptions range in principle from bit switching to frame switching. It is this range that endows frames with pre- and postproduction capabilities. As far as application development is concerned, in a frame environment IDR handles postproduction releases, or postreleases, in exactly the same fashion as prereleases. The only difference is that the number of cycles per postrelease will probably be less than three (because of reduced volatility). Maintenance disappears as a separate mentality and methodology. It is done by the same people, the same tools, and the same techniques.

## Decoupling Application Evolution from Component Evolution

So far, we have discussed the evolution of applications. What about the components reused in constructing the executables of an application? That question was discussed in Chapter 20. For convenience, we include a brief summary of the ideas.

### Component Evolution

The more context-sensitive a component is, the more vulnerable it is to evolutionary pressures. Context-sensitivity falls off as we go deeper into frame trees because frames further from their roots tend to be reused by more frames (contexts), hence are independent of those contexts. This context-stratification is a natural way to decouple the evolution of the various components from each other. But can random mutations to a reused frame be totally decoupled from its user frames?

Many frames are generated from high-level specifications, such as window and report layouts, database definitions, and templates specifying architectural patterns such as client-server. Such derived frames do not need to be "maintained." Moreover, changes to the information contained in these frames is fully decoupled from the SPCs that adapt them.

Manually crafted frameworks constitute an IS organization's standard architectures—system, application, and business. These are read-only to other than author(ized) frame engineers. We want to be able to evolve such frameworks, without affecting any existing systems.

We emphasized in Chapter 20 that reusable components should be stable so that we become proficient with them. We rightly balk at frequent unlearning and relearning. Stability becomes paramount for components that are officially released for reuse. When manual refinements to a standard frame are needed, there are two complementary ways to handle them in order to preserve stability, as explained in Chapter 16.

The first technique puts a "temporary wrapper frame" around the frame in question. The wrapper encapsulates a related set of additions, deletions, and modifications to the wrapped frame. The net effect is the same as if the wrapped frame had been changed. Frames reuse the wrapper as if it were the modified wrapped frame. New executables may incorporate the wrapper. And old executables are, of course, oblivious to the modifications since they do not incorporate the wrapper. The benefits of temporary wrappers are as follows.

1. Over time, a wrapped frame remains absolutely stable.

2. Proposed enhancements are isolated from both the wrapped frame and SPCs.

3. Later, when you consider actually enhancing the wrapped frame, you can easily analyze a wrapper's reusage.

4. Wrappers let you hedge your bet—time will tell which changes have a scope of reuse matching the wrapped frame, and which have more limited contexts of reuse. The latter remain as permanent wrapper frames, and the former may be consolidated with the wrapped frame.

Consolidations are achieved using the second technique, formal version control (using the SELECT mechanism as discussed on page 182). It enables a frame to carry a complete audit trail of its own evolutionary history. It guarantees each executable remains invariant, no matter how much or how often its components have been modified.

Both techniques enable components to evolve independently of the executables in which they are reused. Of course there would be no point in evolving components if no executable ever took advantage. The point is never to force retrofits.

## Handling Retrofits

On the other hand, when a retrofit is warranted, it can be scheduled to suit the business, rather than the technical needs of IS.

For example, suppose users request a change to their billing application, say "detailed time logs should be displayable while composing invoices." Further, suppose that some time after the current billing system was released, one of its components, a frame for browsing single tables, was modified under version control to handle simultaneous browsing of multiple tables. This modification is invisible to the current billing system, but now the users have asked for an enhancement that justifies retrofitting the frame. The users pay for the changes they requested and get the retrofit as a hidden side benefit. How?

- First, do an impact analysis. The frame utilities will report all SPCs whose executables include the table browsing frame. The frame trees will show all possible adaptor frames.

- Second, decide which frame $F$ between the table browser and the SPCs should adapt the table browser. There may be several such frames (at most they are all the SPCs).

- Third, modify $F$ (and any other adaptors of the table browser) to take advantage of its modifications. These *mods* include changing the version symbol in $F$ so it will include the new version of the table browser. Because the frame commands enforce a consistent way to adapt the table browser frame, the retrofit will be the same for all frames like $F$.

- Fourth, assemble, compile, and test all affected executables.

## The Evolution of Purchased Packages

Retrofit problems are the Achilles' heel of software package vendors. Mechanisms such as user-exits are too weak to handle the subtle data-structure and interface modifications that sophisticated customers must always make. Such customers are thus forced to customize packages by direct modification of source code. Expensive and frustrating retrofit problems result when a new version of a package must reintegrate the customers' source-level changes. Customers must either start all over again to reapply their changes or abandon the vendor's upgrades. This is a lose-lose situation—either submit to a treadmill of costly repetitive retrofits or lose the benefits of vendor enhancements.

But were the package assembled from frames, each customer could customize it via its own wrapper frames. When the package vendor releases a new version, most, if not all, of the customizations can be automatically reapplied. And the situation is symmetric. If vendors keep their upgrades in their own wrapper frames or under version control, customers can easily understand and precisely control their use of the upgrades. Customer impacts caused by vendors' new versions are localized to specific customer frames. This decoupling of customer-evolution from vendor evolution converts the lose-lose into a win-win. Customers enjoy new package enhancements while avoiding most of the recustomization frustration. Vendors enjoy additional revenues and happy customer references.

Even if vendor sources have not been framed, it is an easy matter to automatically frame the source by surrounding every block or section of code with BREAK-END-BREAK pairs. So, at least the customer can isolate his customizations. Then, when the vendor ships new sources, they are reframed and the customizations automatically reapplied (or at least those that are unaffected by vendor changes).

## Frame-Based Evolution

Here is what frame-based software evolution provides:

1. Effort reduces from dealing with 100% of each system to the essentially novel 5 to 15%.

2. Components evolve independently from their executables.

3. Components remain stable for long periods, yet proposed enhancements are accommodated.

4. Isolation of proposed enhancements from both custom and standard components simplifies the evolution of both.

5. Deciding which actual enhancements to consolidate can be deferred, pending hard evidence of which are sufficiently reused.

6. Periodic consolidations reduce component proliferation, sustaining an effective information-domain structure.

7. There is a single point of control for retrofitting to a frame. Adaptors of this frame will all retrofit the same way because the customizations must be applied through frame mechanisms, forcing consistency.

8. Software package evolution can gracefully coexist with customer-specific changes.

The sooner the word "maintenance" disappears as a distinct mind-set and methodology, the better. A separate maintenance department is unnecessary and counterproductive. Development tools, techniques, and skills can and should be the same for both preproduction and postproduction.

Moreover, the team that originally developed the system should have long-term responsibility for its evolution. This location of responsibility has two benefits.

1. The team's application expertise grows with time. This expertise increases the likelihood the system delivers real business benefits and avoids frivolous changes.

2. Being responsible for long-term evolution, teams will design systems to make them easy to evolve.

# A
# Statewide
# System
# Uses IDR

## CHAPTER 23

*"Everyone writes and uses frames. Less experienced programmers
write more sophisticated systems without additional work.
After a frame is developed it rarely fails.
Programs built on frames then require less testing."*
Statewide System Project Manager

A s we bring Part III to a close, the experience of a state school system shows how iterative design refinement, based on frame technology and extensive reuse, makes possible a level of achievement not attainable with earlier practices. Here are the key statistics of what was accomplished:

- more than 700,000 lines of source code;
- in 18 months;
- with four developers;
- reaching 93% reuse;
- for more than 700 agencies.

The project manager believes his team of four would have needed more than five years using traditional practices.

## Genesis of the System

Concerned with declining educational standards, the state decided that a little competition would be a good thing. So its legislature passed a law allowing parents to send their children to the school of their choice, and to have their school taxes follow them! That placed upon parents the obligation to make choices. Intelligent choices presuppose adequate knowledge.

Knowledge—aye, there's the rub. To enable parents to make rational choices, the law required schools to report the details of their on-going performance:

- staff and students;
- classes attended and missed;
- marks on tests;
- teachers' salaries;
- book purchases;
- capital costs, and so on.

In all, there were over 300 data items in 25 tables. In other words, for the very first time, the entire state and each local school district were to have an MIS data collection and reporting system. Needless to say, making all this work together promised to be exceedingly elaborate.

The state asked one of its school districts to build the system for deployment throughout the entire state. The software project team would consist of three developers and one consultant. They would have 18 months to go from a standing start (i.e., the date of legislative enactment) to a system in statewide operation.

## Constraints Faced

Unfortunately, the legislation, detailed as it was from a legislative point of view, left many gaps in the requirements from a system point of view. Not only were many specifications unavailable at the start, the requirements were changing weekly. For example, what to disclose to the public was the subject of heated debates between teachers and legislators. For one thing, the system had to protect individuals' privacy. Formally, the state had the responsibility to define data validations and outputs. As a result of these politically hot potatoes, the outputs were not completely defined until near the very end of the project.

The hundreds of school districts in the state already had their own computers, many of them different from those of other districts. They were already collecting some of the data the new law called for, but they had their own data collection formats. These differing formats meant custom data structures for each district all had to be converted to a common format so they could be statistically aggregated in a consistent manner.

Districts varied in size from as small as 200 students to as large as 60,000. Over 700 different agencies were entering data and no new computers were being purchased for data collection or aggregation. Still, the data the parents needed had to be available in time for them to make decisions. As a result, system performance was critical. Moreover, the tight schedule—18 months—left no time to experiment with a pilot system. And the lack of output specs until just before roll-out meant there was no time for beta testing. And, if it didn't work, well, it was like living in a fish bowl surrounded by hungry cats!

## System Strategy

The run-time architecture was straightforward. The raw data (collected both electronically and by tape) were cleaned up and stored in tables (files), which could be corrected and maintained centrally. These tables were revalidated and aggregated in various ways in order to print statistical reports. Figure 23-1 illustrates the construction-time architecture for building the objects that did the revalidations and statistical aggregations.

**Figure 23-1.** Frame architecture for Ohio schools MIS.

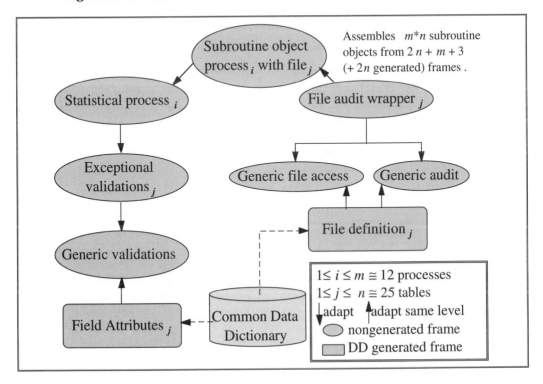

To minimize the need to rebuild parts of the system unaffected by later changes in requirements or design, the developers designed the system as a collection of objects (external Cobol subroutines). Each object encapsulated the transformations from one district's input to the various aggregated outputs, suitable for statistical reporting.

Because input data formats and attributes were not under the control of the system designers and were changing frequently, the team decided to log formats and attributes in a data dictionary. They built a translator to map data-dictionary entries into Cobol frames defining the input (tables and data attributes). They designed a table containing a list of permitted data ranges, so all single-element data-validations could be table-driven at run time. And they designed frames (one per input format) to isolate cross-file data validations and any others too complex to be table-driven.

The rules for aggregating and reporting the data were also out of the team's control, being whipsawed by the back-room negotiations between teachers and legislators. So the team isolated the necessary rules by designing a dozen or so statistical process frames that could be married to the 25 or so source data formats. These two isolation strategies allowed them to frame the rest of the system independent of most changes to data properties and aggregation rules. Each time a change occurred, the data-dictionary translator, together with frame technology, allowed them to reassemble and recompile the affected objects automatically.

The other relevant object subassemblies shown in Figure 23-1 were as follows.

- The generic validations frame, which could be adapted to validate specific data elements against the table of permitted ranges; the data elements were the names and attributes coming from the data dictionary.
- Two generic frames, which audited input files, i.e., cross-checked information in different files.

## System Results

The system, running on a mixture of HP3000s and DEC VAXs, consisted of 382 specification frames. These SPCs embraced 93 programs and 289 subroutines. These Cobol modules were assembled from 146 reusable, non-generated frames. By nongenerated, I mean frames other than those automatically derived from the data dictionary. In all, there was a total of 710,550 optimized ESLOC (no blanks or comments). The 382 SPCs contained 52,250 ESLOC, implying a reuse level of 93%. Moreover, the same data validation frames were reused in the programs that cleaned up the raw data.

An interesting feature of the architecture in Figure 23-1 is the relationship between frames and objects. Three generic frames, plus $2n$ data handling frames (not including the $2n$ that are constructed automatically), plus $m$ statistical frames, can give rise to $mn$ objects. This formula implies that complexity grows only as the square root of the number of objects. One new process results in $n$ new objects; one new data format results in $m$ new objects.

Had this project been done with normal industry productivity, the team of four would have needed over five years. This length of time would have been out of the question in such a highly politicized project.

Now that the system has been in production for several years, the system manager sees two on-going benefits. One is the frame architecture's ease of exception handling in the face of still ongoing changes. Adding data fields or changing attributes usually leaves SPCs unaffected. The other benefit is performance tuning—the frame approach allowed them to reduce run times by 50 to 90% from the system's initial release.

The case study exemplifies the power of IDR to build systems under extremely volatile conditions. Also, the construction architecture highlights the differences between an object oriented design and a framework based on un-encapsulated object components. The ability of the project team to exhibit grace under pressure critically depended on their ability to isolate data structures and methods into separate parts.

# PART

# 4

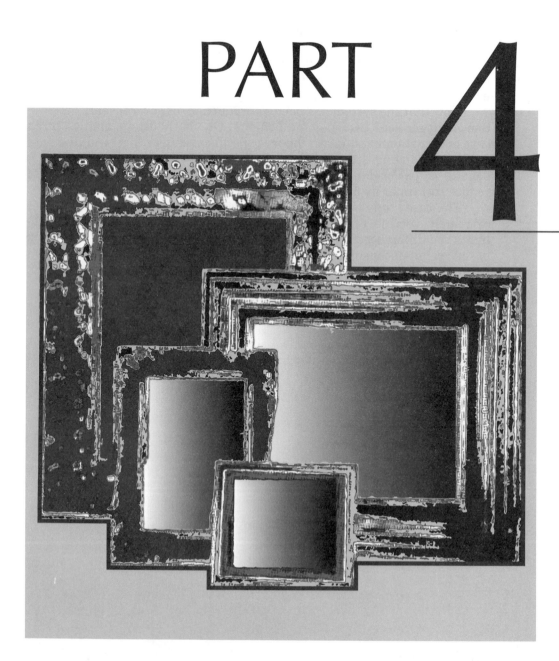

# MANAGING THE TRANSITION

W e have the technological means, the subject of Part II. We know what of reuse-based development processes should be like (Part III). Now we have to get from here to there, from where your organization now is to one organized for systemic and cultural reuse. You have to manage that transition. It doesn't just happen.

Where are you now? It has become quite popular to assess your software organization with capability models, such as the Capability Maturity Levels of Carnegie-Mellon

University's Software Engineering Institute or the International Standards Organization's ISO9000-3. My Organization Fitness Checklist and Reuse Maturity questionnaire enable you to self-check your organization.

Self-improvement involves more than sticking technology Band-Aids on your organization—much more. You have to keep your present organization functioning, for business must go on. At the same time, you must overcome the powerful barriers to change; you must inspire your people with a new vision. It is a tall order. I have seen many failures and a few successes. I may be able to help.

The transition we are talking about affects more than the information systems organization. True, IS constitutes the central nervous system of a reengineered organization.

But all the "stovepipe" functional departments could be joined in a process-oriented pattern of serving the customer.

To make it all work takes people. It takes people at all levels: executives, managers, and staff. It is nice to treat people nice! But there is far more to welding people into the "new organization" than being pleasant. In fact, you may, from time to time, have to arrange for the more stubborn among you to seek out one of the backward organizations that still remain—in which to be stubborn.

My experience indicates that, given strong leadership and vision, people will adapt to the new ways. They want to be more effective. They want to be proud of what their new organization can accomplish. Go gently into that bright future.

# Is Your Organization Ready for Reuse?

## CHAPTER 24

> *God, give us grace to accept with serenity*
> *the things that cannot be changed,*
> *courage to change the things which should be changed,*
> *and the wisdom to distinguish the one from the other.*
>
> Reinhold Niebuhr, 1934

Reuse is a tremendous amplifier—of noise as much as signal. While frame technology makes significant benefits possible in many recalcitrant areas of software design and development, obtaining those benefits depends critically on people's willingness to adopt a reuse attitude, infrastructure, and culture.

The information systems organization can take stock of itself by means of the "Fitness Checklist." It can diagnose the degree to which it needs retooling. Watts Humphrey of Carnegie-Mellon University's Software Engineering Institute has described a way to assess a software organization's capability maturity [34]. His checklist describes five maturity levels: initial (also termed "chaotic"), repeatable, defined, managed, and optimizing. Whether the metaphor is fitness or maturity matters little. The strategic and structural issues are the same. They require the attention of senior managers who are above the fray and able to effect the necessary changes.

We examine IS fitness from three stakeholder perspectives: the self view, the users' view, and senior management's view.

## The Self View

### Size

The size of the software development organization is the first consideration, not only because of its direct effects on the fitness of IS, but because
it causes many of the other fitness issues described below. Burton Napier,
the Canadian Imperial Bank of Commerce's Executive Vice President of
Operations and Information Technology, has stated that many organizations "have so many peasants standing in the field, there is nowhere to
plant the grain."

Given the explosive growth in demand for software over the past couple of decades, it was (and still is) virtually axiomatic for data processing
departments, about to miss a deadline, to hire more people. Back in 1975,
Fred Brooks, in his classic *The Mythical Man-Month*, warned us that this
axiom is completely fallacious [3]. But the industry lacked an understanding of the issues, and lacked the tools for dealing with them. In-house software organizations grew to contain hundreds, even thousands, of employees. Bureaucratic and inefficient, these monsters demand to be fed.

Communications problems grow explosively with the number of people. How many ways can three people hold a meeting (with at least two
people present)? Four. How many ways can 30 people hold a meeting
(with at least 10 present)? Over one billion! Organizations form hierarchies to try to redress the dangers of haphazard communications. A tree
structure provides a systematic channeling of information to relevant
subgroups.

So what's wrong with this picture? Well, consider how tightly coupled
software systems are—a single misplaced period can cause arbitrary damage, which may go unnoticed for months. Then consider that people—
loosely coupled, speaking and working with the usual idiosyncrasies—
must cooperate to build and modify these intricate paragons of precision.
When more than a few developers work in tight synchronization, communicating becomes the primary bottleneck. The costs of this bottleneck are
enormous: modest systems cost millions to implement and take far too
long; demand for enhancements cannot be met; direct-to-indirect labor
ratios are poor; bureaucracy stifles innovation and responsiveness.

In IS, as in computer chips, small is beautiful. Happily, given an effective reuse technology, large development teams are unnecessary. In my
experience, teams of one to four are best. Beyond six or seven, there is
always an opportunity to divide the work to keep the team(s) smaller. As
Burton Napier puts it: "four people can be twice as productive as eight."

I have seen the IS populations of comparable multi-billion dollar companies range from thousands to dozens—two orders of magnitude. At

which end of this range do you think companies are doing more and better with less? People think downsizing is necessary in order to cut costs. This way of thinking is rather like telling a smoker to quit because it saves cigarette money.

## Competence

IS sustains the central nervous system of the whole organization. The competence of its staff, or lack thereof, is paramount because reuse technology amplifies both. Who wants harmful systems even faster?

Bureaucracies tend to drive the competent up or out, leaving the rest to pick up the pieces. Standards of excellence decline to standards of mediocrity, with a hidden agenda of self-perpetuation. Who are the ones carrying the load; who are the unproductive, and the antiproductive?

Fitness would substantially improve if organizations did no more than motivate bright, ambitious people to stay and the rest to leave. Staffing is the single most powerful control point that management has. Offsetting this control are cultures and compensation plans where power and esteem correlate with budget size and "head count." Creating an environment where only the most competent thrive is indeed a worthy challenge. On the other hand, managers and staff alike can be given incentives to achieve better results with less resources. That is what adaptive reuse is all about.

## Morale and Apathy

Is the IS department a pleasant place to work? Do people enjoy their jobs? Are they keen to learn? Do they strive for the greater good of the organization? Or do frustrated people find for one reason or another that they cannot get on with what they need to do? How does IS staff turnover compare to other departments? To software vendors? More importantly, do the leavers tend to be the best performers? The skills they carry away "between their ears" can cripple the organization.

## Specialization

In large organizations, it is common for jobs to become highly specialized. Programmers do not analyze, analysts do not program, and managers do neither.

As people specialize, they have less and less exposure to the business as a whole, and hence less and less relevance to the external world. It gets silly when installing a new software tool requires six people—a tool specialist, an operating system specialist, a workstation specialist, a network specialist, a security specialist, and an operations specialist. At least one of them can be counted on to be in a meeting, sick, or on vacation.

Exacerbating this problem is the policy of rewarding technically skilled people with management promotions. Not only are their technical skills lost to the organization, but the attitude that one can get ahead without knowing much about the business will now be instilled in others.

## Metrics

Sad to say, but most software shops use no objective measures of productivity or quality. Nothing more clearly signals our industry's immaturity. Metrics are the subject of numerous books, such as Capers Jones' *Programming Productivity* [35] and Lawrence Putnam and Ware Myers' *Measures for Excellence* [2]. Objecting to impartial measurement is objecting to sound management. The obvious inference can be drawn.

## Maintenance

Are those who "maintain" production systems other than the systems' builders? Do maintenance programmers tend to be junior? Is peer esteem for maintenance lower than for new development?

A "yes" to any of the above degrades fitness. With the maintenance burden now consuming 70 to 80% of all resources and growing, we will soon be unable to undertake any serious new development. As if 80% maintenance were not embarrassing enough, the world faces the "year 2000."

So-called "legacy systems" are the most tangible expression of the millstones around our corporate necks. According to Gordon Kerr of Hyatt Hotels, 40% of his legacy systems consist of human interfaces, 30% manage data storage. Since component-based tools provide these elements, 70% of his legacy systems are just thrown away.

Positive fitness signs are: using Thomas McCabe's "cyclomatic complexity" to infer the modifiability of your programs, and rewriting programs to improve their modifiability [36].

## Waterfall Methodology

Are CASE or similar modeling tools actually slowing down the life cycle? Is the waterfall model entrenched?

## Culture

Is the organization conservative, risk-averse, oriented to the status quo? Or is it open to new ideas? Does it provide the means for people to innovate without fear of failure? An open climate is essential for any new paradigm to take root and thrive.

Positive cultural indicators involve an interest in reuse and in the common good—having standards that are actually followed; libraries of classes, designs, and/or sources that people are actively reusing; "protocycling," real end-users and developers working together on a routine or daily basis.

I'm bemused by the irony that software's people, who are themselves change agents for the rest of the organization, are themselves so change resistant. We must be prepared to be judged on responsiveness and flexibility. *Carpe diem!*

## The Users' View

### Cooperation

What kind of relationship exists between the user community and IS? Is it one of trust and cooperation, or adversarial? Typically, users do not understand or respect what developers do, and vice versa. Users have been disappointed time and again with systems that are late, over budget, and not what they need. Developers complain that users, never satisfied, are always changing their minds.

With reuse tools and methods at hand, the opportunity exists to escape from this polarity. And escape is vital. Neither users nor developers alone can know all there is to know about complex systems. Nor can that knowledge remain fixed, since the business changes at unexpected times and in unpredictable ways, as does the computer environment. A system can only be as good as the insights contributed by its users and its developers, and shared in a spirit of joint and timely commitment to each other's welfare.

### Ownership

Is there a single owner, an executive who sponsors and accepts the system, whose staff uses it, and who lives with the consequences? There should be.

Bureaucratic IS departments wield de facto monopolistic powers over their internal customers. Do the users willingly accept responsibility and ownership for the systems they use, or do they perceive that IS is imposing systems on them?

Suppose a system has taken many months to develop and is being exposed to the users for the first time. Any significant design issues raised at this stage will be disputed. The loss of so much time, money, expectation, and reputation, and the further delay in obtaining the anticipated benefits combine to make it nearly impossible for anyone to take responsibility for correcting the errors.

## Quality

Quality has many dimensions. The most important three are: relevance to business needs (functionality), ease-of-use, and performance.

1. *Relevance.*  Do delivered systems model how the business should work—not necessarily how it does, or did, work? What does each system contribute to the bottom line, net-net? Is relevance even measured objectively? Xerox, for example, knows that a one percent change in customer loyalty is worth $2.7 million in profits, and it tests its systems against this criterion. Hyatt tracks revenues per available hotel room, percent occupancy, and other success indicators.

2. *Ease-of-use.*  Are simple things simple to do? Is there a smooth learning curve? Are user interfaces natural and consistent? Is information accurate, timely, and presented in useful contexts?

3. *Performance.*  Are peak transaction loads handled adequately? Are interactive dialogues responsive enough? What is the MTBF (mean time between failures)? What is the system availability level? How expensive are the recovery procedures?

The above quality issues are at a point in time. A fourth issue, usually overlooked, is particularly relevant to software engineering quality:

4. *Adaptability.*  How quickly and cheaply can a system accommodate corrections and enhancements? Can systems be modified for a few selected users, without impacting the rest? Adaptable systems can be tried out, then improved, then tried again until they attain the needed level of quality in the first three senses.

   Is malleability sustainable? That is, can a system remain easy to modify even after the original developers have long since departed?

## Backlogs

How long is the backlog of requests for new/enhanced systems? Official backlogs are like unemployment statistics—they mislead because all the people who have given up trying no longer appear to be in need. How big is this hidden backlog?

## Business Risk Sharing

This means more than IS delivering systems on time and on budget. Is it anticipating the needs of the business, realigning itself to seize new opportunities and to meet possible competitive threats? Not getting caught flat-footed is the way IS shares risk with its users. IS must enable, not retard, opportunities to hone the competitive edge.

## The Senior Management View

### Opportunity versus Cost

Does senior management view IS primarily as overhead? A means to cut costs? Or do they also view it as a strategic weapon to leverage the business? Or at least as a resource to generate new revenues, as American Airlines views its Sabre reservation system? Are information systems being used to flatten management hierarchies? Are information-related products and services part of the organization's strategic business plan? Is IS a profit center?

### Budgets

Does the organization take a zero-based budgeting approach to IS? This approach is another reflection of the "small is beautiful" attitude.

Do managers have the "use up the budget" syndrome, common just before fiscal year end? That mentality is a clear sign of a lack of proper incentives in the management ranks.

Does senior IS management do variance analysis to base-line indicators? Some variances are good, some are bad. The important benefit comes from attending to successes and hot spots. Of course, establishing meaningful baselines is a prerequisite. This is where metrics come in.

### Pricing Policies

How are projects quoted for users? Are they fixed bids or time-and-materials, or fixed by progress milestones? If time-and-materials is typical, then it is much more difficult to analyze people's accomplishments, prove the benefits of their work, and get real control over budgeting and productivity.

Rather than roll-your-own, is the first option to buy and tailor non-mission-critical systems? What about systems that are key differentiaters in your organization's markets; does your company buy these too? Are software vendors customizing to the organization's real needs? Are outsourcers responsive enough? Are they cost-effective?

Are IS costs compared to a credible outsourcing vendor's? Projects may still be done in-house, but such sanity checks are healthy, and may indicate need for remedial action.

## Manageability

Senior management's perception of IS often is that of a "black hole," mysteriously consuming ever more resources. IS seems to be a thing apart, unmanageable the way other departments are. Responsiveness and service levels may sag in spite of increased budgets. And senior management is frustrated, as the organization damps out each reform. Do you suffer from the "Chernobyl syndrome," where you are told what others think you want to hear?

Part of the problem may be in the executive suite itself. Does it harbor technophobes who abdicate responsibility, naively hoping that the problems will go away? Is someone in a key position just waiting to retire? Are managers simply managing for their own comfort?

## Focusing on Reuse

In Chapter 4, I introduced the idea of organizational reuse maturity. For convenience, Table 4-1, describing the levels, is shown below in Table 24-1.

**Table 24-1  Organizational Reuse Maturity**

| Level | Name | Typical Reuse | Typical PI |
|---|---|---|---|
| 0 | Ad hoc | 0%–40% | 13–20 |
| 1 | Latent | 40%–80% | 20–24 |
| 2 | Project | 80%–90% | 24–29 |
| 3 | Systemic | 90%–95% | 29–33 |
| 4 | Cultural | 95%–99% | 33–36 |

Typical reuse represents reused lines divided by total-lines (of source code, not counting blanks, comments, and code used as-is). The productivity index, representing process productivity, advances sharply with the level.

Having studied dozens of enterprises that practice reuse with varying degrees of success, I have formulated ten questions that I use to help companies better focus their reuse efforts. See Table 24-2, or visit my web site at http://www.netron.com . For those new to organized reuse (Level 0), the questions serve to prompt thinking about what it involves. For those who have embarked on organized reuse, you can answer the questions and score your organization as follows:

- Question 1. Note that answering (1a) can be tricky. Reuse cannot cross "span of control" boundaries. People on different sides of such boundaries cannot be induced to cooperate. If your organization's total IS population divides into groups who are unlikely to adopt inter-group standards and share components, then restrict your answers to this questionnaire to your group's "span of control."

$$\text{Score: } 10^* [(1b)/(1a) + (1c)/(1b) + (1d)/(1c)]$$

- Question 2. Score: $10^*$(the percentage) as a decimal (e.g., 25% scores 2.5)

- Questions 3–10. Each definite "yes" scores 2, each "no" or "seldom" scores 0; each "sometimes," "partially," "when relevant," or the like scores a 1.

- Total your score.
  Level 1  (Latent):          0–6;
  Level 2  (Project):         7–46;
  Level 3  (Systemic):        47–63;
  Level 4  (Cultural):        64 and above.

**Table 24-2  Ten Questions to Test Organizational Reuse Maturity**

| | | |
|---|---|---|
| **1. a.** | How many software developers are in your I.S. organization? | |
| **b.** | How many are trained in reuse concepts and technology? | |
| **c.** | How many practice reuse in their daily work? | |
| **d.** | How many are expert parts engineers (i.e., design/build reusable parts)? | |

2. What percentage of annual IS Development expenditures are allocated to reuse infrastructure initiatives (tools, training, parts engineering, methodology improvements, promoting reuse, sharing between groups, etc.)?

**3.** Is managing reuse (parts, people, and infrastructure) included in the systems management process, beyond daily project management?

**4.** Do business analysts try to reuse available models when defining system requirements?

**5.** Do software projects take an iterative approach to reuse during development?

**6.** Do you have policies or guidelines related to reuse for the following? Are measurements in place to track them?

| | Policies/ Guidelines | Practices/ Measurements |
|---|---|---|
| Reuse goals and performance against the goals. | | |
| Ownership and responsibility for reusable parts. | | |
| Maturing reusable parts into corporate standards. | | |
| Sharing/selling reusable parts to other organizations. | | |
| Reuse of software parts across projects/departments. | | |
| Estimating project schedules and resources. | | |

**7.** When maintaining legacy systems, is time budgeted for reconditioning programs so that chunks of code are replaced with references to existing reusable parts?

**8.** Are explicit rewards used to motivate managers and developers to reuse software parts?

9. Are programmers and/or teams portable, redeployable to different projects, because they share a common vocabulary of reusable components?

10.a. Has the organizational infrastructure been modified to support the spread of a reuse culture within IS development?
   b. Has reuse become the basis of a centralized/decentralized hybrid organization?
   c. Is the "parts engineering" group managed as a profit center?
   d. Are there software engineering career paths in which parts design and construction achieve compensation rewards and peer esteem commensurate with promotion into management?

## The State of the Practice

For large IS organizations, this checklist can be quite sobering. Unfortunately, average fitness (capability maturity) is low.

The situation is ironic. The systems we develop epitomize well-defined, repeatable behavior, yet the development process is typically at capability maturity Level One—chaotic. The trouble is, software construction has lacked the engineering rigor that software execution has always had. A contributing factor is that management, awash in conflicting approaches and technological diversity, struggles to get its own act together. The resulting tyranny of the technocracy feeds back into itself, making the situation worse.

The relevant software engineering principles are poorly understood. And even when understood, too many organizations lack the will and the discipline to translate them into practice, opting for incrementalism over substantive change. As a result, systems continue to complexify needlessly. This state of affairs not only impairs survival, it perpetuates bloated, labyrinthine IS infrastructures. It is a spiral into oblivion—or outsourcing.

We need to get back to basics. Surround good software engineering technology with a matching discipline, and insist that IS departments sustain adequate ROIs, just as the business as a whole does. There are two sets of issues to deal with: translating sound engineering principles into practice, and managing the transition from current practice. We proceed to these issues in the remaining chapters of this part.

# Key Business Drivers

Too many IS organizations today are buying technology Band-Aids. Judging by the time and money spent on evaluations, acquiring tools seems paramount (Figure 25-1). We fixate on technology because it is well defined, tangible, objective. We take comfort in our burst of due diligence and ignore the hardest challenges of all—acquiring a culture and an infrastructure that harness technology's power to the cost-effective benefit of the enterprise.

Technology merely enables, as we have said a few times. Achieving order-of-magnitude improvements in responsiveness and flexibility depends much more on people's attitudes and skills, supported by good organization. Attitudes are fuzzy, subjective; organizations are exceedingly difficult to change even assuming we know the right changes to make.

Power tools such as frame technology are like sharp knives; in inexperienced hands they can easily do more harm than good. Management's top challenge is minimizing risk while adapting its organization to reap the benefits inherent in new paradigms.

In this chapter and the next, we set forth a strategy for developing a reuse culture and infrastructure, conducive to high responsiveness and flexibility, while ensuring standards and quality.

The path from the status quo to a culture that sustains constant process improvement contains many potholes. The first step on that path

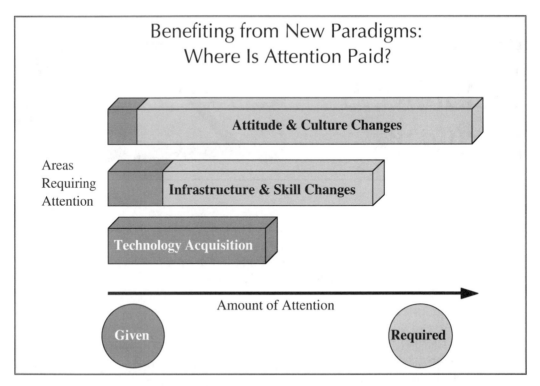

**Figure 25-1.** It's all too easy to fall into the trap of thinking we are home free once we pay due diligence to acquiring new tools.

is to develop a flexible strategic plan, one that articulates a clear and quantified vision of the goals, along with an interative process and a schedule for achieving them. Indeed, the very process for acquiring a culture of adaptability and responsiveness will embody the spirit of what it is trying to achieve.

## Management Commitment

Introducing automation into an organization disrupts its equilibrium. Expected benefits fail to materialize because of reactionary offsets: obsolete thought and work patterns, power struggles, personnel dislocations, fears of the future, and maladjustments to new critical paths. Management's pivotal role in forming a new equilibrium is to:

**1.** identify and overcome barriers to change;
**2.** foster Deming's "kaizen culture" in which everyone [37]:

- avoids waste,
- plans-does-improves-repeats,
- makes what works sharable and reusable;

**3.** identify new work-flow critical paths and support them with appropriate infrastructures.

Changing the status quo demands senior management Leadership with a capital $L$. They alone have the authority to articulate new strategic directions, create and destroy reporting structures, settle turf battles, alter career opportunities, and so on. In the face of an entrenched bureaucracy, evangelistic fervor will not be enough; indeed, if executives merely approve and delegate, the lower ranks damp out real change. It is just another tempest to be toughed out. Successful captains of industry not only champion the initiative, they are prepared to go down with their ships. They lead the charge to achieve tangible net benefits.

## Strategic Goals

Historically, IS has strived to improve an enterprise's operational efficiency, a tactical more than a strategic, business goal. While top management may be aware of IS's strategic potential for business innovation, people are so habituated to IT's chronic lackluster performance, few understand the order-of-magnitude improvements that are within our grasp.

Such a vision is, in fact, an impossible dream for most. Organizations that achieve it do so by taking radical, zero-based approaches. They structure their enterprise to thrive on perpetual renewal and reinvention. Sadly, few enjoy and take pride in doing much better with much less.

Begin with your customers. What are their satisfactions and frustrations? What innovations might bolster demand, remove frustrations, and increase loyalty? How can the enterprise improve service levels at all stages of the relationship, from initial contact through each business transaction step? Answers to such questions will drive the key business processes and hence the systems to support them.

### "Stovepipe" Structure

Most enterprises are organized as a series of vertical "stovepipes": marketing, sales, production, service, accounting, administration, as illustrated in Figure 25-2. Each stovepipe may be internally efficient, while the whole group is not. This global suboptimization reflects itself in reduced resource sharing and in duplication of otherwise reusable system components.

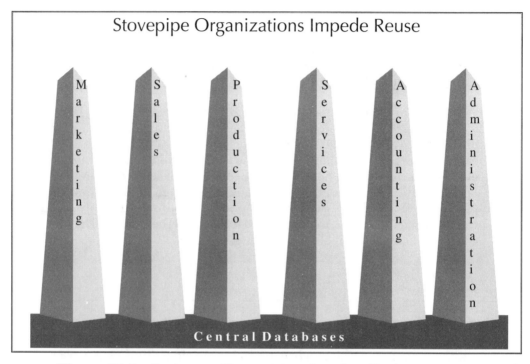

**Figure 25-2.** Customers like one-stop shopping. Business process reengineering finds ways to manage relationships that improve customer satisfaction and efficiency at the same time. Reuse goes up, too.

Customers could care less about internal organizational structure. They want one-stop shopping. Client-server architectures are one way to integrate the stovepipes, creating a seamless work flow while retaining organizational efficiency. A pleasant corollary is the increased scope over which system and software components can be used and reused. We shall explore this topic further in the next chapter.

## Organizational Fitness

Effective innovation, our best survival insurance in a fiercely competitive world, requires superior organizational fitness:

>  *Flexibility* to adapt current assets to new demands without compromising ongoing responsibilities, and
>
>  *Responsiveness* to satisfy those demands quickly.

Fit organizations anticipate changing market conditions, or at least adapt in real time. They occupy market niches that have short half-lives; they quickly tailor products and services for their customers to a level of sophistication that their competitors cannot match.

When talking about fitness and evolution, the organization-as-organism metaphor is useful, but has its limits. An individual organization can evolve, while a single organism cannot. Species evolve over a series of generations. Unfortunately, many organizations act too much like organisms—they lack mechanisms for self-evolution.

While flexibility and responsiveness are common-sense maxims, very few enterprises sustain them in other than burst mode. People become complacent, especially when what they do seems to work again and again. Complacency, in the face of relentless competitive and regulatory pressures, spells the decline of organizations, indeed, entire economies.

## Learning Organization

On the one hand, mechanizing adaptive reuse resonates with the learning organization concept. That is, when patterns work, package them in frameworks so you can automate your success and move on to the next challenge. On the other hand, coping with an uncertain future requires learning by doing. Combining these two lines of thought yields an improvement process that minimizes risk: the process of prototyping innovative ideas by adapting proven frames in novel ways.

Small changes are quick; the risk in a prototype reduces to the time and effort spent implementing its essential novelty. If it doesn't work, we learn from the failure and try again. If it works, we incorporate it into the evolving corporate (frame) assets. And from the modern theory of evolution we know that basing innovation on patterns that already work is far more effective than random mutations [38]. This strategy enables an organization to transcend the individuals making it up—it becomes a true learning organization.

Organizational fitness can be an explicit, enduring principle. The challenge is to capitalize on adaptability, literally and figuratively. Frame technology enables only a literal form. Figurative capitalization requires a major shift in attitudes. Every business unit needs to understand the principle, the means to pursue it, and the urgency of doing so.

## Constant Adaptation

Having described fitness, by what means should one pursue it? This is a trick question. Adopting a "big bang" strategy, a global simultaneous switch to a new status quo, misses the point! A modern enterprise needs to constantly adapt and to respond quickly to a constantly changing environment, not undergo a big bang whose maladaptations risk a big bust. The trick in the question, then, was that the means for achieving adaptability and responsiveness should itself be adaptive and responsive.

Perfect fitness is an unnecessary, unreachable fantasy. The fit with a changing environment will always be imperfect, and the degree of misfit drives the rate of evolution. (The HIV retro-virus actually evolves faster than the body—its environment—can respond with new antibodies. The reason: HIV's genetic replicator produces imperfect copies.) Evolution always involves some dislocations, some rework of the enterprise and/or its products and services.

**A fit organization expects to evolve, and strives to optimize evolution's cost:benefit ratio.**

In a fit organization, every individual, from the CEO to the floor sweepers, understands that her responsibility includes identifying potential improvements, and working toward implementing those that provide the most overall benefit for the least overall cost. Complacency-prone, status-quo people need not apply.

## Forced Evolution

Revolutionary benefits can be accomplished through forced evolution. Change needs to go hand in hand with benefits. Create early momentum with quick "breakthrough" projects. Then demand a pace that is just within your organization's capacity to absorb structural change. The most adaptive organizations thrive in the zone between gridlock and chaos [39].

Forced evolution will be resisted. Organizations, like organisms, possess homeostasis—"the maintenance of normal, internal stability in an organism by coordinated responses of the organ systems that automatically compensate for environmental changes" [Webster's New World Dictionary]. When bureaucracies are squeezed, for example, they, like balloons, simply bulge somewhere else. An organization's strong natural tendency to revert to the status quo has to be actively thwarted. There are a variety of carrot-and-stick techniques, covered below.

First and foremost, create incentives to work smarter. Doing better with less should be the daily objective of all business units, not just IS. Those who talk about doing more with the same resources are endorsing the status quo.

Strategic plans should include a small number of principles that capture the vision that the IS organization celebrates [40]. Small means under ten, a number people can take to heart. A sample: choose technologies least likely to limit your organization's future flexibility. A major U.S. bank, for example, has a principle "to develop applications using standard components shared across platforms." Such principles foster adaptable, rapidly deployable corporate assets; motivate and constrain forced evolution; and help the business units' action plans to be mutually reinforcing.

The plan's implementation schedule should convey a sense of urgency—couple short deadlines to deliverables that stretch people. This time-boxing causes staff to focus on getting things done, rather than on all the reasons things can't be done. At the end of each time-box, progress is measured and publicly confirmed by peers (not superiors or subordinates). And pray that the ghosts of items killed in the quest to time-box don't come back to haunt. Measured progress sustains the commitment to proceed with the next time-box. Conversely, a lack of progress can be detected early, when remedial action can still be effective.

In keeping with forced evolution, increasing reuse maturity should spread through the whole enterprise in staggered-start stages.

- In the first stage, which is relatively short, management uses specific system projects involving small IS groups to demonstrate that the new processes work locally in a repeatable fashion. (Project reuse–Level 2).

- Stage Two creates a reuse infrastructure for standardizing frameworks, architectures, and processes that span more and more of IS. Significant downsizing should be occurring by the end of this stage. (Systemic reuse–Level 3).

- Stage Three, which overlaps Stage Two, begins when non-IS departments undertake strategic business process reengineering (BPR) projects, now supported by a relatively fit IS organization. Stage Three is the steady state of an organization geared to thrive on perpetual self-renewal. (Cultural reuse–Level 4).

Failure to enter Stage Three means IS becomes an engine whose power the rest of the enterprise cannot harness. For example, the head of a large IS department announced he was going to increase capacity by 40% over 18 months and "give half back"—code words for reducing his own staff by 20%. Frameworks, in combination with off-loading mainframe development to personal computers made this goal achievable, a real win-win opportunity. But his peers let him take all the risk. Unless his increased capacity to deliver systems is matched by their commitment to shape them and to manage their benefits, there will be little contribution to the bottom line.

## Accountability Structure

### Steering Committee

Empower a senior-management steering committee to control the enterprise's on-going evolution. While the committee does not steer the day-to-day activities of individual projects, it is nonetheless responsible for setting and enforcing common structures and policies. The committee is a visible symbol of commitment; it should be chaired by the CEO and composed of business unit managers with ex-officio representation from key technology suppliers.

In the early days be prepared to micro-manage. The steering committee will need to meet at least weekly to review status and resolve problems, especially those that affect schedules and/or resources. Its members are "fixers" whose authority is sufficient to quickly resolve any impasses that develop among various subordinate groups. As momentum builds and progress becomes self-sustaining, meetings can shift to biweekly then to a period that matches the evolutionary pressure.

When the pace of solutions is accelerated from months to days or hours, the pace of problems obviously accelerates, too. While the many "nervous Nellies," skeptics and doubters in the organization should be reasonably accommodated, the organization also must make progress. Counter-intuitively, when you feel things are moving too fast, and you want to put on the brakes, go faster!

A formal, prompt problem escalation protocol, culminating in steering committee meetings, should be in place. An escalation protocol ensures that critical path impacts—resource shortages, communications problems, bureaucratic delays, plan revisions—get resolved at the proper level of authority and with appropriate dispatch. Figure 25-3 diagrams the idea. Individuals at different levels of responsibility and authority escalate to the next level any issue that could affect a schedule and that is outstanding at that level for a predefined time period. When an issue reaches a new level, it is formally logged and the clock on this issue is tracked.

The escalation protocol, combined with zero tolerance for "surprises," will immunize the organization against the "Chernobyl syndrome." When lower ranks are loath to report news that reflects badly on themselves, everyone looks bad. Conversely, when an organization institutionalizes learning by collaborative problem solving, a sense of "we are all in this together" can develop.

### Reuse User Group

Complementing the steering committee, this group consists of a representative from each development project. Meeting, say, once per month, reps

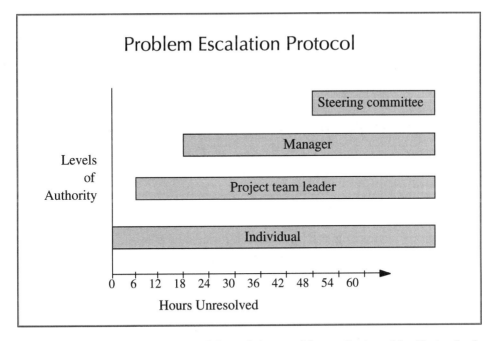

**Figure 25-3.** A formal protocol for solving problems that could affect schedules: Problems are logged and a clock starts. At predefined periods, an unresolved problem escalates. By institutionalizing problem solving, people feel less inclined to indulge in the "Chernobyl syndrome."

share their team's experiences, discuss issues, and bring insights back to their respective projects. Each month, the group designates a different rep to make a short presentation on some aspect of reuse. Such "grass roots" meetings are a mechanism for breaking down "us versus them" attitudes, presenting ideas of mutual benefit, publicly unveiling new frames, presenting productivity and other awards, and sustaining the climate of cooperation so necessary for reuse. IS departments often publish this information in internal newsletters.

## Project Manager Meetings

On this level, people track detailed issues, such as schedules, budgets, sharing frame engineering resources, frame sharing, ownership and promotion, intraproject synchronization, system interface testing, feedback from user JADs, demonstrations and tests, metrics, and coordination with external suppliers.

## Some Potholes to Pave

Many issues transcend individual projects and departments and hence can only find their resolution in the steering committee.

### Power Struggles

Peter Keen details the turf battles that ensue when organizations change information gatekeepers [41]. For IS, this issue is doubly acute:

1. New systems change information flows among user departments;
2. Creating these systems concentrates business knowledge from user departments into IS.

Automating software development increases the velocity of knowledge flow, requiring new relationships among users, developers, and management. The steering committee exists in part to anticipate and head off the resulting power struggles.

Peer rivalries can defeat the best-laid plans. Often the very success one manager has with an initiative ensures that peers won't adopt it! They do not want to be seen following a rival's lead. While there is a role for competition between managers within the firm, their behavior also should enhance the greater good of the whole enterprise.

### Islands of Technology

What is the balance between doing due diligence on new technologies and having "one of everything?" Incompatible tools and techniques can only fragment technical skills, limit personnel redeployability, and require multiple support infrastructures.

If project managers go off on their own technology tangents, how is substantive reuse ever going to happen? The very point of reuse is to ensure cross-group leverage in productivity, quality, adaptability, portability, standards, and complexity hiding. Far better to make one adequate technology work everywhere than always to be at the "bleeding edge" on separate "islands of technology." The acid test of reuse is an organization's ability to standardize on one common infrastructure, development process, and tool set.

Yes, by all means, investigate new technology options. But investigative effort should be in proportion to expected benefits and expected impact, organization-wide. Prior to a detailed investigation, a quick *proof-of-concept* should test a new approach against a list of measurable "hard" benefits. Organizations should not allow obsolete assumptions and modes of behavior, baggage dragged along by the status quo, to constrain the test.

A successful initial test of a technology with potential for universal deployment warrants a more thorough investigation. In particular, a reuse technology must be able to support both current and anticipated technical requirements. Is the technology "open"—compatible with existing architectures? Will it scale up to complex, heterogeneous, cooperative processing requirements? Will giant component libraries be necessary? Will search time affect productivity? Can systems evolve gracefully under pressure—without forcing retrofits or creating a sea of look-alike components?

## Too Many Constraints?

A clever resistance tactic is: "Gee, that's a great idea, but let's make sure we do it RIGHT!" By the time the requisite committees exhaustively define "right," they will have so over-constrained the new idea that it has no chance of success. Masquerading as team players, the resistors can smile and say, "Oh, there's another good idea that won't work here." A very clever ploy.

Technology evaluation groups often have checklists of features they try to tick off: a repository, a GUI, a client-server architecture, object-oriented, and so forth. Rather than this simplistic, fad-prone approach, allow vendors latitude in their features. Allow this latitude only as long as they can demonstrate the benefits of their features and reasonable coverage of risks. In particular, on-time on-budget development of cost-effective systems has never gone out of style—and has never become routine.

## Pre- and Co-requisites

All too often, new technology roll-outs start without proper preparations.

**Education and training.** This is one of the most important investments. New paradigms require a mind-set shift, so tool users, managers, even end-users need a level of understanding that ensures their ability to benefit and/or contribute, depending on their role. Education related to performance also sends a message that the organization wants people to succeed. Equally important, initial training is a reliable indicator of who is likely to succeed. Promptly remove apathetic or change-resistant people before they poison the climate.

Technologies whose learning curves must be climbed in parallel is a problem often hard to avoid. Trying to master a new reuse technology, a new LAN (local area network), a new PC environment, a new GUI (graphical user interface), and a new database schema, all at the same time, can overwhelm people.

One way to mitigate steep learning curves is to bury technological complexity inside reusable components. Such a framework should be laid down prior to a massive roll-out of new technologies. Thereafter, relatively few people will need to be expert in those specific technologies.

**Appropriate projects.** Introduce reuse technology neither by tackling a 200-staff-year project nor by inventing a laboratory experiment. Pick a small project, say 10 to 20 executables, that would be built in any case. You can always subdivide large projects. (Also, refer to Chapter 28 for a discussion of SWAT teams.)

**Hardware.** LAN-based workstations, one per developer, facilitate iterative software development. LAN-based development brings its own set of issues. Is the LAN server controlling the distribution of specifications and components (frames)? How is software being put into production? Is it built only with approved components? Answers to these questions vary from shop to shop and will require some combination of LAN hardware, software utilities, and management discipline.

**Software.**  Will current versions of required utilities work properly together: analysis and design tools, library management utilities, software construction tools, compilers and linkers, configuration management and documentation utilities, test-bed generators, debugging tools, target-environment emulators, impact analysis tools, LAN support, project management and metric tools, and so on? All too often a new release of a utility is incompatible with other vendors' existing releases. This is an important time gobbler to minimize. One simple strategy is to standardize the tools for every developer workstation. Another is to wait until vendors guarantee compatibility with the other tools.

**Facilities/logistics.**  Do SWAT team members have quiet environments where they can work together? Are key users available to answer questions and provide feedback when needed? Are sufficient classroom facilities and mentors available? Five novices per frame expert seems to be about the limit.

## Getting to Systemic Reuse: Lessons from the Real World

The benefits of reuse are proportional to the scale on which it is practiced. Significant productivity, quality, and adaptability gains are obtainable within the scope of individual projects. However, order-of-magnitude productivity gains, corporate quality standards, portable people, high responsiveness to shifts in business focus, and the like are available only by extrapolating reuse across multiple projects and systems. To do this requires embedding reuse into the IS culture and infrastructure, a challenge to test the mettle of all concerned.

Given a successful initial project, how can we roll out reuse to all of IS? Chapter 4 discussed some of the barriers that tend to block the roll-out of reuse technology. Now that you have read about frames in some depth, I can bring out the real-world lessons I've learned about rollingout the technology.

## Technology Islands

Reuse technology is a meta-technology. In this role it glues other technologies together, to integrate them and to hide their complex interfaces. You can integrate GUIs, for example, with COBOL programs by hiding the voluminous API calls in underlying frames. This approach yields both local and global benefits—it improves individual project productivity and quality, and it benefits an organization's investment in other technologies.

## Project Centrism

Because of the make-to-order nature of software applications, project teams are an essential organizational unit. But consider the tension this form of organization creates between local and global priorities. Application developers face potentially unlimited demands to support expanding, changing requirements, yet they also work under severe time and budget limits. These limits put projects under tremendous pressure to reject anything perceived to be non-project-specific, especially an unfamiliar reuse methodology. "What's in it for me?" scoffs a harried project manager.

While organizations should not jam things down project managers' throats, neither should they allow them the latitude to just do their own thing. Quantified savings in time and cost in other projects make it easy for management to show "leadership" with resisters. But having all projects employ a common reuse technology is only a start. There are other project-centric reuse barriers to dismantle. Two warrant particular emphasis.

First, development projects lack sufficient time, budget, and motivation to generalize reusable components beyond the scope of their local needs. How, then, are corporate reuse assets to be created? Chapters 19 and 20 explain how to promote project-centric frames into departmental and corporate standards. Fostering reuse across multiple projects involves capitalizing corporate reuse assets and their administration. It is easy to measure the direct return on investment. The numbers also point out where profitable new investments should be made.

Second, teams engender us-versus-them rivalries, even outright non-cooperation. This adversarial spirit can be lethal to a culture of sharing. Japan's so-called software factories cope in an interesting way [42]. They have quality control groups with the power to stop the release of any software from any project. This veto power compels all project teams to share common quality standards and opens the door to sharing other things, such as reusable components and developers.

But a QC group with veto power can exacerbate the adversarial approach, which is already far worse in Western firms than in Japan. Internecine conflict can be minimized by having QC standards and procedures set by the project managers themselves. They, or an appropriate subcommittee, also can oversee the QC group. And QC testers can be developers, seconded from project duties on a rotating basis.

But wait a minute. Since software's quality and many of its standards are to be packaged in reusable frames, it follows that frame administration is just QC in disguise. In the early days, the focus is on setting standards—coding, documentation, interface, and architecture standards. Then comes framing, testing, and making the results available to all projects. (This work is the corporate investment to which I referred above.) When over 90% of a typical system is automatically assembled from standard, pretested components, development will have much more of a system integration flavor, with everyone playing a QC role.

## Legacy Systems

A question that always comes up is "Frames may be great for new development but what about my legacy systems?"

First of all, systems should not be re-architected unless the economic benefit justifies the investment. Framing "hot spots"—programs that receive a lot of changes—to cool them down is usually easy to justify. Otherwise, let sleeping dogs lie.

For programs that require only occasional changes, the dictum I learned as a Boy Scout applies: "Leave things a little neater than you found them." An entire program can be treated as one large specification frame. Suppose a report program (SPC) needs to be modified. Remove from it all code lines that handle the report, and replace them by one reference to a standard report frame tree. This removal leaves only custom details in the SPC. As a result, the SPC becomes smaller and simpler. Over time, the program becomes easier and easier to change, as more and more of it is hidden in underlying frames.

What about salvaging reusable components from legacy systems? This is a tricky question. Especially in old systems, designed for yesterday's computer architectures, the fragments worth salvaging may be so intertwined with junk, it's a little like trying to extract the cream from a cup of coffee. In these situations, it's much cheaper to rebuild rather than renovate.

On the other hand, tools exist to analyze legacy code and extract the useful bits. Tools also exist to automate framing them. But such frames are only a first approximation. They need to be put through IDR's maturation process, described in Chapters 19 and 20. Is the exercise worth the cost? It's hard to say. Each situation has to be judged on its merits.

When does the time come to reengineer entire legacy systems? It comes when existing frameworks (homegrown or purchased) can remove enough of the sting. That is, the "deltas"—differences between the frameworks and the legacy systems—are small enough to warrant the reengineering cost. Of course, the cart may be beside or even in front of the horse—the need to rethink the business may render the legacy obsolete.

## Lack of Education

Technology roll-out is limited by the rate at which people receive both training and experience. There are synchronization problems here. Classroom knowledge decays exponentially unless applied immediately. Therefore training needs to be just-in-time for project work. Moreover, the availability of sufficient mentors to coach the trainees constrains the rate of roll-out. If mentors double as frame engineers, a danger exists that they will be spread too thin.

One frame engineer should coach three to five apprentices until they become "journeymen," in one to three months. Journeymen are so recognized when they become three times as productive as they were before training. It takes four to six months to turn a good novice into a mentor.

People presuming to be frame engineers should be skilled in analysis and design, and skilled in reusing the frames of others. Acquiring such skills can take several months, depending on the individual and the environment. Coaching and frame engineering emphasize different skills. When people are pressed to play both roles, the mentor's role often can conflict with high-priority frame writing. Economizing on these engineering and coaching resources, given the huge potential ROI, is short sighted.

Mentors and frame engineers may need to be supplied from external sources until the organization becomes self-sufficient. The name of this game is technology transfer, not body shop contracting.

## Lack of Frameworks

Depending on business and IS priorities, system and business architecture work may be accelerated or delayed. As several projects will be needed to mature such frames, the roll-out rate depends on the availability of mature frameworks.

When should you start up a central frame management and engineering group? The quality control aspect, as described above, needs to be started as soon as you make the commitment to multi-project reuse. QC precedes frame management because, in these earliest days, there aren't yet many in-house frame engineers, and project frames have yet to be promoted and certified as department or corporate standards. There is, however, an immediate need to design certification standards, and to take stock of any existing frameable modules—skeleton programs and copybooks. The main constraint on forming this group is to have one or more competent frame architects.

## Obsolete Infrastructure

As I have mentioned, iterative design refinement puts pressure on resolving missing or conflicting requirements. Setting up an infrastructure to support IDR involves difficult changes:

- eliminating layers of specialists through which information gets delayed and distorted;
- forming new reporting structures;
- establishing reuse-related measures of competence and performance;
- creating incentives to do better with less; and most importantly,
- revitalizing direct end-user relationships with developers.

Do a critical-path analysis of IDR-related tasks to estimate min-max cycle times. Zero-base the analysis. Try out the new infrastructure and tune it as experience shows what works and what doesn't.

## Internal Publicity

People like to think that success begets success, that people beat paths to better mousetraps. As the discussion of peer rivalry hinted, spreading a new IS culture can be like trying to light a fire in a pile of wet leaves. One team's success can drive rival teams in opposite (and incompatible) directions. The steering committee has the power and the will to notice and reverse such counterproductive pettiness.

Internal publicity is an obvious, but often neglected, success spreader. The CIO should kick off the reuse campaign with visibility and fanfare. When each project completes, measure the productivity and other benefits, then publicize the story. Be sure to describe any difficulties and how the project overcame them.

Publicly posting quantitative results applies not-so-subtle pressure on those whose own results, based on doing things the old way, cannot measure up to what others are achieving. People like trying to "keep up with the Joneses."

Reward those who achieve quantitative success targets. The rewards are an official, corporate endorsement of the new order of things. Success stories and endorsements, career promotions, awards parties, rah-rah meetings, and system demonstrations are all part of the effort to create and sustain momentum.

The campaign also needs a grass-roots movement. Successful project team members and end-users will be more than willing to help win the hearts of the other troops. Comments like "I could never go back to the old ways" or "If we stop using frames, I quit" or (from users) "This is the best system you ever gave us" can be expanded into testimonials. Grass-roots support is a subjective yet vital component of any campaign to create a reuse culture.

# Reengineering the Infrastructure

## CHAPTER 26

*The Chief Information Officer's ability to add value*
*[in key business areas] is the biggest single factor in determining*
*whether the organization views Information Technology*
*as an asset or a liability. . . . The Chief Executive Officer can help*
*by inspiring a receptive and constructive climate*
*for IT across the organization.*

Michael J. Earl and David F. Feeny

Traditional corporate departments—sales, marketing, production, customer services, accounting, and administration—are likened to "stovepipes": vertically integrated, but horizontally isolated. Customers, fed up with poor service, will switch to companies who can offer "one-stop shopping." By integrating the work flows among stovepipes, we can shorten response times, improve customer satisfaction, create new business opportunities, and strengthen relationships, both internally and externally.

The path to this integration, of course, lies through information systems. In this chapter, we consider first reengineering the business as a whole, then the role that IS plays in this reengineering.

## Reengineering the Business

In a conventional organization, the infrastructures that evolve in the separate departments tend to be incompatible. One result is massive duplications among the stovepipes. In consequence, they share far less information and processes with each other than they should. The key to one-stop shopping is to achieve a proper balance between diversity and commonality.

## Diversity versus Commonality

Diversity is inherent in the differences among various types of customers and suppliers, products and services. But if we look for commonalities, we find that these same entities are much more alike than they are different! All customers purchase; all suppliers sell; sales orders, purchase orders, work orders—all possess many common traits. Even customers and suppliers resemble each other—they all have names, addresses, sales transactions, and so on. Humans naturally emphasize differences, but the diversity we actually need is only about 5%—experience indicates that 95% of systems' components are sharable, reusable.

## Client-Server

How? Provide all lines of business with access to common information and work flows. Figure 26-1 illustrates a three-layer application architecture that progresses from interfaces with external customer and supplier groups, through the major product and service lines of business, to the

**Figure 26-1.**   Client-server architectures are well suited to replacing stovepipe systems with common processes and frame components.

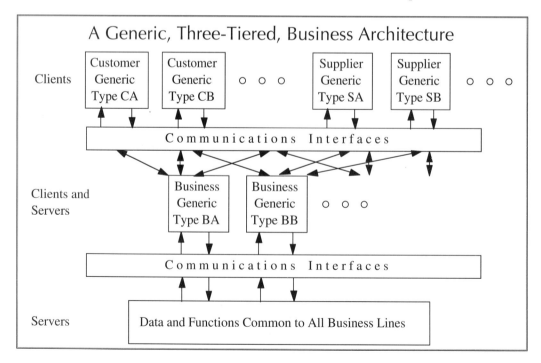

back-office data and processes that are common to all business activities. It is a client-server architecture because, as a network of cooperating processes, each process plays the role of "client" when it requests the services of another process, and plays the role of "server" when it provides a requested services.

These processes may be in distinct processors (e.g., mainframes, work-stations), or they may be distinct executables within the same processor. Figure 26-1 assumes workstations are connected via a communications network (i.e., LANs and/or WANs) to other machines whose processes encapsulate related data and functions. This approach to systems is inherently object-oriented.

## Isolate Change

Notice that the most common elements occur at the bottom layer of this figure, with progressively more specialization in higher layers. The more specialized the element, the more it is subject to change. Layering serves to isolate changes from other layers. In practice, the number of layers depends on how many independent sources of change affect the business. The illustrated architecture suggests that adding or modifying a customer-type seldom affects the business lines or the back-office functions. Conversely, the business can modify or add products and services without necessarily changing the customer/supplier interfaces. The advantages of the client-server approach are many: increased flexibility, shorter time-to-market, more work being done by fewer resources, higher customer satisfaction.

The three client-server layers are glued together by independently evolving technology layers, depicted as communications interfaces in Figure 26-1. Isolating the technology layers allows business analysts to ignore nonbusiness details such as inter- or intraprocessor communications protocols, and logical data view extraction from a distributed database, perhaps with both relational and hierarchical components. By isolating such technical details, the business can get on with what it does best. Because a competitive edge often utilizes technologies not yet mature, being able to buffer the business from their negative aspects is vital.

## Encapsulation

All business processes and information structures are composed of relatively few generic types. The question is: how do we get from the few to the many without drowning in details, which happens when we copy-and-modify? We can (at design-time) encapsulate in frames the generic types. Then, each business specific is an isolated delta from some combination of types.

By avoiding the copy-and-modify approach, you both reduce your organization's apparent complexity and literally have an objective framework for reengineering your business.

An example of a generic process type involves the interactions of a business unit with its customer(s) and supplier(s). See Figure 26-2. This is a model developed by Don Burnstine, which he applies to organizations of all sizes and shapes. The generic "customer" and "supplier" roles can be external or internal to an organization. To deal with customers and suppliers, ADVOR defines five generic activities:

- "Accept" orders from customers,
- "Deliver" products or services to them,
- "Verb" is whatever internal actions are required to produce the goods and/or services of that unit,
- "Order" products or services from suppliers, and
- "Receive" them from suppliers.

When detailing the workings of an actual business, ADVOR is applied at several organizational levels (however, any particular instance may not require all five ADVOR activities).

**Figure 26-2.** This generic process model can be adapted to any business, and to levels within a business. ©Burnstine and Associates Inc. 1991.

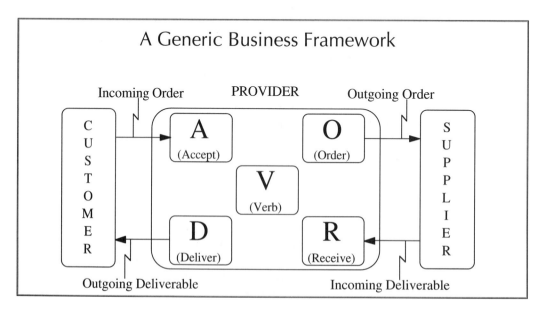

## Reusing Business Process Reengineering in IS Departments

A blizzard of issues surface when transforming a traditional IS shop to a systemic reuse culture. Previous chapters addressed these issues from several angles. Here we add a bit more flesh to some key ideas:

- IS's mandate;
- reuse infrastructure;
- practicing reuse, day-to-day;
- IS's retained earnings.

### Mandate

Our goals are to position IS to anticipate business needs, and to manage the IS function like a "normal" business unit. As we saw in Part III, iterative design refinement is itself a continuous reengineering process, co-evolving frames along with the systems assembled from them. A very important part of IS reengineering, then, is to establish an environment that fosters attitudes and behaviors conducive to iterative refinement. Engendering this environment can be difficult, since the reward system entrenched in many IS shops is not conducive to reuse.

The variable to track is speed of response. A request for a new or enhanced executable should take minutes, not days, to satisfy. Small systems of a dozen or so executables should take a few days to implement; preliminary versions may be built by end-users. SWAT teams should aim for productivity indexes of 25 or more, far above the industry average for business systems of 16.9.

Lest you think such productivity is unrealistically high, the QSM study, described in Chapter 1, reported an average PI of 26.2. Since completing that study, QSM has doubled their database of frame-based projects, and the average has gone up to 26.9! One four-million-line system at the Hudson's Bay Company, for example, described in Chapter 29, was clocked at a PI of 28.7. One of the highest PIs QSM has ever seen is 33.1, set by Automated Financial Systems Inc. They developed, and now market, a check-clearing analysis tool called CSM Plus (see Table 26-1). Beyond the high PI, the project was done in five months and consumed eight staff months. That's a team size average of 1.6 people!

The goal of high speed entails other goals, such as the existence of easily tailored frameworks, and an infrastructure that provides to developers quick clarifications and feedback. These goals, in turn, enable high quality, since mistakes can be caught and corrected quickly. IS's mandate, then, includes integrating well with the rest of the organization.

**Table 26-1  Specifics of Automated Financial Systems Inc. Project.**

| System | "CSM Plus" (Check Services Model Plus) | |
|--------|---------------------------------------|---|
| Description | Enables bank "float analysts" to optimize their daily check-clearing practices. | |
| Total size | 635,363 ESLOC | |
| SPC size | 56,592 ESLOC | |
| Reuse | 91% | If done with industry average productivity |
| Time (detailed design through completion) | 5 months | 51 months |
| Effort | 8 person-months | 83 person-months |
| SPC PI | 22.9 | 16.9 |
| Overall PI | 33.1 | 16.9 |

## Reuse Infrastructure

Chapter 18 explained why a co-located IS organization was superior to either a centralized or a decentralized one. A small, central frame-engineering administration group supports co-located SWAT teams. Their functions and responsibilities were detailed in Chapter 21.

Here, I want to emphasize the distinction between frame management and frame development. While the former should be centralized, the quality of the latter is definitely higher when decentralized. Working in an "ivory tower" leads to elegant frames that are not practical, produced by people resented as elitist by developers.

In World War I, the generals found that they lost fewer pilots when a plane's mechanic had to go for a ride each time it came out of the hangar! So it is in post-industrial manufacturing. Engineers stay involved in day-to-day factory operations [43]. Software engineers, beyond implementing corporate standards, are the only ones who can ensure that their frameworks are current, effective, and reused.

Nor should frame writing be the exclusive purview of frame engineers. All application team members should be encouraged to write frames. This approach not only provides a career path for developers, but application-specific frames often become candidates for promotion into corporate standards.

## Practicing Reuse Day-to-Day

For reuse to become self-sustaining in an IS organization, experience shows that at least 40% of the developers need to be practicing reuse as a daily routine. Below this critical mass, managers have a constant uphill struggle to create a reuse culture. With this critical mass, managers can shift their focus to process improvements (TQM). Such improvements aim to increase reuse beyond what individual projects can achieve.

Unless your IS shop is small, avoid trying to "boil the ocean." That is, achieve a critical mass in one unit before starting another. This strategy avoids the nearly impossible task of drumming up a broad commitment to systemic reuse before enough people have seen the benefits.

For groups who are mostly in "maintenance" mode, the focus should be two-pronged:

1. In the absence of business frameworks, use frames to leave programs "a little neater than you found them," my Boy Scout dictum. This tactic provides incremental benefits. More importantly, it ensures that everyone can hone their adaptive reuse skills, not just those doing rewrites or new development.

2. Begin work on business frameworks, using the iterative processes described in Part III. The cost to reengineer legacy systems goes down as reusable functionality goes up. As soon as the cost becomes less than the benefits of replacing those systems, the first prong has served its purpose. You emerge from the tar pits, hopefully for good.

## Retained Earnings

Systemic reuse cannot be sustained unless some of its benefits are retained. More than once have I seen the very success of reuse come back and bite the people who achieved it.

Here is a typical scenario. A project team reuses frames and attains "fantastic" productivity (e.g., a PI 8 higher than the local average). Because it can "get the job done," the team takes on additional work, as a "favor" to another project. Having done the favor, they discover that they are stuck doing the enhancements (i.e., successful software always evolves, but not by itself). Meanwhile, in the name of reaping the benefits of reuse, the team is downsized, losing members to other projects. The "reward" for good behavior is a kick in the shins.

Another hazardous practice is to let projects create frames without knowing what other projects have done. A corollary is that project frames are not properly matured to be reusable by other projects. For a while, projects lift productivity by dint of their own framing activities. But the ongoing buildup of overlapping, immature components creates drag. Eventually, the worsening lift-to-drag ratio causes reuse to crash.

These two scenarios are manifestations of not protecting the initial investment in reuse. Frames are capital assets, producing an easily measured ROI. They require a capital investment mentality. Treat them as overhead and, like any asset that is not looked after, it withers away. By all means, some of reuse's ROI should be distributed as dividends to the bottom line. But some of the earnings should also be retained, to grow the business of reuse.

We have already described treating the frame management function as an internal profit center. For some, this even becomes an *external* profit center by remarketing the frames to other organizations.

Another mechanism for reinvestment allows a manager to keep a fraction of the budget that she doesn't spend, a fraction proportional to her improved service levels. Hopefully, this positive feedback mechanism further improves next year's service levels, doing better with less.

# Doing Better with Less

## CHAPTER 27

> *Good firms everywhere critique their processes and products*
> *in order to learn from past successes as well as failures.*
> *They measure and benchmark what they do.*
> *They study customers.*
> *And they try to get different parts of the organization*
> *to cooperate and share components.*
>
> Michael A. Cusumano and Richard W. Selby

Putting the information systems department on a disciplined engineering footing is essential to the goal of reengineering the enterprise. Managing this department as a normal business unit has a number of implications regarding the effective use of people, the embodiment of standards in frames, the control of uncertainty in estimating development, and the use of metrics.

## Use of People

"People are everything (well, almost everything)," Fred Brooks observed in material he added to the 1995 edition of The Mythical Man-Month. Of course, frame technology is over in Brooks' "almost everything" category, but to make it work, to make anything in software engineering work, takes people. In fact, much of this Part IV has been about people—how to achieve an infrastructure that supports reusable people and their frameworks. In this section, we look directly at people and particularly at the aspects listed in Table 27-1.

**Table 27-1  People and the Reuse Organization.**

**1.** Direct and indirect IS labor reductions.

**2.** Central engineering management and support.

**3.** Technical information exchanges.

**4.** Replacing the craftsman ethos.

**5.** Generalists replacing specialists.

**6.** Communicating via working models.

## Reduced Direct and Indirect Labor

Because of the automation inherent in frame assembly, small teams of one to four people are able to develop large systems. In this way, development organizations can avoid the severe communications problems inherent in synchronizing the work within large technical groups. That means they can avoid the deep hierarchies needed to moderate the flow of information among hundreds of stakeholders. Like other business units, IS can and should reap the benefits of flattened hierarchies.

## Central Engineering Management and Support

As we have seen, a hybrid centralized/decentralized infrastructure maximizes the leverage of a small number of good technical staff. And, in the spirit of running IS as a profit center, the central group can charge royalties on its frame products to application development projects, and bill them for its support services.

## Technical Information Exchanges

The significance of IS professionals having a common engineering vocabulary cannot be overstated. While software modules interact in extremely precise ways, people are just the opposite. They use vague language, socialize informally, and work as uncoupled, autonomous individuals. The frames they share enable them to use an effective shorthand, and when necessary, to discuss subtle engineering issues with high precision. Or, as one wag quipped: "We are all INSERTs in the great SPC of Life!"

## Replacing the Craftsman Ethos

The antithesis of professional engineering is the solitary craftsman, fashioning individual parts and putting them together, one at a time. An automated component assembly environment combines the outputs of many individuals systematically. The craftsman mentality gives way to a manufacturing ethos. Automated assembly emphasizes standard components and efficient production.

## The Rise of Generalists

Technical expertise such as GUI APIs, LAN and WAN protocols, CICS, IMS/DC/DB, and so on, can be packaged in frameworks. Generalists who are both business analysts and software developers replace non-business-oriented specialists. Such generalists, relying on the frameworks, are competent to map the business domain directly into full-scale, well-tuned software. The fewer intermediaries translating business problems into effective solutions, the less time needed, and the less lost in the translations.

## Communicating via Working Models

Mature reuse environments fundamentally improve how end-users and developers interact. First, there is mutual trust. Second, a combination of JADs and working (pre)releases make for efficient discussion of the deltas between what is currently available to the next (pre)release. Users test drive the system and report their feedback. Developers relate this feedback directly to the deltas that refine the system.

## Use of Standards

The word "standard" has been much used and abused. Depending on the situation, a standard may ensure consistency and efficiency, or it may frustrate and retard. A standard is the last thing one needs if it is inappropriate or cannot be adapted to suit the need.

There are three properties of good software engineering standards:

1. stability,
2. efficacy,
3. flexibility.

## Stability

First and foremost, a standard must be reasonably permanent. A standard cannot happen overnight; it is slowly distilled from multiple variations and alternatives into a form that survives the test of time. Unfortunately, the pace of technological change in IS prevents many so-called standards from stabilizing.

## Efficacy

Second, stability must combine with efficacy. That is, a standard should work as intended and thereby avoid problems and save labor. The more situations in which a rule or structure could apply, the more it qualifies to become a standard. When people ignore a relevant standard, that act is an indication either that they do not understand how it should be used or that it is too hard to apply. In other words, standards should pave a path of least resistance to achieving a goal.

## Flexibility

The third property of successful software standards is flexibility. This property is vital to IS because of the pace of change and the need to make shoes fit their feet rather than the reverse. When people promulgate standards, they often focus on the normal cases; their standards disallow exceptions. Such rigid standards are just not good enough for software systems. Granting credit is a good example of a notoriously judgmental task. Nevertheless, certain standards apply, or else banks would go bankrupt. Can we handle such standards in software?

As first mentioned in Chapter 2, a mature frame epitomizes a stable, efficacious, flexible software standard. Indeed, in a frame environment, executables are nothing but blended combinations of standard components. Frames can ensure that all systems involving credit, for example, automatically apply minimum credit standards, while allowing for optional judgment factors, depending on the application.

## Effective Control of Uncertainty

Lederer and Prasad, through a survey of 120 randomly chosen IS shops, have quantified just how poorly people estimate the time and cost of major software projects [44]. Three-quarters of these estimates are seriously inaccurate, with 84% of these causing cost overruns. Figure 27-1 ranks the leading causes of inaccuracy; what glares at us is that four of the top five causes stem from ill-defined requirements. Clear signs of fuzzy domains are stakeholders disagreeing about requirements, and changing them well before systems go into production. Indeed, as we have emphasized before, IS is really in the business of finding well-defined solutions to ill-defined problems.

## Fuzzy Domains

Why are we in this kind of business? Fuzzy domains harbor endless opportunities to innovate, for those who can penetrate the fuzz. Take customer

| The Top Five Causes of Inaccurate Estimates | |
|---|---|
| Causes | Extent of Responsibility Mean Rating (1-5 scale) |
| Frequent requests for changes by users | 3.90 |
| Overlooked tasks | 3.61 |
| Users' lack of understanding of their own requirements | 3.60 |
| Insufficient user-analyst communication and understanding | 3.36 |
| Poor or imprecise problem definition | 3.35 |

**Figure 27-1.** Lederer and Prasad's partial listing table of reasons for systems to be late.

information systems, for example. At first glance, a CIS is just a file of customer masters to be maintained. But upon reflection, a CIS can be a serious competitive weapon. Properly integrated with other systems, such as order processing, billing, and accounts receivable, a CIS can track customer profiles. Such intelligence enables you to tailor products and services for each customer uniquely. A good CIS can shorten response times, reduce complaints, link up with your customers' own systems, and so forth. The opportunities are endless, but fuzzy, ill-defined.

It is only with the advent of software that serious exploitation of rich but volatile domains became possible. Only software is malleable enough to track the evolution of unstable requirements. Today, the major risk lies not in making systems that work, it's in making the wrong systems. While there can be no substitute for business acumen, navigating fuzzy domains requires systems to be (engineered so they remain) adaptable. This is the raison d'etre of frame technology.

## Risk

In the past, systems had to be designed and built from scratch because we lacked frameworks that were sufficiently adaptable. Risk, measured in time, people, and resources, was proportional to a system's size and complexity. Worse, because requirements are moving targets, sizable systems were stale-dated even as their designs were completed. In hindsight, it's ironic that the software industry thought the waterfall strategy to be conservative, when actually its from-scratch, nonadaptive methods actually increased the risk of solving the wrong problems!

In an adaptive reuse environment, developers base design on proven frameworks; this practice eliminates most traditional design effort because it is redundant. Moreover, new design errors are exposed in early prereleases. Thus, two major risks decline. And confidence increases in project estimates because the proven underlying architecture is well understood, conferring predictability.

Lederer and Prasad found that those who bear the brunt of implementation, the system developers, make the best estimates [50]. Estimates should rely on "documented facts, standards and simple arithmetic formulas." With frame technology, this reliance involves estimating function points: the number of windows, reports, user views of data, and system interfaces, and weighting them in three complexity categories: easy, medium, and complex. See Table 27-2 in the next section for an example.

## Estimating Guidelines

Prereleases limit risk to a fraction of the whole project. When you complete a prerelease, analyze its time and cost estimates in order to improve future estimates. Feedback from each prerelease also reduces the risk of building the wrong system. IDR is very much in the spirit of several other Lederer and Prasad cost-estimating guidelines.

- "Delay finalizing the initial estimate until the end of a thorough study." That study ends with feedback from the first prerelease.

- "Anticipate and control user changes." Negotiate change requests only at the end of a prerelease, so changes cannot affect a current prerelease deadline. Having built key parts of the system, developers are in an excellent position to estimate the cost/benefit of proposed changes, and to renegotiate costs and schedules.

- "Monitor the progress of the proposed project." This is integral to IDR's prerelease strategy.

- "Evaluate proposed project progress by using independent auditors." Lederer and Prasad report less than 10% of the IS departments surveyed follow this common-sense advice. Yet, developers are notorious for faking progress through inaccurate reporting. Each prerelease is eminently testable by users, the ultimate auditors.

## Use of Metrics

Common sense and good business and good engineering practice all dictate that software activities should be measured. As Tom DeMarco put it, "You can't control what you can't measure. Measurement costs money. . . . If you think that cost is high, consider the cost of being out of control." [32] Measuring usually improves things, simply because of the attention being paid (the Hawthorne effect). It is a sad comment on the state of our profession that few shops measure; indeed, they don't know why, what, or how!

Why is the measurement discipline absent most of the time? People openly resist. They resent the extra effort, and they suspect it will be used to judge their personal performances. This is where managers must show leadership. Managers and staff alike must believe in the overwhelming need to reduce project uncertainty and risk, and to ensure a satisfactory return on investment. Modern project management tools exist both to minimize the onerous nature of data collection and to protect individuals. It's time to give these tools a chance. Bite the bullet long enough to produce the job satisfaction that comes with contributing to a profitable, tightly run operation.

### Measurement Payoffs

Especially in the early stages of introducing new tools and methodologies into a traditional systems culture, accumulating a database of objective measurements has three important payoffs.

**1. Metrics improve your ability to estimate project sizes and durations.** Larry Putnam and Ware Myers derived an empirical formula from the statistical measurement of more than 3500 software development projects [2]. The projects represented every type of application domain from business to microcode and firmware. For convenience, Figure 27-2 repeats the formula from Chapter 1.

The equation says that the volume of software produced varies with:

- the effort, measured in person-years (including all direct and indirect labor), divided by a skills factor (ranging from 0.16 for projects under 16K source lines of code to 0.39 for projects over 70K ESLOC—source lines of code not counting comments and blank lines),

- the calendar time (from detailed design to full release), and

- the productivity characteristic of the development process.

- ESLOC = effective source lines of code
  (no blanks/comments)
- time = detailed design to user acceptance, incl.
- effort = staff months
- B = ESLOC related skills factor (0.16 - 0.39 )

$$PI = \log_{1.272} \left[ \frac{ESLOC}{time^{4/3} * (effort \, / \, B)^{1/3}} \right] - 26.6$$

**Figure 27-2.**  The QSM software equation shows that the relationship between project size, development time, and effort determines a productivity value that QSM calls the *process-productivity index.*

What this formula most reveals is that controlling a project's schedule is much more effective than changing its manpower. Allowing more time increases the delivery volume more than linearly. On the other hand, doubling the project team squeezes the schedule by 16%, tripling saves only another 8%! Moreover, there is a minimum schedule beyond which more resources are essentially excess baggage.

The formula is the quantitative equivalent to Brooks' famous dictum: "Adding bodies to a late software project makes it later" [33]. After all, if a man can dig a post-hole in an hour, 60 men cannot dig it in a minute; nor can nine women have a baby in a month.

The productivity index is not output per month or per person-month. Rather, this factor characterizes the productivity of all the factors affecting the software development process: software tools, frames, development methodology, technical skills, management effectiveness, degree of cooperation with users, complexity of the application, and so forth. Noma Industry's process productivity index, for example, based on 16 people cranking out 3.9 million new or replacement ESLOC per year, is 31.3, or ($1.272^{[31.3 - 16.9]}$=) 32 times the software industry norm.

**2. Metrics help determine your return on investment in reuse.** A rational approach to reuse is to show a credible ROI. What better way to do this than to establish a current PI baseline, do a pilot project with component-based reuse, and measure its PI? Since PI is directly related to time and effort, it's easy to calculate the savings, hence the ROI. But don't stop there. Measure your progress on each project and prove to the skeptics that you indeed made a wise choice!

Adding three to the PI more than doubles what you can produce, for a given schedule and cost. Equivalently, increasing the PI by three shortens the schedule by 35%, all else being equal—and does so on every project! Experience shows that when you adopt frame tools and techniques, you can jump your PI, not by three, but by eight or more. That means schedules shrink by 70%, and costs by 84%.

**3. Identify "hot spots" that need management attention.** Compare your measures to norms for your industry, such as those reported by Putnam and Myers, and, most importantly to your own growing baselines. Significant deviations, both plus and minus, are red flags for further analysis. Timely reinforcement of positive deviations and correction of negative ones is one of management's basic responsibilities. To quote Fred Brooks again [33]:

> "The Plans and Control group is the watchdog who renders the imperceptible delays visible and who points up the critical elements. It is the early warning system against losing a year, one day at a time."

Systems must not only be done, but must be seen to be done with high speed, high quality, and low cost.

## Instrumentation Guidelines

### 1. Set Measurable Criteria

Minimum criteria needed to judge each project a success should be negotiated among users, developers, and management in advance. Which criteria are used depend on the needs of the environment and the project. Typical criteria involve:

- functionality,
- performance,
- ease-of-use,
- productivity,
- adaptability (maintainability),
- standards adherence,
- portability.

### 2. Manage Expectations

This guideline is key to the successful introduction of new technology. Publish the success criteria so that both the project team and potential critics know the ground rules, and avoid focusing on irrelevant issues. The criteria should create significant expectations over current experience, yet be modest enough to be exceedable. Initially, your reuse consultants can help you set expectations appropriate to the skills of the team.

Part of expectation management is to explain in advance that changes in requirements are normal, especially when users react to prereleases. Having allowed for rework, and other delays, such as vacations and illness, people should welcome feedback.

## 3. Measure

Metrics need not be onerous to compute. Choose simple, objective, and consistent measures that correlate well with desired goals and benefits. They should be verifiable by others. Here are some useful ones.

### Size- and Complexity-Related:

- Project duration in calendar weeks or months.
- Project effort in person-weeks, -months, or -years, including all direct and indirect labor from the start of detailed design to production release.
- ESLOC.
- Function points. Albrecht and Gaffney developed a simple estimation procedure [45].

First, for each of four types of function—inputs and inquiries, outputs, logical views of data, and interfaces to external systems—estimate how many "simple," "average," and "complex" ones you need.

Second, calculate the total "function points" by summing the counts, as weighted in Table 27-2.

Table 27-2

| Type of Function | Simple | Average | Complex |
|---|---|---|---|
| Inputs & Inquiries | 3 | 4 | 6 |
| Outputs | 4 | 5 | 7 |
| Logical Data Views | 7 | 10 | 15 |
| External Interfaces | 5 | 7 | 10 |

Estimators weight each type of function in terms of their judgment of whether it is simple, average, or complex.

Third, estimate ESLOC from total function points. Capers Jones has provided estimated conversion factors for various languages [35]. For COBOL and Fortran, his factor is 106; for C, it is 150. But you should derive your own conversion factors by counting your own project functions and SLOCs. Table 27-3 illustrates.

**Table 27-3  Example Derivation of Source Lines of Code from Function Points.**

| Type of Function | # x Simple | # x Average | # x Complex | Total |
|---|---|---|---|---|
| Inputs & Inquiries | 3 x 3 | 10 x 4 | 2 x 6 | 61 |
| Outputs | 10 x 4 | 10 x 5 | 10 x 7 | 160 |
| Logical Views | 0 x 7 | 5 x 10 | 2 x 15 | 80 |
| External Interfaces | 0 x 5 | 3 x 7 | 2 x 10 | 41 |
| Total | | | | 342 |

Estimated Cobol ESLOC = 342 x 106 = 36,252.

**Productivity-, Time-, and Cost-Related:**

- Using the process productivity index the (Putnam-Myers formula given in Figure 27-2), you can use the estimated ESLOC and number of project staff to estimate each prerelease time, allowing for rework and other time losses. You can also do after-the-fact measurements and understand how your estimates relate to actuals. After a few projects, the reliability of estimates should improve.

- Ratio of indirect-to-direct labor costs. The overall ROI depends on factoring in the indirect costs.

**Adaptability-Related:**

- Average defect removal time.

- Given the perennial need to evolve the requirements, we also need to measure the average user-request turnaround time.
    One danger here. Powerful tools make it easy to be too responsive to requests. Those concerned must exercise judgment and care to ensure that system changes make business sense. This is one reason

it's so important that developers understand the business context in which their systems work.

**Quality-Related:**

- Defects per developer per month, where a defect is a specific deviation from the specification. Requirements are incomplete and defective, too. But requirements defects indicate quality only weakly, as they are less under the control of developers than of users who, in turn, are at the mercy of changes in business and technology.

- User surveys of system functionality, ease-of-use, and performance. Allow plenty of room for free-form comments and suggestions.

Doing better with less is a consequence of all the foregoing discussions. It is people who apply their business knowledge to create systems that satisfy business needs and opportunities. It is proven standards, consistently applied, yet tailored to fit each system's peculiarities. Above all, it is the ease with which systems can be changed as needs and opportunities change. Although the quantitative aspects of quality can and should be measured, quality is mostly an intangible—the smiles of satisfied users.

# Alleviate Staff Insecurity

## CHAPTER 28

> *Changes in culture are what make the shift*
> *to processes so difficult. . . .*
> *It takes a lot of time to win understanding*
> *and acceptance of major changes.*
>
> Paul Allaire (CEO, Xerox)

Security and self-esteem depend on believing you have some control over your own destiny. Organizations intent on a reuse culture, downsizing their IS departments, force people to change or lose their jobs. Forced change generates insecurity because people feel they have no control.

Sensitive managers can do much to alleviate such stress:

- Present the changes positively, explaining each person's new role;
- Answer questions forthrightly—people appreciate candor;
- Encourage constructive suggestions and participation as change agents;
- Emphasize all the things that won't change!

Having installed powerful reuse tools, we cannot merely teach programmers when to press what buttons. In many environments, programmers consider new tools little more than gadgets. Gadgeteers become addicted and spend time doing frivolous things. With graphical modeling tools, for example, people often diagram themselves into oblivion, creating reams of details that turn out later to be irrelevant or wrong.

We fail, not for lack of good technology, but because we are blinded by our habits. We treat software as a kind of hardware, confuse use with reuse, ignore the duality of data and process, design from scratch, ignore metrics, on and on. We can't hope to improve without replacing old habits with better ones. To accomplish this systemically requires an intensive, ongoing campaign to educate, train, and coach. This campaign involves staff at all levels within IS, and users, too.

## Career Paths

In a reuse culture, people become most valuable when they understand both business and software engineering. Today, those individuals are rare indeed, and yet the remedy is straightforward. There should be professional career paths for people who have the aptitude and aspire to be software engineers. There are two kinds:

1. Applications engineers adapt existing frameworks into evolving application systems. They combine the business analyst and application programmer skills. These skills don't embrace the details of CICS, graphics APIs, or client-server architectures. They are experts about the business and about how to apply frames in order to hide the routine, but voluminous, technicalities.

2. Frame engineers create and evolve the frameworks that application engineers reuse. Engineers working on systems architecture correspond to traditional system architects. Those framing business rules are ex(cellent) application engineers.

Like any engineering profession, the peer esteem and remuneration of software engineers should keep many of them in the profession, rather than in management.

## Professional SWAT Teams

For our purposes, an ideal SWAT team is a small group of professionals, skilled with reusable tools, who work with users to build and evolve cost-effective systems. SWAT teams exist within those business units that will be primary users of the application being developed; this arrangement reflects the principle of co-location, advocated in Chapter 18. Chapter 21 details how a SWAT team participates in the iterative design refinement process.

## Team Skills

Ideal SWAT team members are results-oriented application engineers, skilled at:

- asking pertinent questions that clarify basic business and systems issues;
- recognizing patterns of similarity, suitable for framing;
- designing evolvable, fine-tunable systems, based on proven models;
- implementing and testing with reuse-based tools;
- negotiating cost-effective changes with end-users.

## Team Quality and Size

The quality of your IS staff is by far your most important variable. It is well known that productivity varies by a factor of 10 or more between average and top programmers. Amplify that range with powerful tools and you put out a very strong signal or even more noise. A few excellent people can support a large organization. Conversely, a horde of mediocre gadgeteers can crank out more than enough fully functional junk to put you out of business.

Good people tend to be scattered around large organizations, fully committed to local responsibilities. Their managers will be understandably reluctant to release them. The steering committee may have to resolve conflicts between existing priorities and the critical need to jump-start the new reuse culture with top people.

Just how small is a small SWAT team? A reuse-intensive organization of one-person SWAT teams can produce an average of 20K ESLOC/team/month (of which less than 5% needs to be hand-crafted). No team should have more than three or four engineers. The need for interpersonal communication grows very rapidly with team size, creating negative productivity. This relationship is empirically reflected in the productivity equation discussed in Chapter 27.

A large system can be produced by a small team as a series of prereleases. Also, the larger the system, the easier it is to split into loosely coupled subsystems. Then splitting larger teams into smaller ones, working in parallel, considerably shortens the schedule. The productivity equation shows that two equal, independent teams are almost 60% more productive than one combined team. And because the subsystems are loosely coupled, the cost of the extra interfaces is well justified, both in net time saved and in design modularity.

The need for small teams puts emphasis on combining all the skills listed above in single heads. By doing so, the need for interpersonal communication and synchronization dramatically shrinks. At the outset, team members may not be generalists, hence larger teams are unavoidable. But the professionals described here emerge from a steady focus on your recruiting, education, and training. Your very ability to recruit top people is enhanced by the prospect of working with other top professionals in a leading-edge environment.

### Team Spirit

When beginning the transition to systemic reuse, a SWAT team sees themselves as pioneers. They gird themselves for slings and arrows in order to:

- blaze trails through a forest of status quo and doubt;
- identify and cope with obstacles blocking efficient team functioning;
- establish trust relationships with frustrated and skeptical end-users;
- become coaches, role models in rolling out reuse technology to the less enthusiastic practitioners.

## Education and Training

Becoming a professional software engineer entails following a process familiar to all professions, be they doctors, dentists, electricians, plumbers, or engineers.

In addition to technical training, people need to understand how reusability changes the development process (IDR), and what is expected of them in terms of using and writing frames. Project managers need to understand SWAT team organization; the role of frame engineers; how to coach novices, schedule projects, and estimate costs in a frame context; manage expectations; expedite requirements clarifications; and negotiate user requests for change.

Everyone—IS managers, developers, and even users to some extent—should get an introduction to the concepts of adaptive reuse and IDR. Managers attend seminars in topics including IDR project management, how to deploy and use metrics, change-management issues and practices. Developers get detailed technical training, which we now discuss.

### Just-in-Time Training

Synchronizing theory with practice may be difficult at times, but, unless reinforced, detailed technical knowledge decays exponentially. This decay wastes the valuable resources of trainers, trainees, and classrooms. It loses opportunities to be productive elsewhere and frustrates everyone involved.

## Please, No "Laboratory Experiments"

Avoid projects invented simply for training purposes. That's the intention of classroom exercises. Remember, the hardest issue is breaking old habits. Artificial projects generate little enthusiasm and no commitment. In such a setting, the skeptics and change-resisters focus on the wrong issues and put down the new ideas. Old habits are not broken.

Real projects proceed regardless. They have hard deadlines, *the shorter, the better*. There is nothing like a short deadline to clarify the mind, and to cause you to seek help when stuck. Short deadlines also produce quicker feedback, leading us to intercept problems before they cause much damage. "Quick hits" also reinforce the commitment to achieve the reuse vision.

If a project is large, cleave out a modest piece for quick implementation. Such cleavages exist and should be made in any case. Remember that software scaffolding is part of the IDR process.

Don't be deterred by claims that projects are "not far enough along" to be candidates for reuse. If your goal is to speed up the status quo by an order of magnitude, here is an opportunity to force the issue! It's the projects that are well underway that should be avoided.

## Coaching

Other trades call it apprenticing, interning, postdoctoral studies, articling. The idea is the same. A novice works with an expert on real work to learn pragmatic skills.

Fresh out of an introductory course, a little knowledge can be dangerous, like a sharp knife in the hands of a child. Novices often confuse their new-found powers with mastery. They jump into the deep end and, if not rescued, may quickly flounder. Enthusiasm evaporates into frustration and they start blaming their new tools. By far the most effective way to shorten the path to true mastery is to apprentice with an expert who is prepared to explain "why" as well as "how"—a mentor or coach.

Besides organizing the work and acting as a role model, the mentor coaches both pro- and reactively:

- Preventing frustration is often just spotting an obvious error or offering a simple tip. Help at critical moments sustains an apprentice's original enthusiasm and teaches effective problem-solving strategies.

- Constructively criticizing a solution highlights subtle issues to do with optimizing performance, adaptability, portability, style, and so forth. Having just solved a problem, the apprentice is most receptive to its finer points.

Ideally, a mentor is devoted to coaching, not to deadline-driven work such as frame engineering. In reality, the two kinds of work are often done by the same person. Production work conflicts with teaching, and the personality of a good frame engineer may not fit that of a good mentor. If resources allow, one full-time mentor should be able to work with four or five apprentices, possibly in adjacent SWAT teams.

Apprentices typically are at least as productive right after initial training with frame tools as they were before. After a month of on-the-job coaching, they should be at least three times as productive. At this point, an apprentice becomes a practicing journeyman, and active coaching normally ceases. Further productivity increases result primarily from writing and deploying additional frames.

Journeymen with frame engineering potential take advanced training, then write project-level frames with guidance from an expert. At some point, depending on demand and experience, the journeyman achieves master application- or frame-engineer status, able to lead SWAT team projects, engineer frames, and/or act as a mentor. Frame architects are the master level for frame engineers. They coach other frame engineers, design reuse policies, standards, and architectures, and are responsible for the integrity of the corporate frameworks.

## Changing the Relationships with Other Departments

It is often said that users care not how a system is built, only what it does. This belief is harmful. Given the conflicting constraints inherent in modern applications, users ought to become big champions of IDR because it caters to their own unfolding understanding of what they really need. The harder problem is to not cater to frivolous (or worse) requests. The need for trust and synergy among users and developers cannot be overstated.

### Symmetrize the End-User Relationship

Being able to quickly convert revised designs into revised systems means users do not forget, lose interest, or find the business has changed by the time the system is built. That quickness requires users to be an integral part of the IDR process.

Unfortunately, in many large system environments, developers wield de facto monopolistic power over users. It is a kind of tyranny of the technocracy. It creates disaffected users who, in spite of paying for the systems that IS builds, feel that IS is inflicting the systems upon them, and who certainly feel no pride of ownership.

Recently, some organizations have rebounded to the opposite extreme: a kind of tyranny of the users. Management hopes that programming can be eliminated and that end-users will inherit the earth. Neither tyranny works terribly well. Yes, users make good critics, but developers should be systems architects, not users. Yes, users should feel pride of ownership, but developers should be responsible for technical standards and integrity, not users.

Neither group knows enough by themselves to build high-quality software systems. Only users know details about the way the business works that are critical to meeting the existing needs. Only developers know details about the way software works that are critical to its integration with existing structures, its performance, and its adaptability to future needs.

The acronym GIGO (Garbage-In-Garbage-Out) has long been used to explain what comes of misusing information systems. But GIGO also applies to the misuse of software engineering tools. As I said in Chapter 18, meta-GIGO occurs when users and developers do not complement each other's knowledge when shaping the inputs to those tools.

Let's bring down the barriers between developers and users; get them trusting each other, cooperating in a timely way to refine their mutual understanding of the system they are jointly trying to build.

## User Intermediaries

Many large organizations have evolved groups of people who presume to speak on behalf of end-users. The rationale is that end-users don't have time to spend designing systems, and may not be sufficiently technology-literate to articulate their real needs for automation. Thus the enterprise nominates surrogate users, intermediate between end-users and software developers.

Is this a good idea? On the surface it sounds like a great idea—a strong lobby group that can talk peer-to-peer with the techies. The real users can then get on with running the business. In the days of large centralized IS shops and long software development lead-times, the presence of permanent intermediaries might be a useful counterbalance to the monopolistic power such shops wield. The problem is entrenchment. Over the years, entrenched intermediaries have become power groups, wielding as much power over end-users as the techies did! Consider a typical scenario.

> A business-unit manager, many levels removed from the "coal face," contemplates a new system. IS and the surrogate users, who are mostly business analysts, hold initial discussions. Together they spend several months defining the requirements. The real users may hear rumors but are not involved because they are busy. Anyway, they feel intimidated by "the experts."

Then many more months go by, and little is heard from IS as it grinds away. Much later, IS informs the surrogates that the system is ready for "user-acceptance" testing. Several more months go by while IS defends itself against the surrogates' expectations. Meantime, these expectations have evolved so far from what IS has built that the surrogates refuse to accept the system without some major changes. Finally, the surrogates do introduce some end-user "guinea pigs" to the system. These long-ignored bystanders then start "whining" that the system is a step backwards from the status quo.

Now, the surrogates, who have polarized their positions in heated arguments with IS, are not about to admit that they didn't understand the requirements. So, more pitched battles erupt. Everyone is unhappy with a system in which so much time, money, and ego have been invested that saving face and careers forces its deployment with cosmetic changes.

Sound familiar? What's wrong? The surrogates became noise in the channel! What started off as a plausibly useful group now has negative utility. Not only is morale low, but the enterprise blew its budget building the wrong system.

Intermediaries are still a good idea, as long as they remain current with the business. One way to ensure this is to rotate the people back into the field after a year or two, replaced with fresh experts. There are also a great many facilitation roles that need playing. Let's replay the above scenario with some changes.

The business-unit manager responsible for managing the benefits of the system he envisions contemplates a new system. Application engineers (who are also business analysts) and key end-users, handpicked by user-intermediaries for their knowledge of requirements, hold initial discussions (approved by the business-unit manager). Together they spend a week or so in the end-user environment(s), defining the major requirements as extensions and exceptions to existing demonstration frameworks.

Then three or four weeks go by, as an on-site SWAT team adapts frames to implement the most important requirements. One end-user is seconded to the project to answer questions on the spot and to design the user-interfaces using WYSIWYG editors. This early prerelease is tested by end-users, using test data sets and environments devised by the intermediaries. The SWAT team incorporates requirements changes over the next week or two. Intermediaries begin user documentation, and the revised prerelease is formally accepted.

This process repeats for several more prereleases, until a sufficient amount of the system can be put into production. Intermediaries plan the roll-out of the system. This roll-out entails training, pilot system deployment, cut-overs of office procedures, and the like. Further postreleases are built, then deployed with the help of intermediaries in a similar manner.

There is no shortcut to understanding the real requirements. But the two greatest time-wasters of the past—designing from scratch and analysis paralysis—can be banished with IDR. Bringing real business experts into the process is the shortest, and kindest, cut we can take.

# What Next?

## CHAPTER 29

> *Things should be made as simple as possible,*
> *but not any simpler.*
>
> Albert Einstein

The past half-century has seen the rise of the computer-dominated world. In the last decade, we have lived through the tremendous expansion of personal computers. In this decade we are in the midst of business process reengineering, the replacement of mainframes by client-server systems, and the commercialization of the Internet. And the end is not yet in sight.

We can expect the continued spread of microprocessors into more and more products, as well as into the control of the home and business buildings. We can expect a surge in network capabilities that will bring all kinds of information everywhere. We can expect more of the activities of business, industry, and government to be brought under computer control.

Moreover, the capabilities of computers will spread in directions that we cannot presently foresee in concrete detail. Sales and financial transactions, suitably protected by encryption, will become network-resident. Intelligent agents will seek out whatever we are concerned with, without our having to know how to navigate what is already a very complex cyberworld. Antivirus agents will run through the network, detecting and bringing back for study new viruses, destroying old ones. Human capabilities will be amplified manyfold.

There is a Catch-22. All these activities have to be programmed. There are hundreds of billions of lines of code extant. These new activities will take hundreds of billions more. Where are the analysts, designers, programmers, and testers to come from?

Long ago, in the childhood of the information age, when you lifted the phone, a human voice said, "Number, please." There were no dials on the phone instruments; there were no automatic switches in the telephone exchanges. The telephonization of the entire world, a sage guesstimated, would take more young women to operate all those exchanges than were then alive. We needn't pursue this story. You know what happened—transistorized computer-like switches. But they require tens of thousands of programmers.

## Three Paths Ahead

Programmers who have been surplused by downsizing believe there is no shortage of programmers. Managers trying to hire the very best, those current in the latest technologies, think otherwise. Perhaps both are right. Be that as it may, three possibilities face us.

### Program from Scratch

We might continue to expand the number of programmers. Capers Jones estimates that "about 1,750,000 people in the U.S. derive their salaries directly from work associated with software" [16]. Worldwide, he believes there are about 12 million professional software personnel. Of course, this number is a tiny fraction of the five to six billion people now alive. Many of them are children, or illiterate, or at best somewhat short of the level of education and ability that good programming requires.

On the one hand, continuing on the program-from-scratch course will slow down the advance to the future. Big projects take years to complete now and are mostly late and over budget when they do complete. Defects in code will continue to be numerous, leading to serious troubles as computers and their programs take over more of the world.

On the other hand, program-from-scratch would be a continuation of present practice. The hierarchies comfortable in the existing programming world would not have to change their paradigm. Unfortunately for them, the comfort of these hierarchies does not seem to be foremost in competitive minds.

### End-User Programming

In fact, a great deal of what we used to call "programming" has already been transferred to users. The Basic language derives its name from that thought. The spreadsheet is an example of do-it-yourself programming. Jones estimates "there are perhaps 10,000,000 managers, engineers, architects, accountants, and other knowledge workers [in the U.S. and more than 30,000,000 worldwide] who know enough about programming to build end-user applications with spreadsheets and other tools." Just as, once upon a time, the telephone companies invented the dial telephone and the automated network, and transferred the duties of operators to the users.

## Reuse

There are so many paths to reuse that Yogi Berra's insight comes to mind: "When you come to a fork in the road, take it."

The world is certainly taking the first fork on this path: packaged software. Whenever vendors can sort out some function and sell it for $25, or even thousands of dollars, that is much cheaper than programming it yourself.

Some businesses are also taking the second fork: outsourcing. Again, vendors use the same programs over and over for different clients. But many businesses are not taking this fork. Systems specialized to particular business processes do confer competitive advantage.

The third fork is the little black book or the bottom desk drawer. Individual analysts, designers, coders, and testers use work they or their nearby associates have already done. We call it "experience." It seems hard to get beyond about 25% reuse on this fork.

The fourth fork calls for management intervention—setting up domain analysis, reuse groups, repositories, financial incentives. This fork can get reuse up to around 50%, sometimes more, sometimes less, depending on the amount of push management gives it. This fork is the first one that involves a change of paradigm. It requires forethought, new organization units, capital investment, time, and change. Only a few organizations are doing much along this fork so far.

The fifth fork is object-oriented technology. In theory, already programmed objects can be reused by means of the inheritance mechanism. Only a few organizations have had much success trying to reuse objects:

1. Learning object-oriented analysis, design, and programming is difficult. The learning process takes people out of production for quite a while. Yet, whole organizations have to convert at pretty much the same time. You can see the conflict here between bread-and-butter (bringing in current dollars) and cakes and cream (more effective reuse).

2. Lower objects in the hierarchy inherit the qualities of higher objects, but generally have no way of implementing the "same as, except" principle. This inability to subtract operations leads to thousands of objects, each differing from the next by only one or two operations.

**3.** This large number of objects exceeds the ability of programmers to keep track of what they have available. They often find it preferable to reprogram some function rather than hunt for the object where part of what is needed may already exist.

**4.** In execution, objects call what they need from another object by means of messages. Messages take time—even more time if the message has to be passed through a series of objects to reach the one with the needed operation.

## Frame Technology

Where do we stand then? What are the characteristics we need to make reuse work?

**1.** The ability to adapt existing solutions with the "same as, except" faculty. If a programmer can subtract, as well as add, capabilities, she needs far fewer objects.

**2.** The ability to congeal reusable design and code in a few hundred frames, rather than tens of thousands of objects.

**3.** The ability to make these adaptations at construction time, rather than run time, allowing the resulting code to execute much faster.

**4.** The ability to wrap valid legacy code in a frame, enabling "bread-and-butter" work to carry on as usual.

**5.** The ability to rework wrapped legacy code to improve its efficiency, when schedules permit.

Frame technology embodies the forgoing abilities.

### Experienced Users

Frame technology is not a new, untried idea. On the contrary, it has been in use since 1980. More than 150 organizations have applied it across a gamut of applications, including telecommunications, utilities, retailers, distributors, and aerospace.

Recently, I queried 11 organizations that had been using frame technology for an average of six years. These organizations were in insurance, credit reporting, manufacturing, government, banking, agribusiness, education, and software itself. Table 29-1 lists their principal characteristics.

All but one of these eleven organizations reported that information systems is "very strategic" to their operations. It is the "very heart" of their business.

**Table 29-1**

| Organization size: | 3,000 to 20,000 people |
|---|---|
| IS size: | 11 to 800 |
| Number of developers: | 7 to 275 |
| Number of management levels: | 1 to 5 |
| Percent maintenance: | 15 to 50% |

The broad range in size of the organizations surveyed illustrates the scaleability of frame technology.

The developers at these organizations, both the frame engineers and the application developers, were mostly in their 30s. They had, typically, three years of computer science education, though some had up to eight years. Turnover was generally very low, in the range of zero to 10%. Parts of these organizations employing frame technology reported lower turnover than parts not yet using the technology.

There were multiple platforms in these organizations: IBM MVS CICS; DEC VAX; HP; RS6000; AS400; PCs. The programming language employed was overwhelmingly COBOL: 86%. (However, frames may be used with any programming language.)

The IS function was centralized in most of these organizations, with the hybrid form of organization in the rest. The latter organizations stressed the importance of centralized standards and frame-support services, even though project execution is decentralized. Half the organizations use no intermediaries between the users and project staff. The other half have up to 100 people doing this work.

The trend in these organizations is away from purchased software packages, except for functions considered to be commodity services, not strategic to the business. This trend is counter to that in industry as a whole. The reason is that frame technology creates an alternative to the traditional make or buy-and-modify decision. These organizations buy-and-add. For instance, they can buy an 80% solution, a generic framework, adding their own special, proprietary twists to the package, using the techniques of frame technology.

At the time of the survey, each company had an average of 45 systems installed using frame technology. They were using iterative design refinement. Four of the eleven organizations had reached "critical mass," that is, more than 40% of their developers were using frames. At about this level, the use of frames becomes institutionalized. It becomes "the way things are done around here."

## Introducing Frame Technology

These companies typically introduced frame technology with a one-week course leading into an immediately following project. During the project, an expert coached the novices in how to apply what they had learned in the classroom to the project specifics. I emphasize that what is learned in the course be applied straightaway, under guidance, in a real project. Within a month or two, the novices generally become self-sufficient users of the frame technology tools. Some time after that, given interest and aptitude, some of the developers can take advanced courses, leading to a frame engineering career.

The management role ranged from mild encouragement to forced reuse. Centralized frame engineering ranged from none to fully established. What I have reported here is my view of 11 organizations using frame technology to various degrees. Obviously, they are scattered along the reuse maturity levels. All are enjoying a degree of success with the technology, but only a few have reached the highest maturity level. The fact that they are scattered along the reuse maturity scale supports our contention in Parts III and IV that changing software paradigms is not easy and takes time.

Generally, I find that some smaller companies, say, those with fewer than 20 developers, have reached the upper levels of the scale in a year or two. For one thing, small companies cannot afford to have less than competent people. For another thing, large companies tend to have been in existence for a long time—long enough to have their traditions entrenched. Few bureaucratic IS organizations have attained Level Three so far. None has reached Level Four.

One large company ($12 billion in revenues a year) did reach Level Four in about two years. The reason was that it already had the necessary motivation, people, and culture. It was not bureaucratic!

## Business Processes

In the early years of the computer revolution, information systems organizations were fully occupied in automating particular tasks attached to the existing functional organization of business—engineering, manufacturing, marketing, and so forth. Enormous cost reductions were possible and were achieved. Everyone was happy. In later years, vendors found that they could sell packaged versions of these functions, often with hooks enabling the package to be adapted—to a degree—to the needs of a particular company.

Now, the world of business (and even many governments) is coming to see that its processes should be focused on the customer. The art of business process reengineering is devoted to this goal. Focusing on process chains takes business knowledge, not just knowledge of how to operate computer systems. Fundamentally, however, it is the computer and the software systems that animate it that make the process chains possible. All the people along the chain work off the same database of information. Client-server systems are one expression of this goal.

The process chain certainly differs from industry to industry. At the present state of knowledge, it differs from company to company. On the one hand, some of the outsourcing companies are developing systems that can be applied to more than one company. More commonly, they just take over the existing staff and procedures of the company they are serving.

On the other hand, frame technology enables companies to combine standard frames from a vendor (at least 70% of the entire system) with their own expertise. Using the frame approach, they adapt the purchased functionality. They retain full control over the additions or changes they make. In this way they can process engineer more expeditiously and less expensively, retaining the competitive edge of systems specialized to meet their own needs.

## Hudson's Bay Company

The story of one of the companies using frame technology epitomizes the experience of all of them. . . .

Hudson's Bay Company, established in 1670, is Canada's oldest corporation and also its largest department store retailer. Throughout its major operating divisions, The Bay and Zellers, Hudson's Bay Company covers the Canadian retail market across all price zones and from coast to coast. It accounts for approximately 40% of Canadian department store sales; almost 8% of all retail sales other than food and automobiles. The Bay operates more than 100 stores, covering over 16 million square feet of floor space, and Zellers operates 300 stores covering over 21 million square feet. They service these stores from seven major distribution centers (two in Toronto, two in Vancouver and three in Montreal). In 1994, the company enjoyed record sales of almost $6 billion (Cdn) and record profits.

Hudson's Bay Company has been using frame technology since 1992. They have about 150 people doing systems development work across both Zellers and The Bay. About a quarter of these have some proficiency in frame technology, have applied it in a number of major projects. HBC is well on its way to achieving systemic reuse (Level Three).

Originally, QSM analyzed about 20 HBC projects in order to establish a historical process-productivity-index baseline. These projects averaged a PI of 18, well above industry average. HBC now uses QSM's measurement tools, such as SLIM, to estimate and track all projects. Interestingly, they compare each completed system's overall PI to the PI of its specification frames. SPC frames, of course, contain custom details and carry a lower PI. The jump from the SPC PI to the overall PI is consistently about eight. Even better, both sets of PIs have been steadily rising.

We focus now on national purchase-order management system (NPOMS), the largest frame-based project HBC has done to-date.

## National Purchase Order Management System

This system is The Bay's enterprise-wide, core retail system for buying and managing merchandise for all its stores. Replacing seven regional and two corporate systems that were 10 to 25 years old, it consists of six subsystems:

1. Vendor database management
2. "Open to buy" planning and management (enables buyers to keep track of purchasing power by product category)
3. Purchasing management and Item creation
4. Receiving and Distribution (checking, tracking, and movement of goods)
5. Payment processing
6. Administration

Electronic data interchange is an integral part of NPOMS, including purchase orders, advance shipping notices, payment remittance notices, elimination of paper invoices, and eventually, checks and payment receipts.

The project team, consisting of IS and business experts reporting to a senior management steering committee, kicked off the project in October 1993. Using a high-level business reengineering strategy defined by Peggy Macek, Director, Bay Merchandising System, the project team had a quick start to the system development life cycle (SDLC). This team was also instrumental in subsystem testing and roll-outs. They were successful because: their relevant business experience was extensive, they responded rapidly to requirements gaps and miscommunications, and they co-located and synergized well with the system construction team.

The technical design teams, one per subsystem, began in parallel to determine the requirements. These groups were innovating many new concepts, and reengineering the fundamentals of their business. But would these ideas work? They used prototypes to answer this question, one prototype per subsystem. "Prototypes were the only way to move quickly from concepts to something practical," according to Moses Levy, NPOMS IS project manager.

By testing the critical ideas to see if they worked, they were able to refine the vision and strategy accordingly. Examples:

- They decided to create a centralized system to mirror the highly centralized buying function (three distribution centers supply all Bay stores).
- One of the initial requests from HBC's business communities was to deliver a system with PC/GUI features, and distribution capabilities in the distribution centers. At the time (1993), they were not convinced that the benefits outweighed the risks for a large, mission-critical system. So, capitalizing on their existing mainframes and 3270s, they used COBOL frames to build a CICS/DB2 system.

They extracted frames from the prototypes and embedded them in the frame architecture for the full system. To offset the lack of GUI, several frames were developed for scrolling, selecting, and sorting information, and displaying dynamic menus. About six business-rule frames were constructed to handle security, transaction updates, and audit control reporting.

Figure 29-1 illustrates the run-time architecture. Each executable is either a menu or a program that handles a screen transaction. There is one program per transaction and each screen appears in either of Canada's two official languages, English and French.

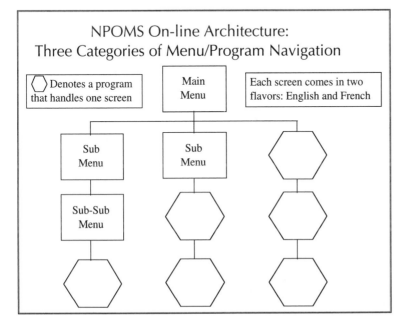

**Figure 29-1.** At run time, the on-line portion of NPOMS is organized by a menu hierarchy. There is one program per screen-based transaction, in English or French.

Figure 29-2 illustrates the framework that composes each program. The hierarchies are composed of three frame categories: NPOMS business rules, HBC standard frames, and Netron standard frames. Certain frames are selected or not, depending on the specific needs of a given program. The SQL frames are a good example of separating the table definitions and the table operators into separate frames, so they can be independently reused.

The IS project and construction teams' peak staffing was 38 people made up of full-time and consulting staff. Most of the team had limited exposure to frame technology, but a significant hurdle was imbuing them with a reuse mind-set (not inventing from scratch). In addition, the in-house people had to learn to use PC development workstations. The combined effect was a relatively steep learning curve. Netron's role was to focus on the run-time and construction-time architectures and to coach the frame novices, offering tips and weekly reviews. They audited what people were doing and critiqued their solutions. They used the learning curve to

**Figure 29-2.** Each NPOMS program is composed from three frame categories: NPOMS business rules ( ⬜ ), HBC standard frames ( ⬜ ), and vendor standard frames ( ⬛ ). Each box is a frame or subassembly.

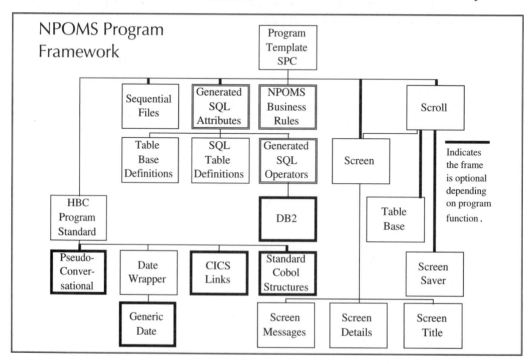

shape the roles of the team members. Those who were less adept at frames got involved in designing test scenarios, prototyping, and testing.

## Project Technical Constraints

NPOMS uses a complex of over 320 DB2 tables, some having as many as 60 million rows. Part of the challenge was the significant amount of business reengineering that was going on in parallel with trying to design NPOMS. Performance and fail-safety were also critical.

The Bay handles up to 30,000 carton movements per day, requiring subsecond response times when scanning carton and item bar codes. Should this part of the system go down, 300-500 distribution center employees become idle. Noncritical business functions required sub-two-second responses 95% of the time.

Reuse was key to HBC's approach. They not only needed to get the system built quickly, but it had to substantially increase the existing functionally, have high performance, enforce common standards (including look and feel to end-users), hide complexity, integrate new technologies, such as RF scanners (wireless bar code readers), and adapt to changing requirements. Each subsystem, since it has gone into production, has been enhanced "almost daily" with new features and functions.

## Major Milestones

All six subsystems have been put into production: Vendor management and the major Administration functions were delivered into production in 1994, Open-to-buy in February 1995, Purchase Orders in April/May, Receiving and Distribution in July, Payments in September. These subsystems amount to 5.2 million ESLOC. Phase II, enhancements currently under development, will bring the total ESLOC to over 6 million.

QSM reports that the four subsystems completed in 1995 jointly represent 3,988,000 new or modified ESLOC, which were detail-designed, developed, and fully tested over 17 months, and consumed 358 staff-months of effort. The four subsystems contained a total of 519,000 SPC lines (with a PI of 20.2), implying a reuse factor of at least 87%.

To quote QSM, "requirements were modestly turbulent, at 30% to 35%. Normally, PIs suffer with this amount of turbulence, and defects found and fixed tend to be high." Yet in the first-month reliability (mean time to defect) was normal, and the overall PI was 28.7.

## Bottom-Line Benefits

When this PI is translated into time and effort, the comparisons are remarkable. Let's grant (for a moment) that the same number of people attempted to build the same system using HBC's pre-reuse productivity (PI = 18). Then 6.4 years would have to elapse from detailed design to roll-out! And the project would consume some 1,600 staff-months. At the current cost per staff member, NPOMS would save over $11 million in development costs. Even more significantly, NPOMS, by being put into production 60 months sooner, would contribute a further $12 million in benefits. Not bad for one system.

Given the highly competitive nature of retailing, a 6.4 year project is completely out of the question. Instead, HBC would simply get a much smaller system, thereby losing the corresponding business benefits. As Moses Levy expressed it: "We delivered five times more functions than [we] ever thought possible. Frame technology enabled us to meet our objectives and avoid unnecessary complexity. Not including a GUI has not hurt us. We are well positioned for the year 2000. By opening up the power of EDI, we've shortened order cycles and improved the quality of order data, reducing labor-intensive exception handling."

As I've noticed in other successful frame environments, the very power of reuse can be carried to a fault. Moses Levy again: "The ability to drive out so much new functionality so quickly caused the demand [for change] to grow tremendously, both in volume and in sophistication."

But the ultimate confirmation of success came from the users, with reactions like, "This is the nicest system you ever gave us."

That is a good "bottom line" with which to end this book. Private organizations have to make profits; governmental bodies have to live within legislative appropriations. In both, it is "users" who have to achieve these ends. They can do that more successfully with the kind of systems that frame technology makes possible.

# References

[1] Ira Grossman and Michael C. Mah, "Independent research study of software reuse (using frame technology)," Technical report, QSM Associates, Pittsfield, MA, September 1994, 75 pp.

[2] Lawrence H. Putnam and Ware Myers. *Measures for Excellence: Reliable Software on Time, Within Budget*. Englewood Cliffs, NJ: Prentice Hall, Yourdon Press, 1992, 378 pp.

[3] Frederick P. Brooks, Jr. *The Mythical Man-Month: Essays on Software Engineering*. Reading, MA: Addison-Wesley, 1975, 195 pp.

[4] Barry Boehm, "A spiral model of software development and enhancement," *Computer*, May 1988, pp. 61–72.

[5] James Martin. *Rapid Application Development*. New York: Macmillan, 1991.

[6] Allan J. Albrecht, "Measuring application development productivity," *Proc. Joint Share/Guide/IBM Application Development Symp.*, October 1979, Share, Inc. and Guide International Corp., pp. 83–92.

[7] Scott Guthrey, "Are the emperor's new clothes object oriented?" *Dr. Dobb's Journal*, December 1989, pp. 80–86.

[8] Survey results as reported in the *Newsletter of the Connecticut Object Oriented Users Group*, P.O. Box 230464, Hartford, CT 06123-0464, September 1995.

[9] James A. Stikeleather, "Making the transition to object technology," presented at the Symposium on Engineering the Enterprise with Object Technology, October 1995, Toronto, ON, Canada.

[10] Peter Naur and B. Randall, eds. *Software Engineering: Report on a Conference Sponsored by the NATO Science Committee*, 1969.

[11] Mary Shaw, "Prospects for an engineering discipline of software," *IEEE Software*, November 1990, pp. 15–24.

[12] William Kent, "A simple guide to five normal forms in relational database theory," *Communications of the ACM*, February 1983, pp. 120–125.

[13] Bev Littlewood and Lorenzo Strigini, "The risks of software," *Scientific American*, November 1992, pp. 62–75.

[14] M. L. Dertouzous, "Communications, computers and networks," *Scientific American*, September 1991, pp. 64–69.

[15] Computer Science and Technology Board, National Research Council. *Keeping the U.S. Computer Industry Competitive*. Washington, DC: National Academy Press, 1990.

[16] Capers Jones, "End-user programming," *Computer*, September 1995, pp. 68–70.

[17] C. W. Krueger, "Software reuse," *ACM Computing Surveys*, vol. 24, no. 2, June 1992.

[18] Marvin Minsky, "A framework for representing knowledge," in *The Psychology of Computer Vision*, P. Winston, ed. New York: McGraw-Hill, 1975, pp. 211–277.

[19] I. Kanter, "Undecidability principle and the uncertainty principle even for classical systems," *Physical Review Letters*, January 22, 1990, pp. 332–335.

[20] Michael Conrad, "On design principles for a molecular computer," *Communications of the ACM*, vol. 28, no. 5, May 1985, pp. 471–472.

[21] Peter Coad and Ed Yourdon. *Object-Oriented Analysis*, 2nd ed. Englewood Cliffs, NJ: Prentice Hall, Yourdon Press, 1991, 232 pp.

[22] Peter Coad and Ed Yourdon. *Object-Oriented Design*. Englewood Cliffs, NJ: Prentice Hall, Yourdon Press, 1991.

[23] Grady Booch. *Object-Oriented Analysis and Design with Applications*, 2nd ed. Redwood City, CA: Benjamin-Cummings, 1994, 589 pp.

[24] Robert A. Frosch, "A new look at systems engineering," *IEEE Spectrum*, September 1969, pp. 24–28.

[25] Eleanor Rosch and Barbara B. Lloyd, eds. *Cognition and Categorization*. Hillside, NJ: Lawrence Erlbaum Associates, 1978, 328 pp.

[26] George Lakoff. *Women, Fire, and Dangerous Things*. Chicago: University of Chicago Press, 1987, 613 pp.

[27] Edward Yourdon and Larry L. Constantine. *Structured Design: Fundamentals of a Discipline of Computer Program and Systems Design*. Englewood Cliffs, NJ: Prentice Hall, 1979, 473 pp.

[28] C. J. Date. *Relational Database: Selected Writings*. Reading, MA: Addison-Wesley, 1986.

[29] W. Kim F. Lochovsky, eds. *Object-oriented Concepts, Databases, and Applications*, Addison-Wesley, Reading, Ma, 1989.

[30] Anthony Crawford. *Advancing Business Concepts in a JAD Workshop Setting: Business Reengineering and Process Design*. Englewood Cliffs, NJ: Prentice Hall, Yourdon Press, 1994.

[31] Gustav J. V. Nossal, "Life, death and the immune system," *Scientific American*, September 1993, pp. 52–62.

[32] Tom DeMarco. *Controlling Software Projects*. New York: Yourdon Press, 1982, 284 pp.

[33] Bennet P. Lientz and E. Burton Swanson. *Software Maintenance Management*, page 73, Addison-Wesley, Reading, MA, 1980.

[34] Watts S. Humphrey. *Managing the Software Process*. Reading, MA: Addison-Wesley, 1989, 494 pp.

[35] Capers Jones. *Programming Productivity*. New York: McGraw-Hill, 1986, 280 pp.

[36] Thomas McCabe. "A Complexity Measure." *IEEE Transactions on Software Engineering*, vol. SE-2, no. 4, December 1976.

[37] Masaaki, Imai. *Kaizen; The Key to Japan's Competitive Success*, McGraw-Hill, 1986.

[38] Manfred Eigen, "Viral quasispecies," *Scientific American*, July 1993, pp. 42–49.

[39] Stuart Kauffman, "Antichaos and adaptation," *Scientific American*, August 1991.

[40] Harvey Gellman. "Do You Have Principles?" *Inside Guide*, June, July, August 1992.

[41] Peter G. W. Keen, "Information systems and organizational change," *Communications of the ACM*, vol. 21, no. 1, January 1981, pp. 24–33.

[42] Michael A. Cusumano. *Japan's Software Factories: A Challenge to U.S. Management*. New York: Oxford University Press, 1991, 513 pp.

[43] Ramchandran Jaikumar, "Post industrial manufacturing," *Harvard Business Review*, November-December, 1986.

[44] Albert L. Lederer and Jayesh Prasad, "Nine management guidelines for better cost estimating," *Communications of the ACM*, vol. 35, no. 2, February 1992, pp. 50–59.

[45] Allan J. Albrecht and John E. Gaffney, Jr., "Software function, source lines of code, and development effort predictions: A software science validation," *IEEE Transactions on Software Engineering*, vol. SE-9, November 1983, pp. 639–648.

# Glossary

We have briefly defined terms used in frame engineering or in this book. It is not a glossary of all the terms encountered in the software field.

**Abstraction.** Extracts the properties essential to some purpose from properties that are irrelevant to this purpose. For example, a disk drive may be viewed as a collection of logically addressed files, not as a physical device requiring a specified voltage from a power supply.

**Adaptability.** The extent to which a component can be modified for reuse, either by adding or subtracting capability.

**Adaptor frame.** A frame with the ability to select and modify the properties of other frames. The same as an **ancestor frame**.

**Analysis.** The process of determining relevant requirements. The "what of a problem."

**Analysis paralysis.** Refers to the tendency to agonize over requirements and specifications so long that the system is out of date before it is completed.

**Ancestor frames.** With reference to a given frame, the frames above it in the hierarchy, up to and including the specification frame. The same as an **adaptor frame**.

**Application generator.** Provides source code in response to inputs specific to a particular application. The inputs are in a language easier to use than source code, often something close to a natural language.

**Application program interface (API).** The calling interface between executable layers in a run-time environment.

**Archetype.** The original pattern or model of a category. A "best example" of a subdomain or category.

**Architecture, system.** The architectural stratum containing generic adaptable components for interfacing to devices, screens, reports, databases, operating systems, network protocols, and so forth.

**Architecture, application.** The architectural stratum containing generic adaptable components for processing (data entry, update, enquiry, reporting, etc.) and data (transaction types, master-record types, parameter tables, and so forth.).

**Architecture, business.** The architectural stratum containing generic adaptable components that specify the rules and data structures that model applications specific to a business.

**Assembly.** A tree or lattice of frames, designed for the purpose of constructing source modules. The process of composing frames into a source module.

**Binding.** The act of assigning a value to a variable in a module.

**Black box.** A component with known inputs and known outputs; that is, a specified interface to other components that carries out defined functions, but whose internal functioning need not be known by the user.

**BREAK.** A frame parameter whose default value is a contiguous block of related lines in a frame. A break-name identifies this block to ancestor frames. The default value (which may be null) is called *frame-text*. An ancestor frame can customize the frame-text by using INSERTs. Terminated by END-BREAK.

**Brittle.** As delivered software is corrected, enhanced, and modified, it tends to lose its capacity for easy changeability; that is, it becomes brittle.

**Business analysis.** The process of scoping the software requirements from the point of view of business, not technology, down to the function-point boundary.

**Business process reengineering**. Recasting an organization from a functional format to a flow of work through business processes, such as bringing a product to the marketplace, receipt of product by customer to collection of invoice, procurement of raw materials to delivery to customer.

As an overhaul involving discontinuities, reengineering imposes heavy strains on the organization's information systems. Frame technology can ameliorate this strain.

**Capability maturity model.** An assessment of an organization's effectiveness in producing software, developed by the Software Engineering Institute at Carnegie Mellon University for the U.S. Department of Defense. An assessment results in an assignment to one of five levels:

1. Initial; 2. Repeatable; 3. Defined; 4. Managed; 5. Optimized.

**Category.** A subdomain of similar elements.

**Child frame.** With reference to a given frame, the frame immediately below it in the hierarchy.

**Class.** A collection of objects with similar structure and behavior. Often used interchangeably with the term *object*. A subdivision of a domain.

**Code generator.** A software product that accepts rules, decision tables, diagrams, or other representations of high-level design, sometimes in forms close to natural language, describing activities in a limited domain, and outputs implementing code.

**Co-location.** The practice of working at the end-user site with a dotted-line relationship to the local management, while retaining a solid-line relationship to the central information systems group.

**Compiler.** A program that translates source code into executable code, not statement by statement, but as a whole.

**Component.** A general term for a section of a source module or an executable module that is part of a system. Frames are components of source modules.

**Conceptual model.** A macroscopic description of a software system providing information to justify and estimate a project and to project a schedule of prereleases.

**Construction time.** The time at which a programmer or a computer program, such as a frame processor, constructs a source module. The time during which the properties of executable modules that are invariant at run time can be varied.

**Construction interpreter.** An agent, such as the frame processor, that assembles a source-code module, and during that process implements the variations specified in frame commands by a frame engineer.

**Construction-time variability.** The ability to modify a component at the time a program is being put together, rather than at run time.

**Context.** Pertaining to the extent to which a frame is affected by its situation. The topmost frame in a frame hierarchy—that is, the specification frame—is context-specific; the intermediate frames are context-sensitive in varying degrees; the lowest frames are relatively context-free.

**COPY.** A frame command that suspends processing of the current frame until the specified frame has been processed by the frame processor. The specified frame is identified by a "frame-name" embedded in the COPY command. In general, it is terminated by END-COPY.

**Copy-and-modify.** A time-honored, but ineffective, method of reuse. Find a similar program and edit a copy of it to fit the new requirement.

**Copybook.** A piece of COBOL data or procedural code usually intended for reuse as is.

**Cousin frames.** All frames having a common ancestor other than a parent frame.

**Data.** One of the two main content items of software, the other being functions (methods, operations).

**Data model.** A network of relationships among data tables.

**Data structure.** One of the two elements of a class or an object, the other being methods or operations. The data are arranged in a structure suited to the methods. The data within a frame are arranged in a data structure.

**Data types.** Data structures may be divided into categories, for example, a set of similar customer record structures. If the pattern of similarity can be formally expressed, that expression is called a *data type* (not to be confused with abstract data type). Frames express data types.

**Default value.** The value of a parameter built into a frame that is used unless an ancestor frame assigns a new value to the parameter. Assigning a new value is one of the ways in which a frame is adapted during reuse.

**Delta.** A small difference between two things, as a delta to an archetype, or a change that enables a frame to accommodate a new requirement. A set of additions or subtractions that convert an archetype into a different example in the same category.

**Descendent.** With reference to a given frame, the frames below it in the hierarchy, down to the leaf nodes.

**Design.** The practice of satisfying relevant requirements—the "how" of a problem's solution.

**Design template.** A generic version of one or more specification frames that express a type of program or system, such as data entry, report, or client-server. Used as the basis for constructing a particular specification frame or system of such frames.

**Development time.** The duration, extending from the start of detailed design to the attainment of full operational capability, ready for use by the customer. Does not include feasibility study, conceptual modeling, high-level design, or maintenance stages.

**Domain.** A field of activity, such as an application domain or an information domain with a distinct subject matter of concern to users. Domains can be broad or narrow in scope.

**Duality.** In general, a pair of concepts that have corresponding properties. In software engineering, construction time and run time have corresponding properties.

**Dynamic binding.** Resolving linkages (bindings between methods) during execution, as opposed to static binding, where linkages are resolved prior to execution.

**Dynamic model.** A model for which an interpreter exists that can translate the model into an output that simulates, emulates, or changes states in a manner similar to the real entity.

**Effort.** Person-months or person-years devoted to a software project. Includes all development staff: analysts, designers, programmers, coders, integration and test-team members, quality assurance, documentation, supervision, and project management.

**Element.** One of the parts into which a whole may be resolved by analysis. An entity that belongs to a given set.

**Encapsulation.** Hides the elements of an abstraction, especially the data structures, that the user does not need to know in order to use it; the encapsulated object's interface provides only the information the user does need to know, such as the interface characteristics and the results that the object provides.

**Engineering.** The disciplined application of scientific knowledge to resolve conflicting constraints and requirements for problems of immediate practical significance (Mary Shaw[10]).

**Entropy, software.** The evolving lack of order or coherence in a software system as it ages, resulting from the way in which changes are made. "Fixes" tend to increase system disorder until a point is finally reached at which the system no longer operates reliably.

**ESLOC.** Effective source lines of code—total lines minus blanks and comments.

**Execution.** The running of machine code on binary hardware. Information not expressed in machine code can also be said to execute if some interpreter machine code, during its execution, processes the information.

**Executable.** A software module that can run on a binary computer. More generally, a module that can be compiled and linked to run on a binary computer, or a module that can be interpreted by an executable interpreter.

**Expression.** A string in a frame delimited by quotes, apostrophes, spaces, or parentheses.

**Fifth normal form.** Relational database theory employs a number of guidelines, called *normal forms*, for record design. Fifth normal form is a generalized version of second, third, and fourth forms. It covers cases in which information is reconstructed from smaller pieces that can be maintained with less redundancy.

**Frame.** A component in any programming language that can be reused, not only as-is, but as adapted by other frames to fit a new application. A frame contains (1) program commands and variables and (2) frame commands and variables. The frame commands can add to or subtract from other frames' capabilities as the application requires.

**Frame command.** A command embedded in a frame that sets forth the information needed to adapt frames. These commands implement the concept "same as, except."

**Frame, corporate.** Frames used widely throughout a corporation or similar multiapplication domain.

**Frame, division, department,** or **project.** Frames used less widely than corporate, throughout a smaller portion of an organization.

**Frame engineer.** Carries out standardizing, developing, and encouraging the use of frames across a number of projects or departments.

**Frame hierarchy.** Frames organized into assemblies and subassemblies for the purpose of constructing software modules.

**Frame owner.** "Ownership" refers to the organization entity or manager that creates or maintains a frame. Royalties for the reuse of the frame may accrue to the owner.

**Frame processor.** A tool that executes the frame commands in a hierarchy of frames, producing a program in source code. Whereas a compiler turns source code into machine code, a frame processor turns a hierarchy of frames into source code ready for input to a compiler.

**Frame repository.** One or more libraries of standard frames, design templates, and architectures centrally maintained by frame administration.

**Frame technology.** The frame processor, its supporting utilities, and a frame repository.

**Frame-text.** Any text that has (or can have) frame commands embedded in it.

**Framework.** One or more frame assemblies that collectively define an architecture for constructing run-time systems.

**Framing.** Converting use-as-is information into frames.

**Function.** One of the two main content items in software, the other being data. Functions transform data, hence functions are static in the presence of their data.

**Function type.** Functions may be divided into categories, for example, a set of similar batch processes. If the pattern of similarity can be formally expressed, that expression is called a function type (not to be confused with abstract data type). Frames express function types.

**Function-point boundary.** The level of business analysis at which function points (inputs, outputs, inquiries, master files, and interfaces) become evident to business analysts. A count of function points is a metric proportional to the quantity of software produced.

**Generality.** An expression of the number of contexts, situations, applications, domains, and so forth in which a component is reusable.

**Generic.** Referring to all the members of a category; in particular, a frame with attributes common to a category of applications that can be modified to fit a specific need within that category.

**Genotype.** The genes transmitted from parent to offspring. In similarity analysis, the abstractions of a component that, like genes, specify how to make that component.

**Graininess.** Refers to the size of software components. Excessively small components may result in a sea of look-alikes that are difficult to manage and lead to poor program performance. Components that are too large may be difficult for a programmer to adapt to a specific need.

**Gray box.** A strategy that normally hides the content of a component, but makes it available for inspection when needed to make necessary changes.

**Hybrid organization.** An organization combining two parts: a centralized information-systems structure and decentralized projects. The central part supports reuse across multiple departments and projects.

**Infrastructure.** The basic, supporting framework of an organization. For effective reuse, a software organization should have a single, common infrastructure, for example, common methods and tools.

**Inheritance.** Enables one class to make use of attributes or capabilities from another class, while supplementing that inheritance with additional functions. Cannot easily select or subtract inherited attributes or capabilities. Inheritance establishes a hierarchy of classes based on abstraction relationships.

**INSERT.** The part of the COPY frame command that customizes a BREAK. It can replace the BREAK's default frame-text, or insert frame-text before and/or after the default.

**Instance.** The result of a frame command taking a generalized property and making it specific; that is, instancing an attribute to an instance of the general case.

**Interpreter.** Commonly refers to a program that carries out the instructions of a module as if the module were being executed on a binary computer. Used in this book more broadly as an agent capable of interacting with a module according to a set of fixed rules.

**IS.** Information systems.

**Islands of technology.** Multiple incompatible software tool sets scattered across an IS organization, making it infeasible for the organization to reuse components or to have portable developers.

**Iterative design refinement.** The process of creating a solution to the current requirement by use of reusable components and then iterating this solution by modifying and adding to the components as the participants learn more about the requirements of the problem. IDR is reuse across time. Abbreviated IDR.

**Joint application design.** A group process, led by a neutral facilitator, to expose the issues and develop a consensus solution to some business or technical issue. Abbreviated JAD.

**Lattice.** A mathematical term for an acyclic graph. Whereas in a tree each node can have at most one parent, a lattice node can have more than one, but loops are not allowed. Frame hierarchies are usually lattices rather than trees.

**Leaf node.** The most generic or context-free frames at the bottom of a frame hierarchy.

**Look-alikes.** The components resulting from the reuse technique, which multiplies the original component into many similar, but slightly different, versions.

**Macro.** A module containing a body of code that is copied during compilation or assembly when invoked by name. It is not readily modified during invocation.

**Maintenance.** Operations, such as correction of defects, enhancement, or revision of program code after delivery.

**Message.** In object-oriented languages, a request at run time, consisting of the name of the addressed object, a method name, and the arguments needed by the method. The request invokes an operation.

**Metamodel.** A model of a model. If an executable module, for example, is a model of external reality, then the specification of the executable is a metamodel.

**Method.** In an object-oriented language, an operator that manipulates an object's data.

**Module.** A set of symbols—instructions, data, text, graphics—that is referenced as a unit.

**Multiple inheritance.** Inheritance from two or more parents.

*n***GL.** *n*th generation programming languages. COBOL and Fortran are third generation.

**Object.** A group of data structures and methods (or operators), bearing a name and playing both noun and verb roles. An object draws most of its capabilities, particularly its methods, from its parent class or a chain of ancestors, through the inheritance mechanism.

**Object instance.** A class may give rise to many objects, each having the same operators, but providing a different data storage area, as, for instance, a bank-account object reproduced for many account holders. Each such object is called an object-instance.

**Object orientation.** A programming technology characterized by abstraction, encapsulation, inheritance, polymorphism, modularity, hierarchy, and messages.

**Object-oriented languages.** The concept of object orientation dates from Simula-67 and Smalltalk-72. Now there are more than 60 of these languages. C++ and Smalltalk are the leading languages providing object-oriented capability.

**Parameter.** The term we apply to variables at construction time that are to be bound at this time.

**Parent frame.** With reference to a given frame, the frame immediately above it in the hierarchy.

**Phenotype.** The observable appearance and behavior of an organism resulting from the interaction of the genotype and the environment. In software, the behavior of executables.

**Polymorphism.** (Greek for "many forms.") Refers to the ability to use methods that have the same name but different behaviors.

**Postproduction release.** A version of a software system that replaces a version that is already in production. Also called a *postrelease*.

**Preproduction release.** Also known as *prerelease*. A version of a software system that could be, but has not been, put into production. Usually, it is too incomplete to do so.

**Production release.** The first version of a software system that is ready to be put, or already has been put, into production.

**Productivity, conventional.** Delivered source lines of code per staff month.

**Productivity, process.** A numerical measure, or index, of the software product produced during the development time by the effort expended. This index reflects management practices, technical methods, software environment, skill and experience, and complexity of the application type.

**Program.** A representation of fixed algorithms in a readily changeable, or soft, form.

**REPLACE.** A frame command that *conditionally* assigns a value to a frame variable (parameter), overriding the default value or assigning a value where the default value is undefined. The condition is that this variable has not already been assigned by an ancestor frame.

**Return on investment.** The profit generated by an investment, expressed as a percent of the investment. Abbreviated ROI.

**Reusability.** The dual of usability. A module's reusability rests upon three factors: (1) usability; (2) generality (scope of applicability); (3) adaptability (ease-of-use).

**Reuse.** As used in software, reuse is the process of adapting a component in order to make it usable.

**Reuse maturity levels.** Divides software organizations into five levels of maturity with respect to the achievement of reuse by employment of frame technology: 0. Unaware; 1. Latent; 2. Project; 3. Systemic; 4. Cultural.

**Reuse steering committee.** A committee of senior executives with representation from user departments and the information systems department with the clout to set policies, induce behavior and attitude changes, and remove barriers.

**Root.** The source element of a tree. In the case of a frame hierarchy, the root frame, which is the specification frame, is at the top and the structure grows downward.

**Run time.** The time at which a computer executes a module of code.

**Same as, except.** "This problem is the same as that one, except...." The concept underlying the problem-solving strategy of taking an existing solution and adapting it to handle a new problem.

**Scaffolding.** Stubs or mock-ups that supply data to or take data from a prerelease version in test, periodic build, or preliminary operation.

**SELECT.** A frame command that acts as a case statement at construction time, using relational operators. When any of the specified relations are true, the frame processor picks up the corresponding frame-text. Terminated by END-SELECT.

**Sibling frame.** Child frames with a common parent frame.

**Single inheritance.** Inheritance from one parent.

**Skeleton code.** A software component with "holes." A programmer copies and "fleshes" in the holes to adapt the skeleton to a particular use. This is a form of "copy-and-modify" reuse.

**Source module.** The module resulting from the assembly of a hierarchy of frames by a frame processor.

**Specification frame.** The topmost frame in a frame hierarchy that specifies how to adapt the rest of the structure to assemble a source module. It is the least generic, most context-sensitive frame in the hierarchy. Abbreviated SPC.

**Software engineering.** The application of formal methods in the cost-effective development (analysis, design, construction, and evolution) of cost-effective software systems.

**Stakeholders.** The parties to a software project—IS people, management, related departments, users, customers.

**State.** Referring to an object or a component, the collective value of its variables or attributes at a specific time.

**State transition rules.** The logic in a program that defines how the state of objects or components is to change.

**State transition diagram.** Represents the state transition rules in diagrammatic form, facilitating analysis.

**Static model.** A partial model that lacks information needed to mimic the behavior it is modeling.

**Stovepipe.** Refers to the vertical organization structure of marketing, production, engineering, and so on, in contrast to the horizontal structure envisioned by business process engineering.

**Subroutine.** A component activated at execution time, or run time, by a call-return.

**SWAT team.** Skilled with Advanced Tools team (James Martin.)

**System.** This term has been widely applied to everything from atoms to stars with living systems in between. In software, it is a set of components with relations between them that carry out a purpose. Often analysts encounter difficulty in determining just where to set the boundary between the system at hand and everything else.

**Time-boxing.** Setting a time deadline with the understanding that functionality may be omitted in order to meet it. A means for implementing prerelease prioritization: developing the critical components first.

**Total quality management.** A company-wide effort to improve quality, or service to the customer, in every respect. TQM tends to be incremental, improving quality in small steps, unlike business process engineering, which attempts giant strides.

**Tree.** A directed graph of nodes in which no node can have more than a single parent.

**Usability.** A module's usefulness rests upon three factors: (1) functionality (ability to carry out its duties); (2) efficiency (performance time, computer size, memory size); (3) ease-of-use (complexity of interface to other modules or user).

**Use-as-is.** Refers to using a component as it is, in contrast to reusing a component in a same-as-except manner.

**Validity.** The ability of a software system to satisfy the current need.

**Var.** A frame variable to which a REPLACE command assigns a value.

**Waterfall model.** A software approach that assumes that development proceeds in one direction from requirements through specifications, functional design, detailed design, coding, unit test, system test, and delivery.

**WHILE.** A frame command that causes the frame processor to emit a variable number of versions of similar text, controlled by frame variables. Terminated by END-WHILE.

**White box.** A software component with a specified interface to other components that carries out defined functions, whose internal functioning is available to and can be changed by the user.

**Wrapper frame.** Frames in the middle layer of a frame hierarchy that hide the reuse complexities of more generic frames.

# Index